TO LIVE
OR TO PERISH
FOREVER

TO LIVE
OR TO PERISH
FOREVER

Two Tumultuous Years in Pakistan

Nicholas Schmidle

Henry Holt and Company
New York

Henry Holt and Company, LLC
Publishers since 1866
175 Fifth Avenue
New York, New York 10010
www.henryholt.com

Henry Holt ® and ⓗ ® are registered trademarks of Henry Holt and Company, LLC.

Distributed in Canada by H. B. Fenn and Company Ltd.

Library of Congress Cataloging-in-Publication Data

Schmidle, Nicholas.
  To live or to perish forever : two tumultuous years in Pakistan / Nicholas Schmidle.
     p. cm.
  ISBN-13: 978-0-8050-8938-7
  ISBN-10: 0-8050-8938-1
  1. Pakistan—Politics and government—1988– 2. Pakistan—Description and travel.
3. Schmidle, Nicholas—Travel—Pakistan. I. Title.
  DS389.S36 2009
  954.9105'3092—dc22
  [B]   2008048373

Henry Holt books are available for special promotions and premiums.
For details contact: Director, Special Markets.

First Edition 2009

Designed by Meryl Sussman Levavi

Map by Jeffrey L. Ward
Printed in the United States of America

1 3 5 7 9 10 8 6 4 2

For Rikki
And for my parents

Wouldn't we all do better not trying to understand, accepting the fact that no human being will ever understand another, not a wife a husband, a lover a mistress, nor a parent a child? Perhaps that's why men have invented God—a being capable of understanding. Perhaps if I wanted to be understood or to understand I would bamboozle myself into belief, but I am a reporter; God exists only for leader-writers.

—THOMAS FOWLER, in *The Quiet American* by Graham Greene

Contents

INTRODUCTION: LAND OF THE PURE   1

1. "TO THESE GUYS, YOU ARE ALL INFIDELS"   15

2. "SELL YOUR LUXURY GOODS AND BUY A KALASHNIKOV"   28

3. "DON'T SPEAK ENGLISH IN PUBLIC"   41

4. "LEFT ALONE IN A CAVE OF TIME"   56

5. "IT JUST SOUNDS AWKWARD TO CALL MYSELF A PAKISTANI"   69

6. "WHAT WAS WRONG WITH PAKISTAN?"   100

7. "WE HAVE ACCEPTED THE CHALLENGE"   117

8. "THE BLOOD OF OUR MARTYRS WILL NOT GO TO WASTE"   131

9. "IF YOU DON'T LET US LIVE IN PEACE
WE WON'T LET YOU LIVE IN PEACE"   156

10. "This Barbed Wire Stands in the Way of Democracy"   173

11. "Made Like a Sandwich"   190

12. "No Mercy in Their Hearts"   205

Epilogue: "The Fear Factor Spoils the Fun"   220

Notes   239

Acknowledgments   243

Index   247

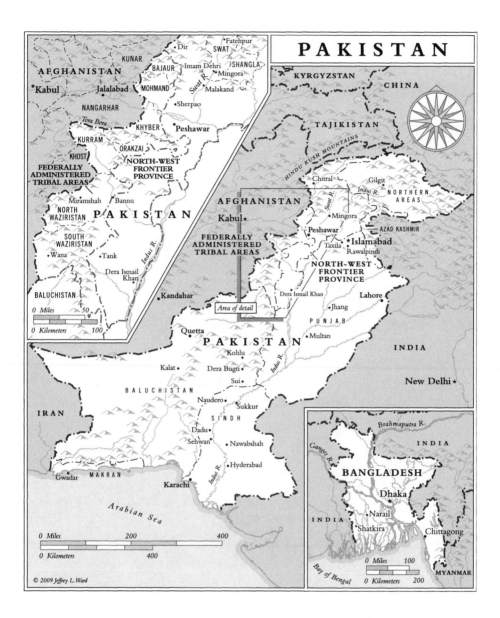

PAKISTAN

AFGHANISTAN

KUNAR
Dir •Fatehpur
SWAT
BAJAUR •Imam Dehri SHANGLA
MOHMAND •Mingora
*Kabul •Jalalabad Malakand
NANGARHAR •Sherpao
Tora Bora
KHYBER •Peshawar
KURRAM
KHOST ORAKZAI
FEDERALLY NORTH-WEST
ADMINISTERED FRONTIER
TRIBAL AREAS PROVINCE
•Miramshah Bannu
NORTH PAKISTAN
WAZIRISTAN
SOUTH
WAZIRISTAN
•Wana •Tank
Dera Ismail
Khan
BALUCHISTAN
Indus R.
0 Miles 50
0 Kilometers 100
•Kandahar

KYRGYZSTAN
CHINA
TAJIKISTAN
HINDU KUSH MOUNTAINS
Chitral Gilgit NORTHERN
Indus R. AREAS
AFGHANISTAN Swat R.
Kabul★ •Mingora
FEDERALLY Peshawar AZAD KASHMIR
ADMINISTERED Taxila ★Islamabad
TRIBAL AREAS Rawalpindi
NORTH-WEST
FRONTIER
PROVINCE
Dera Ismail Khan Lahore
Area of detail •Jhang
PUNJAB
Quetta PAKISTAN •Multan
Kohlu INDIA
Kalat • Dera Bugti •
Sui
Indus R.
BALUCHISTAN
Naudero New Delhi ★
•Sukkur
S I N D H
Dadu•
Sehwan• •Nawabshah
Indus R.
•Hyderabad
IRAN
Gwadar MAKRAN
Karachi

Arabian Sea

0 Miles 200 400
0 Kilometers 400

Brahmaputra R.
INDIA
Ganges R.
BANGLADESH
Dhaka
★
•Narail
INDIA •Shatkira
Chittagong
Bay of Bengal
0 Miles 100
0 Kilometers 200
MYANMAR

© 2009 Jeffrey L. Ward

TO LIVE
OR TO PERISH
FOREVER

LAND OF THE PURE

THE COPS CAME FOR ME ON A COLD, RAINY NIGHT. FOUR OF THEM, HOODS pulled over their heads, stood in the driveway of my home in Islamabad.

"Are you Mr. Nicholas?" one asked.

I nodded.

The senior officer who did all the talking was tall, clean-shaven, and looked familiar; we had met a few weeks earlier at an antigovernment student protest.

"What's the problem?" I asked, my tone sounding partly curious, and yet anxious. Why would the police come to my house three times in one afternoon? When they had stopped by the first two times, I had been out, and was alerted to their visits by our *chowkidar*, or guard.

Now it was raining hard. We stepped under a cloth awning that covered part of the driveway to get out of the rain. The sound of water rushing off the end of the awning and splashing loudly into puddles made it difficult for me to hear.

"I have orders to take you and your wife to the airport," the officer said. "Your visas have been revoked."

2 | TO LIVE OR TO PERISH FOREVER

What?

The officer repeated himself and added, "You must leave Pakistan immediately." He handed me a piece of paper. The document, printed on Ministry of Interior letterhead and covered with signatures from representatives of various police and intelligence units, stated in clear, concise language: my wife, Rikki, and I were being deported.

I looked up from the paper and stared at the officer, stunned but not wholly surprised. For a while, I had suspected that something was amiss. I knew, for instance, that my phone was being tapped. A friend had told me that whenever he called me, the conversation always began with three distinct beeps, the signature sound of a wiretap coming to life, and as of a couple weeks earlier, I had not been able to receive calls from the United States. Moreover, just a day earlier, an intelligence agent from the Inter-Services Intelligence, or ISI, showed up in the flesh. He relayed a message through our chowkidar that Rikki and I were "living in Pakistan illegally"—and that I was "writing against Pakistan."

The cloak-and-dagger shenanigans and subtle intimidations related to a story I had written for the *New York Times Magazine* profiling a new, more radical generation of Pakistani Taliban. I had spent months traveling to regions under their control, and had even passed an afternoon inside a Taliban-run camp. I expected a certain amount of harassment from the intelligence goons, as they often paid courtesy visits to foreign journalists who had reported on sensitive subjects from sensitive areas. Fanatic rebels in the North-West Frontier Province certainly met this condition. Dealing with the agencies seemed to be as much a part of the job as securing a visa, arranging interviews, and actually writing the stories. But a visit from the police suggested something official—and far more serious—than the normal spook routine.

I asked the officer for a minute to consult with Rikki and ran upstairs with the deportation notice in hand. We had been living in Pakistan for nearly two years, renting a two-bedroom apartment in a large house owned by a Pakistani family. We considered Pakistan home. Rikki attended the International Islamic University, the first non-Muslim American to ever enroll. She also worked as the nutritionist at a five-star hotel in Islamabad, where her obese clients included cabinet ministers, prominent businessmen, and senior bureaucrats. Whatever problems she encountered at the university could usually be resolved with a simple phone call from one of her clients at the hotel. So when I burst through the door, out of breath, ranting about how the police were prepared to bundle us off to the airport in the next hour, Rikki promptly yet calmly replied, "Have you called Majed?"

Majed, whose real name I can't disclose, was probably Rikki's largest client. During their first session, Majed told Rikki that he could reduce the amount of food he ate, but that he would have trouble cutting back on the four or five scotches he drank every night while playing bridge with his buddies. I assumed his bridge partners comprised an influential bunch; Majed, who was himself related to the prime minister at the time, had been in and out of government for years. He had told Rikki to call him at any hour, that no favor was too large. "Call him," she now urged.

"Majed? Hi, it's Nicholas. Sorry to bother you tonight, but I have a small problem. There are four police officers standing in my driveway right now, and they say that our visas have been canceled and they going to kick us out of the country."

"Huh?" he replied, sounding slightly preoccupied. I rehashed the details. He related the story, in Urdu, to someone else on his end. He came back on the line. "Listen, I am playing bridge with Tariq Aziz," Majed said in a calm, unflappable tone. (At the time, Aziz was President Pervez Musharraf's national security adviser.) "Why don't you give the phone to the seniormost officer, and I'll give the phone to Tariq. Don't worry. He'll take care of it."

I handed the phone to the tall, clean-shaven officer and told him who was waiting on the other line. I thought about flashing a smug grin, but realized it might seem cocky — and a little premature.

The officer lifted the phone to his ear. He introduced himself. Aziz did the rest of the talking.

"Yes sir," the officer said into the phone. "Yes sir...Yes sir...Yes sir...Yes sir..."

The officer returned my phone and apologized for the disturbance. Then he and his hooded colleagues turned, walked down the driveway, and disappeared into the dark, rainy night. I ran back up the metal stairs that led to our second-floor apartment and, having thrown open the door, announced: "Majed came through. Big time."

Connections meant everything in Pakistan. If you knew the right people, things worked out. If you didn't, you wound up on a one-way flight to Dubai on a rainy Tuesday night. But connections were a double-edged sword, and knowing the wrong people could land you in more trouble than knowing the right people could get you out of. Besides folks like Majed, I also knew plenty of rebels in Baluchistan and Taliban fighters in the North-West Frontier Province, too. Majed's bridge partners, in other words, had saved us from packing our entire apartment into suitcases that night, but the deportation notice, covered with signatures from this-and-that intelligence agency, suggested that the state machinery had been set into motion against us. According to official government correspondence, we were living in Pakistan illegally. And wandering around without valid papers was foolhardy and stupid, if not outright dangerous.

We woke up the next morning to more rain. Low clouds spread across the verdant mountain ridge outside our windows.

I called Majed again. He had just gotten off the phone, trying to find more about our case.

"I can't do anything more," he said. "This is *way* above my head. We asked the police to leave you alone, but this is above them, too. You should really leave the country for a bit."

"Did anyone give any reason for why this is happening?"

"They said something about the Taliban, your trips to Baluchistan, and your coverage of the Red Mosque. But that's all I know," he said.

I hung up and bought the first two available seats on the next outbound flight. Forty-eight hours later, on the morning after my twenty-ninth birthday, we were soaring above the Hindu Kush Mountains — and out of Pakistan.

I WENT TO Pakistan in February 2006, hoping to learn something about this troubled, nuclear-armed country, and about myself. I wanted to become a journalist, but most newspapers were closing their foreign bureaus, not opening new ones. And with next to no formal experience, magazine editors weren't exactly lined up outside of my door, eager to dish out international assignments. In the rapidly changing landscape of American journalism, it seemed like the only way for an inexperienced hack like myself to try to make a name — and potentially a career — was by patching together fellowships and grant money, going somewhere newsworthy, and then praying for good luck.

The Institute of Current World Affairs was my ticket. ICWA, as it is better known, is a foundation that sponsors two-year writing fellowships around the world. Their cash flowed from toilets. Back in the 1920s, Charles Crane, the eldest son of the plumbing magnate by the same name, invested $1 million into a startup fund called the Crane-Rogers Foundation, later dubbed ICWA. The foundation survived the Great Depression and subsequent wars, and continued to send two or three people into the field every year. It operated almost like a venture capitalist fund; they sought applicants younger than thirty-five who showed an interest in foreign affairs and displayed sufficient room to grow. Seemed like a perfect fit. If there was one thing I had, it was plenty of room to grow.

In June 2006, the ICWA board selected me as a Phillips Talbot Fellow. Talbot, who turned ninety years old that same weekend, had spent the 1940s as an ICWA fellow in pre-Partition India. He began his career as a cub reporter at the *Chicago Daily News* in the late 1930s before being tapped for a fellowship. He went on to write several books, become an assistant secretary of state, the American ambassador to Greece, and the president of the Asia Society. I had big shoes to fill. Before I shipped off, Talbot and I had several conversations, and he told me stories from his own time in South Asia facing accusations of being a spy. While Indian Communists tagged him an imperialist agent of the United States, officers in the British Raj accused him of working to undermine their government based on Talbot's contacts with Gandhi, Nehru, Jinnah, and, to some extent, Indian Communists. This seemed to be a common theme for ICWA fellows abroad.

"The Institute of Current World Affairs?" people often asked me. "What is it? Some sort of CIA cover?" In the past, foreign governments had imprisoned even Fulbright fellows — who are relatively well known in international circles — on charges of espionage. An obscure foundation like ICWA, I would soon discover, raised even more suspicions.

I arrived in Pakistan by accident; my fellowship was intended for Iran. I had spent the previous summer studying Persian at Tehran University, and proposed a fellowship to the ICWA board that involved my reporting and writing about ethnic minorities (Kurds, Azeris, Baluchis, Arabs) there. But shortly after ICWA granted the fellowship, the people of Iran spoke, and chose Mahmoud Ahmadinejad as their new president. Ahmadinejad was a hard-liner whose vitriolic anti-American rhetoric dwarfed even that of his predecessors, who had themselves made chanting "Death to America" a staple of public life. Overnight, the prospects of the Iranian government giving an American a two-year visa to drift around and write about the country's ethnic problems seemed, well, pretty dim.

Five months after I first walked into Iran's pseudo-embassy in Washington (the two countries severed diplomatic relations in 1979 and housed "interests sections" in other countries' embassies), an official there finally leveled with me. "Nicholas, this is never going to happen," he said. "Maybe you should think of going somewhere else."

But where?

Afghanistan? Too much war. ICWA funded fellowships that featured hardship, poverty, and an occasional brush with conflict, but they shied away from sending fellows into war zones where a kidnapped American could fetch tens of thousands of dollars.

Central Asia? The 'Stans sounded intriguing, but I figured that getting drunk on fermented mare's milk with two dozen of my closest Kyrgyz friends six nights a week might get really old, really fast.

What about Pakistan? If I had my demographic facts straight, they had some ethnic problems of their own, right? What if I just took my fellowship proposal for Iran, and replaced "Pakistan" with "Iran"? After some convincing, the director of ICWA signed off on my new destination.

A couple of months later, I stumbled into Pakistan.

I CRAMMED TO make up for lost time, first by attempting to call up every Pakistani in the D.C. capital area, and then reading anything I could find about Pakistan's history, culture, people, and religion. I soon learned about Chaudhry Rahmat Ali, the man who coined the name "Pakistan." Rahmat Ali belonged to the cast of characters—along with Mohammad Iqbal, the intellectual dubbed Pakistan's "national poet," and Mohammad Ali Jinnah, a gaunt, sickly barrister—who helped to form Pakistan. Historians regarded Jinnah as the founding statesmen and Iqbal as the founding philosopher. Rahmat Ali, however, enjoyed less influence *inside* Pakistan (he was living in England during the Partition) and most accounts of Pakistan's creation have confined him to a secondary role. "Official Pakistan," wrote a columnist in *Dawn*, an English-language daily newspaper, "has apparently treated Rahmat Ali as the lunatic uncle who has needed to be locked up secretly in the attic."

Rahmat Ali's fame stemmed from a 1933 pamphlet he penned titled "Now or Never; Are We to Live or Perish For Ever?" He opened the treatise:

> "At this solemn hour in the history of India, when British and Indian statesmen are laying the foundations of a Federation Constitution for that land, we address this appeal to you, in the name of our common heritage, on behalf of our thirty million Muslim brethren who live in PAKSTAN —by which we mean the five Northern units of India, viz.: Punjab, North-West Frontier Province (Afghan Province), Kashmir, Sind and Baluchistan—for your sympathy and support in our grim and fateful struggle against political crucifixion and complete annihilation.

Thus, the name PAKSTAN made its debut. But it was more than just an acronym for the composite Muslim-majority provinces in northern India. In Urdu, "Pak" means "pure," and thus "PAKSTAN" meant "Land of the Pure."

Rahmat Ali might have coined the name, but he wasn't the first to pitch the idea of combining Punjab, the North-West Frontier Province, Sindh, and Baluchistan into a single political entity. Three years before Rahmat Ali's pamphlet circulated, Iqbal, acknowledged as a towering intellect even in his own day, had proposed this imagined configuration, which was to fall under the umbrella of an All-India Federation. But Rahmat Ali wanted total independence from India. An upstart student radical, twenty years junior to Iqbal, Rahmat Ali noted, with due politeness and respect, that his demand was "basically different" from the one forwarded by the revered philosopher and poet. "There can be no peace and tranquility in the land if we, the Muslims, are duped into a Hindu-dominated Federation where we cannot be the masters of our own destiny and captains of our own souls," Rahmat Ali wrote.

Rahmat Ali described the fate of Indian Muslims as having arrived at an apocalyptic intersection: "We are face to face with a first-rate tragedy, the like of which has not been seen in the long and eventful history of Islam." What happened to the days when they were "custodians of the glory of Islam in India and defenders of its frontiers"? he wondered. Rahmat Ali added, in closing, "We have a still greater future before us, if only our soul can be saved from the perpetual bondage of slavery forced in an All-India Federation. Let us make no mistake about it. The issue is now or never. Either we live or perish for ever."

SINCE RAHMAT ALI issued his ultimatum — "to live or perish for ever" — this question has remained foremost in the minds of Pakistanis. Millions died during the communal riots that punctuated Pakistan's violent birth pangs in late summer and early fall of 1947. Jinnah, the slender and sophisticated lawyer, succumbed to tuberculosis just thirteen months after founding the country. An assassination in 1951 felled the first prime minister. Civil war tore the country in half in 1971. Military coups staged in 1958, 1968, 1977, and 1999 all promised to "save the nation" from depraved and corrupt civilian leadership, while all eventually becoming depraved and corrupt military dictatorships. In 2007, pro-Taliban insurgents employed dozens of suicide bombers in a terror campaign that killed nearly one thousand people — including former prime minister Benazir Bhutto.

But what else, besides chronic instability, defined Pakistan? Everything I read and heard from the leading roster of Pakistani experts sounded pretty stark: over a period of sixty years, the country had lunged from one crisis to the next, triggered by coups, countercoups, snap elections, and a whole smattering of contorted political configurations. Just keeping track of names and election years was enough to daunt even the most dedicated history buff; serving heads of state, at various points, called themselves prime minister, president, general, chief executive, governor-general, field marshall, and martial law administrator. From what I gathered, there were a few essential things to know about Pakistan: the army was perpetually in charge, the intelligence agencies were a brooding and ubiquitous force, the Islamists threatened to take over, ethnic problems portended more Balkanization, corruption plagued human interaction, and a modest arsenal of nuclear weapons all combined to make Pakistan the most dysfunctional — and most dangerous — country in the world.

And yet, I desperately wanted to understand not just theories about

Pakistan and how it operated, but Pakistanis and how they lived. I craved the tactile experience of Pakistan—anticipating the burning summer heat, the greasy, spicy food, the horrendous, maddening traffic—and the unexpected conversations with unlikely partners. These cravings led me to befriend, upon arriving, a radical cleric (who later became an enemy of the state and was killed), to pine for the smell of tear gas (because it assured me that I was sufficiently close to the action), and to sneak into a Taliban camp tucked in a valley near the Afghanistan border to witness a public lashing. (None of this required any special cunning or skill on my part; oftentimes, I would simply take public buses to places far from home and then start asking questions.) When I first arrived, I even sought out seedy hotels. In Karachi, I used to stay at a musty low-rise just because it seemed more *authentic*. After a bombing at the Karachi Marriott Hotel in March 2006, a Pakistani friend joked to me that my hotel might have been the safest in the city, owing to the fact that "al-Qaeda stays there when they're in town."

There were plenty of things that I would have never found in a book and would have to learn on my own. Like the hazards of *pan*, a chew made from betel leaf. In Karachi, many men—and some women—passed time by packing a wad into the side of their mouths, which they gnawed on like a cud, extracting a red juice that stained their teeth and lips. Every so often, when their mouths filled with juice, they spat. No one warned me about how bus passengers leaned their heads out of the window and, without looking, would spit a thick, arching trail of red, minty juice down below. Exposed pedestrians and passing motorcyclists told horror stories.

Pan presented a second dilemma for me—of being mistaken for blood. When I arrived in Pakistan, the country convulsed with riots and protests against the allegedly blasphemous cartoons published in several European newspapers, including one that depicted the Prophet Mohammad with a bomb stuffed in his turban. Islamists had poured into the streets, attacking anything they thought represented the decadent West. They burned banks and KFCs, along with hundreds of cars and motorcycles. Paramilitary Rangers parked their pickup trucks, equipped with machine guns, in front of every Pizza Hut and McDonald's in Pakistan. After a day cooped up inside my hotel, I ventured out for a walk.

I had gone about a hundred yards when I noticed crimson-colored splotches on the sidewalk and roads. I assumed bloodied rioters, or perhaps dead chickens, left the splotches.

I eventually returned to my hotel and spent the next three days convinced that Karachi was the bloodiest city in the world. Then, one afternoon, while descending a flight of stairs, I noticed that the same shade of red that I saw everywhere in the streets also stained the walls of the stairwell. I spun around quickly to face a Pakistani friend. "It's *pan!*" I exclaimed, feeling a profound sense of relief. The streets, after all, were not paved with blood, and butchers didn't just drag their headless chickens through the alleys. I was humbled. I had a lot to learn.

OVER THE COURSE of twenty-three months, I traversed Rahmat Ali's "PAKSTAN," with the exception of Kashmir, the "K" that never joined. But I did travel to Bangladesh, which Rahmat Ali proposed calling Bangistan and which acceded to Pakistan in 1947. (It seceded twenty-four years later.) My travels took me as far south as the coast of the Arabian Sea and as far north as the glaciers and towering peaks bordering China. I journeyed to the border of archrival India, west to the restive tribal areas, and everywhere in between. Pakistan covered a landmass larger than Utah, Colorado, and New Mexico combined. Diversity characterized its land and its 170 million people. A friend once quipped that there wasn't just one Pakistan, but that each province represented its own, distinct Pakistan. This book is—in part—my humble attempt to explain the many identities and histories that exist throughout Pakistan.

The two years that I traveled through Pakistan were a particularly turbulent time. President Pervez Musharraf lost his mojo, and the Taliban gained theirs. Lawyers in black suits protested in the streets, and former prime minister Benazir Bhutto was assassinated. "You are really seeing history in the making," my grandfather once told me on the phone. "But what's the problem with that place?" Everyone could see Pakistan making daily headlines with riots and bombs. But why? Why were the Islamists such a threat? Why did tensions between the country's many ethnic groups never disappear, as Rahmat Ali and Jinnah and Iqbal had hoped? How did Osama bin Laden and his al-Qaeda henchmen make their home in the tribal areas, with so many people looking for them? And why, more than seventy years after Rahmat Ali first proposed the question, did Pakistanis, on a daily basis, still face an existential dilemma: to live or perish forever? I tried to consider these questions during every journey and every interview. I hope any answers provided are of some use, for all of our understanding.

SINCE RETURNING, people have often asked me how I got around the country—how I accessed places, like Taliban camps, where no other foreigners hung out. After all, at more than six feet tall, with blond hair and fair skin, I couldn't exactly pass for a Pakistani. So I did what I could, wearing local clothes, adopting local customs, and learning Urdu. I had showed up in Pakistan speaking enough Urdu to start, but never quite finish, a conversation. Within a few months, however, I was reading Urdu newspapers, watching Urdu television, and traveling on public buses without a translator. Throughout my time in Pakistan I was amazed that—and never fully understood why—people were so inviting and generous with their time. Some felt compelled by cultural customs of hospitality. Others wanted to get a message out. Many, I suspected, were just intrigued by the presence of a tall, blond American who spoke Urdu and ambled about in a *shalwar kameez*, the ubiquitous baggy-pants-and-tunic outfit.

But Pakistani culture was about more than language or clothes. It thrived on connections and contacts, evinced by Majed's intervention on our behalf the night when the police showed up. Not all of my friends, however, were the kind that I would have brought home for Christmas. Considering that my father is a Marine general and my younger brother a Marine lieutenant, I can say with some confidence that Abdul Rashid Ghazi would not have been a welcome guest at the family dining room table. Ghazi, a pro-Taliban leader in Islamabad, ran Lal Masjid, or the Red Mosque, with his brother. In July 2007, the siblings gained international notoriety when they staged a rebellion in the center of the capital that lasted ten days and led to hundreds of deaths, including Ghazi's own. Yet I learned more from Ghazi, and he opened more doors for me, than perhaps any other single person.

My relationship with Ghazi dated back to the spring of 2006, when a Pakistani journalist who was well acquainted with the jihadis mused: "If the Taliban ever come to power in Pakistan, Ghazi could become the *amir*." (*Amir* is the Arabic word for commander.) His prediction stuck with me; who wouldn't want to meet a future leader, right? Previously, the government had charged Ghazi with orchestrating a terrorist plot to bomb the Parliament, Army House, and U.S. embassy. After multiple suicide bomb attacks in London on July 7, 2005, Tony Blair pressured Musharraf to crack down on the militant madrassas in Pakistan. (One of the bombers had spent time in one just before the attack.) Musharraf ordered troops to barge into Ghazi's all-female madrassa one night. The raid turned into a fiasco, and the next day newspapers printed pictures of bloodied girls. Ghazi emerged as a leading figure in the underground, pro-Taliban movement coalescing in Pakistan.

But to meet him I needed a reference first.

The intermediary would be Khalid Khawaja, a former intelligence officer, air force pilot, and self-described confidante of Osama bin Laden. On at least one previous occasion, involving the *Wall Street Journal* reporter Daniel Pearl, Khawaja had tried to facilitate an American journalist's meeting with Islamic militants. Following Pearl's kidnapping and murder, which Pearl's wife suspected Khawaja of being involved in, a tarnished reputation now preceded him. I met Khawaja for lunch one day at an upscale café in Islamabad. I notified several people beforehand, so that if I never returned, people would know whom I was last with. Khawaja showed up on time. He was wiry thin, with a long beard and intense, vibrating eyes.

"Why do you want to meet Ghazi?" he asked.

I said I wanted to understand more about his thinking, his vision for the future, and the Taliban.

"After Musharraf, whenever that may be, Pakistan will be like Iran was in 1979," Khawaja said. "The only difference will be that, after our revolution, there will be no U.S. embassy left."

Khawaja made me feel very uncomfortable, and I was eager to hurry through lunch and get to the point. "So, can you introduce me to Ghazi?"

He said he would try. Then he stared across the table into my eyes. "But if I tell you that Ghazi is not available, don't go trying to meet with him anyways behind my back. You understand?"

"Yes, of course."

"I told Daniel Pearl that Sheikh Gilani"—the jihadi ideologue Pearl was trying to meet when kidnapped—"was off-limits, and not to try meeting him. But he still tried," Khawaja said. He shrugged his shoulders, as if being kidnapped and killed was a logical, mild consequence of side-stepping him. I took the statement as a threat, went home, and waited for Khawaja to call. A week later, he did.

"Ghazi has agreed to see you."

I FIGURED THAT if Khawaja paid deference to Ghazi, then Ghazi must be one radical dude. The first time I visited him at the Red Mosque, I told Rikki to send out a search party if I wasn't home in an hour. When I got there, I was led from a reception area through a narrow alley to Ghazi's residence. Two madrassa students, in their twenties, blocked the entrance to Ghazi's door. They were sharpening a sword, one gripping the handle while the other rubbed a stone up and down the blade.

My escort, another madrassa student, spoke up. "Ghazi is expecting him," he said. The two parted. Ghazi opened the door. He looked a bit — of all people — like Jerry Garcia. He wore oval-shaped, wire-rimmed glasses, had a gray, fist-length beard, and sported curly hair that flipped wildly around his ears and neckline. Ghazi even had the former Grateful Dead front man's easy smile and chill demeanor.

"Are you going to use that sword on me?" I joked, hoping that Ghazi could appreciate humor. He laughed. Before long, we were talking about his meeting with Osama bin Laden in Kandahar, back in 1998. My mind flashed between Khawaja, Pearl, the sword, and Osama. My gaze drifted to the Kalashnikov propped against one wall, and the pistol lying on the pillow beside Ghazi. He noticed.

"Relax, my friend," he said. "Jihad is a defensive system. You should sit here now and feel safe. Do you?" I swallowed a lump in my throat. "It would be different if you had come in, holding a weapon and making demands that: 'I want to meet Ghazi.' Then I would be a different man. But these are Islamic values. I have given you refuge. I have given you my word. You are in my protection."

Of course, bestowing confidence in a guy who boasted of palling around with bin Laden in his heyday carried certain risks. But Ghazi was more articulate than any other Islamist I had met in Pakistan, and spoke — in English — as though he had nothing to hide. I found his candor and contacts invaluable. When I once asked him about his links with

Abdul Rashid Ghazi, in his office at the Red Mosque, in April 2007. Photo: Nicholas Schmidle

the dangerous jihadi organization—Harakat ul-Jihadi Islami—that spawned most of the others, he responded, "We know each other well. We have a good relationship. They love me. And I love them."

Connections with someone like Ghazi could take you deep into a situation, or be able to get you out of one; dropping such a name in one place could save your life, and in another put it in further danger. But these were risks worth taking. Pakistanis had faced the dire option—"to live or perish for ever"—for decades. If I wanted to understand their country, I would have to do the same.

CHAPTER 1

"TO THESE GUYS, YOU ARE ALL INFIDELS"

THE THOUGHT OF BEING KIDNAPPED CROSSED MY MIND MORE THAN once. We trailed a member of an outlawed Islamic militant group back to his madrassa. He said we would never find the place on our own and so he offered to lead us there. Rafi drove and I sat in the passenger seat. I had met Rafi, a fortysomething journalist, about an hour earlier at the Karachi Press Club. The club teemed with hacks, drunks, and charlatans, no matter the time of day. I was never sure exactly how to classify Rafi who, during later excursions, sipped from a bottle of booze stashed in the backseat of his car. But he knew Karachi well, and he brought another pair of eyes—and years of experience—to detect when something was off. That, and he had previously met Qari Shafiqur Rahman, a member of Sipah-e-Sahaba. Rahman rode on a motorcycle a few meters ahead of us. Sipah-e-Sahaba, or Army for the Companions of the Prophet, was one of the biggest Sunni jihadi militias in Pakistan.

A few minutes earlier, we had all rendezvoused in front of a small, oil-splattered garage and auto parts store beside the main road. "We are here," Rafi said into his phone, to Shafiqur on the other end. "In the blue car."

Shafiqur steered onto a dirt path behind the garage that connected to a maze of unmarked tracks in a bedraggled slum of Karachi. At each juncture, Shafiqur swiveled his husky frame to check that we were still close behind. While this gesture was somewhat comforting, with each passing minute, and each new turn, I became more and more lost, confused which direction we had come from or how we would get out. I wish I could have been relaxed enough at the time to appreciate the trip as a metaphor for my experience in Pakistan—led by strangers into an ever more mystifying labyrinth. Instead, as Shafiqur took us deeper into the slum, I wondered anxiously—though perhaps more sensibly—where we were going and what awaited us there. Four years earlier, Daniel Pearl had been kidnapped and killed while seeking out jihadis in Karachi. His ghost hovered over the city.

Shafiqur sputtered past rows of drab, baked-mud homes with rivers of sewage flowing nearby, and he eventually parked his motorcycle in front of a one-story brick structure. He hopped off his bike and stood, a man of medium height, wearing a white shalwar kameez and crocheted prayer cap. He pointed to a sliver of shade against a building for Rafi to park under.

"Should I say that I am Canadian or something?" I asked Rafi, just before we opened the doors.

Rafi laughed. "It doesn't matter. To these guys, you are all infidels," he said. "And anyway, it will be interesting to see his reaction when we say that you are an American."

SHAFIQUR, as it turned out, considered Americans, Canadians, and all other "crusaders" legitimate targets, but he saved most of his vitriol for Shi'ites. His outfit, Sipah-e-Sahaba, had carved out a niche for itself among the myriad jihadi groups in Pakistan by campaigning to make Pakistan an explicitly Sunni state. (Sunnis make up roughly 80 percent of Pakistanis, with Shi'ites comprising about 15 percent.) They branded Shi'ites as *kafir*, or infidels, and frequently killed them.

Theological differences had split the Islamic community into Sunnis and Shia more than fourteen hundred years ago. A fight broke out after the Prophet Mohammad's death, in 632, over who should succeed him as leader of the Muslims. Those who became known as Sunnis argued that the title should be given to one of the *sahabas*, or companions, of the Prophet; they nominated Abu Bakr. Those who became known as Shi'ites contended that the Prophet had already tapped Ali, his son-in-law, for the role, and that Mohammad wished to keep the leadership within the family. Shia Ali, or the Party of Ali, lost the debate. The first three caliphs, or leaders, came and went, but Ali remained out of power. When he finally did assume the title of caliph, a chunk of Muslims refused to acknowledge his rule, and the schism widened. A Sunni assassin eventually stabbed Ali with a poison-tipped sword.

Twenty years after Ali's death, with the Shi'ites committed to armed opposition against the majority Sunni leadership, Ali's youngest son, Hussein, set out to avenge his father's death. The Shia believed that Hussein belonged to the same infallible lineage of imams, or leaders, as did the Prophet Mohammad and Ali. And so, as legend goes, Hussein mounted a white horse along with seventy-two of his male and female followers and marched toward Kufa, a city in modern-day Iraq where his rivals sat. On the way, a detachment of nearly four thousand Sunni warriors met Hussein in the desert, near the Euphrates River, outside of a town called Karbala. For a week, the larger army besieged Hussein's camp, denying them access to water. On the tenth day of the Islamic month of Muharram, Hussein led his withered, outmanned force into battle. Hussein was killed, and his forces lost everything—including the horses, the women, and the children. To this day, Shi'ites consider Karbala the final, decisive break between the two communities.

Sunni Arabs soon began expanding their empire beyond the Arabian peninsula. In 711, a teenage Arab general named Mohammad bin Qasim landed his invading force on the beach near present-day Karachi, along the coastline of the Arabian Sea, and quickly proceeded north up the Indus River. Qasim was more interested in seizing on economic opportunities, however, than religious ones, and a few hundred years later, Shia missionaries swept into the area, proselytizing their own interpretation of Islam. The pendulum swung back and forth for centuries, as Sunni and Shia preachers competed for followers. Those who attracted the largest following, the Sufi mystics who arrived from Central Asia and the Middle East, straddled the ideological line between Sunni and Shia beliefs. They often synthesized local religious and cultural traditions, such as Buddhism and Hinduism, with Islamic precepts.

During the period of the British Raj in the nineteenth century, a handful of new sects within the Sunni tradition emerged. Some historians contend that this development reflected the British goal to divide and conquer their colonial subjects. Three out of the four dominant sects of Sunni Islam in modern Pakistan—Deobandi, Bareilvi, and ahle-Hadith—formed in the late nineteenth century. Contemporary Sunni militancy in Pakistan, exemplified by the Taliban and groups such as Sipah-e-Sahaba, all trace their ideology back to Darul Uloom Deoband, a madrassa in Deoband, India. From the outset, the Deobandis have been virulently anti-Shia. They deem the Shi'ites adoration of Ali, Hussein, and the other imams as *bi'da*, the Arabic term for "innovation," suggesting deviance from orthodox beliefs.

Despite the historical tensions, sectarian differences played little role at the time Pakistan came into being. For instance, Mohammad Ali Jinnah, the country's founding father, was a Shia. "The Muslim League was as Shia as it was Sunni. It was a common movement. There was no rift in the early years," explained Husain Jafri, a political scientist at the Aga Khan University in Karachi. I asked him how these tensions escalated to the point where they are today. "You can't separate sectarianism in Pakistan from global politics."

Jafri described the Islamic Revolution in Iran as the starting point. In early 1979, Ayatollah Khomeini overthrew the shah of Iran. Khomeini touted the significance of Iran's revolution, and emboldened Shi'ites around the world to overthrow their own leaders. Pakistan's Shia minority seemed eager to follow his lead. To counter the spread of anti-American, revolutionary Shi'ism, the United States had teamed up with Saudi Arabia, Iraq, and Pakistan, an effort that even included arming Saddam Hussein in his war against Iran. "After the downfall of the Shah, the Americans would do anything to stop Khomeini," Jafri added.

Pakistan's military dictator at the time, General Zia ul Haq, promoted an assertive Islamization agenda at home, one tailored for Sunnis. For instance, he made prayers compulsory in government offices. What's the big deal, you ask? Well, Shi'ites pray differently from Sunnis, and they pray fewer times a day. Therefore, when they didn't show up for mandatory prayers, co-workers suspected that they were either insufficiently pious or infidels. That was just the beginning. In 1980, Zia imposed *zakat*, an annual 2.5 percent tax, specifically spelled out in Sunni theology. Shi'ites already paid their own kind of religious duty, directly to the ayatollahs. They weren't happy about getting double-dipped, and they marched on Islamabad. Zia eventually conceded to their demands and waived the zakat requirement for the Shia community.

Meanwhile, jihad raged against the Soviet army in Afghanistan, heavily supported by the United States, Saudi Arabia, and Pakistan. Besides the obvious goal of expelling the Soviet army, the Americans, Saudis, and Pakistan's Sunni establishment saw another opportunity in arming and training young men for jihad. Part of the indoctrination process in the jihadi camps along the Afghan border included a reassessment of who—or what—constituted a true Muslim.

Afghans fighting alongside the Soviet army? Infidels.

Kashmiris supporting the Indian army's occupation of Muslim-majority Kashmir? Infidels.

Shi'ites acting at the behest of Iran? Infidels.

"You can't just tell these guys, 'Go to Kashmir! But don't go to Karachi,'" a political analyst in Islamabad once told me. In other words, upon being brainwashed into the ways of jihad, these young men simply couldn't be reintegrated into a peaceful society. Was a neighbor who missed his prayers preoccupied? Or a Communist? A Shia? By the middle of the 1980s, with Pakistan awash in funds, rigid ideologies, and growing anti-Shia sentiments, Sipah-e-Sahaba was formed.

In February 1995, just before prayers at dawn, Sipah-e-Sahaba militants overran a Shia mosque in Karachi. They were heavily armed, and swiftly rounded up the fifteen worshippers present. The gunmen ordered them to line up against a wall and to remove their wallets and wristwatches. They sprayed the lineup with bullets, tossed the watches and wallets into a bag, and left. Eleven years later, I asked the brother of one of the victims if he thought Sipah-e-Sahaba was gunning for someone in particular; several prominent doctors and businessmen were among those murdered that morning. "They didn't have any idea who was inside," he said. "They just knew they were Shia."

When the Taliban took over Afghanistan in 1996, Sipah-e-Sahaba congratulated them and offered their support. A few years later, as the Taliban conducted purges against the Hazaras, a Shia minority who lived in the central highlands, Sipah-e-Sahaba members reportedly participated in the massacres. (The Hazaras reside in the region around Bamiyan, the site of the Buddhist statues the Taliban later demolished.) "The Taliban had a very good government," Shafiqur told me. "What was their mistake? Why are they being punished now? They were doing good work."

Following the American invasion of Afghanistan in the autumn of 2001, the distinction between the Taliban and sectarian outfits like Sipah-e-Sahaba grew ever more muddled. Evidently, both believed that Mullah Omar, the head of the Taliban regime that ruled Afghanistan from 1996 to 2001, and his cohorts represented the model form of governance. Soon, reports circulated of Sipah-e-Sahaba members training in camps throughout Pakistan's tribal areas, preparing to cross the border and fight against American and NATO forces. Suddenly, they all became anti-American insurgents. They shared constituencies, too. Every Friday outside of the Red Mosque in Islamabad, teenage boys hawked jihadi newspapers in one hand and copies of Sipah-e-Sahaba's treatise in the other.

Meanwhile, sectarianism became one of the world media's most common vocabulary words, owing to the situation in Iraq, where Sunnis and Shias were killing one another in droves. Sunni leaders warned about Iran's aspirations to achieve regional hegemony and create a "Shia crescent" across the Middle East, extending through Lebanon, Iraq, northern Saudi Arabia, Bahrain, and Iran. In February 2006, a suicide bomber, belonging to the Sunni-run al-Qaeda in Iraq, destroyed the al-Askari mosque in the city of Samarra, one of the holiest sites in Shia Islam. The bombing sparked violent retaliations in Iraq—and throughout the rest of the Middle East. In the aftermath of the Samarra bombing, I wondered if sectarian tensions that originated in the Middle East would, once again, be felt in Pakistan. Would Saudi Arabia and Iran begin fighting a sectarian proxy war in the streets of Karachi? To find out, I wanted to meet those who represented both sides of the sectarian divide. Sipah-e-Sahaba, at the vanguard of Sunni sectarianism in Pakistan, seemed a good place to start.

HAVING LED US into his one-room madrassa, Shafiqur seemed delighted to hear that I was an American. He promptly got on the phone and called for a couple of chicken salad sandwiches, a plate of samosas, and cold 7UPs to be delivered. "We have a guest who has come from far," he said into the phone. As we sat on the floor, I asked Shafiqur some basic questions—the closest thing I had to icebreakers—about the madrassa.

How many students? More than a hundred.

When did it open? 1999.

He seemed relaxed, so I steered the conversation toward jihad. Apparently, Shafiqur noticed that my tone had changed somewhat. His own voice doubled in volume. "What is wrong with jihad?" he asked. "We teach jihad as part of our teachings of the Holy Quran. Jihad is used to bring peace to the world, like the Taliban brought peace to Afghanistan. And if anyone usurps our rights or threatens our faith, then there will be jihad."

"What about the Shia? Do you consider them a threat to your faith?"

"I don't consider Shia as Muslims," Shafiqur replied, without a pause. "They are kafir."

Shafiqur then reached into his desk and removed a stack of photographs, which puzzled me a little, since ultraorthodox Sunnis typically consider depictions of the human body to be *haram*. But Shafiqur proudly flipped through the photos, which showed him standing beside Sipah-e-Sahaba luminaries from Jhang, a town in central Punjab where Sipah-e-Sahaba originated. A sign hangs over the entrance to the Sipah-e-Sahaba mosque there saying: IT IS FORBIDDEN FOR SHIA TO ENTER, OR FOR SHIA TO BE MENTIONED INSIDE THIS MOSQUE. Most of the leaders in the pictures were now dead, victims of assassination by Shia hit squads.

One of Shafiqur's students walked into the room. The boy was in his mid-teens, with eyes the color of mahogany. His family lived in Punjab. I asked why he came all this way to attend Shafiqur's madrassa.

"Quran is everything to me," he said, either not quite understanding my question or just reciting his own prepared answer. "Since I started reading the Quran, I stopped watching cartoons. I have no wish to be a pilot or an engineer. I will become an *alim*"—Islamic scholar—"like my father one day, inshallah."

Rafi spoke up and asked the boy, "How do you feel in the presence of this American?"

"I feel fine, because he is also made by Allah. He is a guest, and deserves the same treatment other guests would receive," the teenager said. The even tone of his voice and maturity of his answer shocked me.

"But I also have strong emotions against the Americans. I have read the newspapers and know what they do to Muslims," he continued. "And one day, I will become a *mujahid*"—or holy warrior.

Shafiqur looked at me with a wide, satisfied smile. Clearly the boy was one of his prized pupils.

Rafi asked the boy what he was waiting for; there were plenty of opportunities for jihad at that very moment.

"I am too young to be recruited now," he replied. "But when the time is right, someone will come to me, and inshallah, I will go to jihad."

THE SHIA HAVE their own militant wings. In October 2003, suspected Shia opponents gunned down Azam Tariq on a highway outside of Islamabad. Tariq had led Sipah-e-Sahaba for more than a decade. News of his murder fueled days of rioting and led to Islamabad's only cinema being burned to the ground. A year later, on the anniversary of Tariq's death, hundreds of Sipah-e-Sahaba supporters gathered to pray and commemorate his life in a park in Multan, a city in Punjab, not far from Jhang. As they bowed their heads, a car bomb ripped through the crowd, killing more than forty people. Again, Shia extremists were blamed.

Sectarian attacks had proceeded like this for years. It seemed a self-perpetuating and endless cycle. Local Sunni extremists blamed Iran for funding Shia groups, and local Shia extremists blamed Saudi Arabia for funding Sunni groups like Sipah-e-Sahaba. Yet the longer I spent in Pakistan, the more I realized that these ideologies were being hardened without any encouragement from outside. Sunni friends of mine, who dressed in suits and held respectable jobs, casually described Shia as apostates. And prominent Shia businessmen, like one I met in Karachi, used cell phone ring tones that blared an extremist preacher disparaging the sahaba for not recognizing Imam Ali's right to lead the Muslim community in the seventh century.

In January 2002, former president Pervez Musharraf outlawed Sipah-e-Sahaba, along with a handful of other jihadi organizations, including the Shia militia, Sipah-e-Mohammad. "Religious militias calling themselves Sipahs, Jaishes, and Lashkars cannot exist parallel to the army," Musharraf said at the time, referring to the various Arabic words for "army" used by the jihadi groups. "Our army is the only Sipah and Lashkar in Pakistan." By banning Sipah-e-Sahaba, Musharraf closed their offices, froze their funds, proscribed their publications, and forced prominent members like Shafiqur underground. In many cases, however, the banned groups simply changed their names and resumed their activities;

Sipah-e-Sahaba was renamed Millat-i-Islami Pakistan, or the Islamic Nation.

Musharraf also hoped to cool sectarian tensions by overseeing the formation of the MMA, a coalition of Islamist parties created just before the October 2002 parliamentary elections. The MMA, or Muttahida Majles Amal (United Action Front), consisted of six parties—five Sunni and one Shia. Ijaz ul Haq, the minister of religious affairs, told me one day in his office that though "they might differ politically at times, the MMA has done a good job of bringing the sects together." Ijaz was the son of General Zia ul Haq. The irony of his appointment to such a cabinet position was lost on few; father had built thousands of madrassas and fostered sectarianism, while son now tried to eradicate sectarianism and reform the madrassas. To gauge Ijaz's own sincerity, I asked him if he ever attended communal prayers at Shia mosques, perhaps as an act of solidarity and goodwill. "I go to the mosque for personal, emotional satisfaction," he told me. "I won't go to a Shia mosque myself. I can show my respect for Shia in other ways."

Not everyone was convinced of the MMA's accomplishments. Allama Abbas Kumaili, a respected Shia preacher in Karachi, told me that the MMA was "just a photo session." "They have no Shias in the assembly. And while they claim to represent all, they are still dominated by one sect." Kumaili wondered how the government could trumpet any record of success at normalizing sectarian relations when Shia leaders, including the chief of the one Shi'ite party that belonged to the MMA, had been assassinated. Every year during Ashura, Sunni extremists bombed Shia processions, killing dozens each time. (Ashura, the tenth day of Muharram, marked the day Shi'ites believed that Imam Hussein died near Karbala.) During the Shia processions, Sipah-e-Sahaba activists walked alongside, yelling obscenities and cursing the Shia imams. Sipah-e-Sahaba, in turn, claimed that Shi'ites disgraced the names of the sahaba during such marches. The processions often attracted violence.

Kumaili told me about a big Shia gathering the following week. He would address thousands of people there. "Meet me at my house," he said, "and you can come."

I KNEW I had reached close to Kumaili's home when I saw the giant black flag in the middle of the road. Shi'ites usually wore black to show their perpetual state of mourning for Ali, Hussein, and the other imams. Kumaili lived across the street from an *imambargah*, a congregation hall where Shia gathered for special ceremonies. The imambargah shimmered from thousands of tiny mirrors that lined the exterior walls. Concrete roadblocks had been laid in front of the imambargah and throughout the neighborhood. Over the past few decades, as sectarian violence had increased in Karachi, the Shia bought all the property around their mosques and imambargahs. Predominantly Shia ghettos now existed throughout the city. This way, during Muharram, locals could better identify outsiders—and potential suicide bombers.

Posters of Ayatollah Khomeini and Ayatollah Khamenei, his successor in Iran, were plastered on walls at a couple of intersections, another giveaway that I had entered a Shia neighborhood. I later asked Kumaili about his relationship with the Iranian regime.

"Since I was not educated in Qom," he said, referring to the famed city south of Tehran where Shia clerics often studied to become ayatollahs, "the Iranians don't expect much from me. Besides, when we were being killed, where were they? None of them raised their voice for us. No Iranian leader ever supported us."

But surely, I thought, he would at least concede that Iran's revolution had been a landmark achievement; almost all Shi'ites, if not most Muslims, did.

"What did we, as Pakistani Shia, get from this revolution?" he asked rhetorically. "Sipah-e-Sahaba never existed before this revolution. Ever since then, we have just been killed."

Kumaili's oldest son greeted me at the door when I entered the home and, before even introducing himself, handed me a Palmcorder. "You know how to use it, right?" he asked. I stared back at him quizzically.

Kumaili, who was getting dressed in a room down the hall, overheard our conversation. He popped his head out, wearing a black cloak and a lambskin cap, to try to clarify the matter. He stood well over six feet, with a bulbous nose and large, floppy ears. "I told the hosts of today's event that you are a Canadian videographer making a documentary," he said. In the neighborhood where we were heading, a few American journalists, suspected of being spies, had reportedly been beaten up in the past. "So I thought you should have a video camera."

"But"—I fumbled about for an answer for a second, as I really didn't like the idea of fibbing about my identity, but wanted to show respect to Kumaili—"can't we just say that I am an American journalist writing a story?"

Kumaili eventually conceded, and told his son to keep the Palmcorder. We soon loaded into several cars, led and trailed by heavily armed police trucks. Amid the wail of sirens, Kumaili told me about the two assassination attempts he survived, both of which he attributed to Sipah-e-Sahaba. "I know my name is still on their hit lists," he said.

Posters of the bearded faces of Iranian leaders greeted us when we arrived at the Shia neighborhood of Jaafar-i-Tayyar. As an individual, Kumaili might have had reservations about the Iranian regime, but Shia politics in Pakistan were invariably connected to Iranian politics. One poster showed the face of Ayatollah Khomeini floating in the heavens; a lightning bolt shot from a cloud and incinerated an American flag. In the center of the neighborhood, American and Israeli flags had been painted on the ground so that everyone who passed would stomp on them. Next to the flags someone had painted DOWN WITH THE USA, reminding me of the anti-American murals in Tehran.

Kumaili ducked into a home to rest for a few moments before he began to speak. Black curtains covered the windows of the home. Inside, a painting hung on the wall depicting Imam Hussein with dark, flowing locks and what looked like mascara around his eyes. Another painting portrayed Hussein astride his white horse on the edge of a cliff, looking out over the ocean at a setting sun. Lance wounds covered the horse, as if they had just emerged from battle. The sky and the water were both the color of blood oranges.

A dozen neighborhood leaders and student activists soon joined us. The students belonged to the Imamia Student Organization, a radical Shi'ite student party. While we sat drinking tea, the conversation briefly turned to Sipah-e-Sahaba. One of the students mentioned that the Sunni outfit had been quiet in Karachi of late. He asked Kumaili if he knew why.

"They are quiet," Kumaili replied, "but don't be deceived. Nothing has changed. They are still around. They are just waiting." (One month later, bombers tried to assassinate Allama Hassan Turabi, a prominent Shia politician in Karachi. Just two months after that, a suicide bomber killed him.)

Soon the door opened and a man announced that Kumaili could

speak whenever he desired. Kumaili stood up, adjusting his long black smock and straightening his black lambskin cap. He led us through the door and out into the crowd, past young boys wearing strips of white cloth, dotted with fake blood, around their heads. The day marked the last of the forty-day period of mourning when Shi'ites remember the death of Imam Hussein. Holding an exterminator's jug and hose, a man circulated through the crowd, spraying rosewater into the air. Having pushed through the crowd, Kumaili eventually scaled the *minbar*, a small podium. His speech focused on the seventh-century narrative of Hussein and his followers being slaughtered in the desert. "We can never forget the sacrifices that Hussein made!" he exclaimed.

Then I heard a sniffle. And some weeping. I was sitting in the front row, so I tried to be subtle as I looked for the source of the crying. I turned around to find thousands of grown men with tears running down their cheeks. I had heard that Shi'ites were emotional compared to their Sunni counterparts, but I watched with amazement as Kumaili, in reciting the story of Hussein, brought to the crowd fresh outrage and grief from as far back as the seventh century. The man beside me banged his fist against his forehead.

Evening soon fell, and the afternoon light faded to black. Kumaili finished his sermon as sobbing worshippers dried their tears, stood up, and moved to the center of the neighborhood, where the American and Israeli flags had been painted—and where a towering black flag fluttered in the gentle sea breeze wafting through the city. Dozens of shirtless young men gathered around the flagpole to sing a haunting, lyrical version of Hussein's martyrdom, a cappella, in Urdu: "Oh Hussein, oh Hussein! Karbala is with us forever!"

The shirtless ones began beating on their chests with closed fists. The thud and thumps of slamming against their breastbone, coupled with the crashes of smacking fists against skin, created what sounded like a rolling, pummeling line of bass drum hits and cymbals. Their chests quickly turned pink and began to bruise. They sweated. Some bled. These were the same young men who, forty days earlier on Ashura, had performed self-flagellation and whipped themselves with chains. Their backs showed the scars to prove it. Puffy, torn skin crisscrossed their shoulders.

"Ugh! Hussein! Ugh! Hussein" they chanted.

I looked through the viewfinder of the camera on my dinky cell

Children wearing headbands splattered with fake blood at the *majles*, or congregation, where Allama Abbas Kumaili spoke. PHOTO: NICHOLAS SCHMIDLE

phone, doing a pitiful impression of a Canadian videographer. As I leaned on the tips of my toes, marveling at the crowd of men, I felt a tap on my elbow. A fat teenage boy wearing all black stood beside me. He asked me what I was doing there.

"I am a friend of Allama Abbas Kumaili," I replied.

I was wearing a black shalwar kameez, like everyone else, and answered his questions in Urdu. He cocked his head sideways, apparently more than a little confused.

"Where are you from?" he asked.

"America."

"Are you a Muslim?"

"No. I am a writer."

In the frank manner that would only occur to the very young, he had just one more question — or, I should say, an invitation.

"Do you want to become a Shia?"

CHAPTER 2

"SELL YOUR LUXURY GOODS AND BUY A KALASHNIKOV"

OUR MOTORCADE BLAZED THROUGH THE CONGESTED STREETS OF Karachi. We were roughly a dozen vehicles in all, five or six of them sedans carrying politicians and the other half pickup trucks transporting a squad of commandos whose uniforms were comprised of cargo pants and black T-shirts that read, across the back, No Fear. They sat, four or five per truck, huddled under the enclosed bed. AK-47s rested on their laps.

In each truck, one gunman stood with his head and chest poking through a hole cut in the top. To protect against common hazards like low-hanging telephone wires and flying bricks, he wore a motorcycle helmet. If another vehicle drifted too close to our caravan, the helmeted one aimed his assault rifle at the driver, who then often swerved away or slammed on the brakes. We, meanwhile, raced on.

Farooq Sattar and I sat in the backseat of a black Toyota Camry, near the front of the convoy. Sattar, who has cork-board-colored hair and a well-kempt beard of the same hue, wore a gray blazer over a plaid shirt. He had a professorial demeanor, but in a boy wonder sort of way, which meant that despite his fifty years of age, he could have passed for forty. The air conditioner fan muffled the wail of the police sirens. Sattar's personal bodyguard, a mute character of medium frame with a beard and a baseball cap, sat in the front passenger seat, tapping his fingers against the banana clip of his Kalashnikov. We were driving to a funeral.

Sattar, a member of the National Assembly and the parliamentary leader of the Muttahida Quami Movement, shoved a stack of manila files behind the rear window. His MQM, an ethnic party made of those people whose families migrated from India in 1947, practically ruled Karachi. They dominated the ballots and the streets. "Sorry for the clutter," he said. A box of tissues, some socks, a tie, and a pair of dress shoes sat on the hump between us. "I am constantly moving, and always keep an extra outfit with me," Sattar said. He changed his socks. The bodyguard passed back a couple of apple juice boxes, which we sipped on the way out of town.

AT THE NORTHERN outskirts of Karachi, a sprawling, seaside metropolis of fifteen million, we passed a cluster of apartment blocks in a neighborhood called Suhrab Goth. Men covered in dust stood on the sides of the road and stared. The paved highway broke up and turned to rubble, forcing our motorcade to slow down. Sattar's bodyguard lifted the tip of his gun from the floor mat and leaned it against the window. Sattar slurped the last of his apple juice and, continuing to look outside, said, "We were ambushed here once."

On the roof of several buildings, a black-and-white-striped flag flew taut in the strong wind. The flag belonged to Jamiat Ulema-e-Islam, one of Pakistan's most prominent Islamist parties. Its simplicity—striped, with no lettering—was appealing. I thought to myself that if I ever ruled an outlaw pirate state somewhere in the South Pacific, that would be my flag.

Suhrab Goth was populated mostly by Pashtuns who originated in Afghanistan and the North-West Frontier Province. Many of them worked in the transport business, ferrying cars, cattle, guns, grain—and anything else that needed to be shipped from Karachi's port to the northern parts of the country. They were generally pious and conservative, and often aligned with one of the Islamist political parties, either the Jamiat Ulema-e-Islam or Jamaat-i-Islami. Since the late 1970s, the Islamists had been steadily making inroads into power; the line between government, Allah, and the economy increasingly blurred. People's ethnic and political affiliations often protected business interests, and vice versa. When the jihad kicked off in Afghanistan in the early 1980s, millions of Afghan refugees fled to Pakistan. Many settled in Suhrab Goth.

Sattar belonged to another class of migrants, known as *mohajirs*. After the Partition of India in 1947, the term "mohajir" designated those Urdu-speaking Muslims who moved from India to Pakistan. Most of the mohajirs settled in Karachi. In 1984, Sattar helped form the MQM, originally named the Mohajir Quami Movement (Mohajir National Movement). At the time of the party's founding, Karachi was an ethnic tinderbox. Mohajirs, Pashtuns, and native Sindhis all competed for influence and resources. The spark was lit in 1985, when a passenger bus driven by a Pashtun hit and killed a mohajir schoolgirl. Mobs of mohajirs immediately descended on the scene of the accident. They torched the bus, and rampaged through the city, burning dozens more. Since Pashtuns dominated the transport business, vandals considered every bus a fair target. A journalist who lived in Karachi at the time counted fifty-five burning buses in the following days. "After this, it basically became a turf war," he told me. "The MQM said: 'We are the chiefs. We are willing to negotiate if you accept, but Karachi is ours.'"

The MQM held its first public rally a year later, in August 1986. Altaf Hussein, Sattar's boss and the overlord of the MQM, mounted a stage set up in Karachi's Nishtar Park. Thousands cheered as Altaf rehashed the sacrifices mohajirs had made in the past and the ones they would have to make in the future. Masked gunmen flanked him on either side and fired their Kalashnikovs into the air. This combination of celebration and militant bravado—or "fun and violence," as one anthropologist has termed it—would become the MQM's signature. In the middle of the speech, a monsoon broke through the clouds and unleashed a fierce downpour. Altaf said later, "It was resolved on that day that if the rain could not deter our determination, then the rain of bullets would not even force us to leave the ideology and the struggle."

Two months later, a caravan of MQM supporters, making their way to Hyderabad for the party's first rally outside of Karachi, were ambushed near Suhrab Goth. A gun battle broke out between mohajirs and Pashtuns. It wasn't the first, and wouldn't be the last. Sattar, a political prodigy at the ripe age of twenty-six, crouched for cover and escaped unhurt. Others were less fortunate, and several people died. The survivors, wearing blood-soaked clothing and driving cars pierced with bullet holes, eventually reached their destination in Hyderabad.

Altaf had been in Hyderabad for several days and insisted on going ahead with the rally. In his speech that night, Altaf said the mohajirs had always worked hard, with the belief that Pakistan was their spiritual destiny. Their success had allowed them to buy new TVs and VCRs. And yet, in their new homeland, they were still being abused. "We have come in peace. But we were attacked. We will give them tit for tat," he said. "Sell your luxury goods and buy a Kalashnikov!"

When Altaf finished speaking that evening at around 8 P.M., his followers dispersed, still enraged by the violence earlier that day near Suhrab Goth. While Altaf had pushed them to think of themselves as engaged in an eternal struggle by urging them to "come as followers of Imam Hussein," the grandson of the Prophet Mohammad martyred in the seventh century, the swelling ranks of MQM faithful were optimistic that their new leader, Altaf Hussein, would finally deliver the respect and entitlements they felt they deserved. Soon. And with force if necessary.

But before they did anything else, they had to right the day's wrongs. After the rally in Hyderabad that evening, a group of mohajirs approached a Pashtun shopkeeper and requested a glass of water. They were baiting him. The merchant refused. Within minutes, MQM supporters had looted the man's store and burned it to the ground.

ONCE WE HAD passed Suhrab Goth, the road improved and Sattar relaxed. We munched on coconut-crusted shrimp skewers, packaged for the trip, and sipped another round of juice boxes. The scrubby desert landscape on either side of the road seemed to roll on forever. Small villages, no more than a few dozen square mud huts, cropped up here and there. A single minaret stood at half-constructed filling stations, a scene that repeated itself up and down the highway.

I had met Sattar at the MQM headquarters in the Federal B Area of Karachi earlier that afternoon. The headquarters, better known as Nine-Zero, used to be the residence of Altaf. (The last two digits of his phone number were "Nine-Zero.") Whitewashed apartment blocks lined the surrounding streets. Billboards modeled Altaf's face more than they advertised products, and the MQM's white-, green-, and red-striped flag fluttered from lampposts, traffic lights, and car antennas. Sputtering Suzuki hatchbacks circled around a dried-up fountain the color of rain clouds. A sculpture of a clenched fist rose from the top of the fountain, meant to symbolize something like the resilience or fortitude of the mohajirs' struggle. In MQM territory, one always assumed that the fist was supposed to be Altaf's.

A security perimeter encircled Nine-Zero, and checkpoints, consisting of either a drawn chain or a lowered metal pole, blocked all the roads leading to the headquarters. Armed guards manned the posts. They waved me through, walked me onto the premises, and led me into a waiting room. Photographs of Altaf adorned the walls. Two clocks hung side by side: one set for Karachi time and one set for London time.

Sattar entered the room and introduced himself in the third person. ("This is Farooq Sattar, nice to meet you.") His eyes bulged, reptilian-like, so that they cast dark circles below and his thin lids seemed stretched to the point of breaking. Sattar, a medical doctor by profession, was the most senior MQM member living inside Pakistan. He had been mayor of Karachi at age twenty-eight. I found him extremely thoughtful and bright, totally at odds with the MQM's thuggish image. He talked about making the MQM a more inclusive party, one that appealed to the downtrodden masses across the country, not solely to mohajirs. And yet Sattar was a glorified estate manager—ostensibly in charge, but powerless.

Altaf, who had fled Pakistan in the early 1990s, ran the MQM—and, by extension, Karachi—by remote control from his town house in London and had managed to create a spooky omnipresence. Sattar constantly carried two phones with him: one for personal matters and one for the party. The personal phone displayed a photograph of Sattar's smiling wife and two teenage daughters; the party phone featured a close-up of Altaf's jowls. Hamid Haroon, the CEO of *Dawn*, a Karachi-based media conglomerate, told me in his office one day that Altaf knew about everything happening in Karachi. He advised me to proceed cautiously when investigating the MQM. "If you're snooping around and Altaf doesn't like it, and he doesn't want you to get out of bed... you won't," Haroon said. "To treat the MQM as a political party would be disastrously dangerous." It was closer to a hybrid between a gang and a cult. The MQM required new initiates in the party to recite an oath and swear their allegiance to Altaf:

I swear by my mother that if any conspiracy against the MQM or Altaf Hussein or any act harmful to them comes into my knowledge, I shall immediately inform Altaf Hussein or other main leaders, even if the conspirator be my brother, sister, mother, father, any relative or friend....I swear I shall accept Altaf Hussein's decision as final in any matter and obey all his decisions. If I disobey any of his decisions, I must be regarded as a traitor. I swear that I have and I will have blind trust in party leader Altaf Hussein.

In the early 1990s, when a splinter group challenged Altaf, calling itself MQM-Haqiqi (The Real One), one MQM parliamentarian described any betrayal of Altaf as being "more shameful than raping your own mother, sister, or daughter."

SATTAR AND ALTAF, like millions of other mohajirs, were both raised on tales about the horrors of Partition. On August 14, 1947, the British government relinquished control over the subcontinent, which led to the creation of independent Pakistan, India, and, eventually, Bangladesh. The weeks and months after the Partition were to have been a time of ecstasy, but widespread murder, rape, and torture prevailed instead. In the late summer and fall of 1947, Hindu families living in Muslim-majority Pakistan boarded trains heading east for India, while mohajirs, as Muslims living in Hindu-majority India, headed west. Along the way, members of either opposing faith frequently boarded one another's train cars long enough to light a match, start a fire, and transform them into rolling morgues. The trains often eased into their destinations reeking of death.

The Sattars moved from Gujarat, a state in India bordering Pakistan. Altaf's parents migrated from Agra, the site of the Taj Mahal. Altaf later called the Partition of India "the biggest blunder in the history of mankind." According to him, it divided "blood, culture, brotherhood, [and] relationships." The mohajirs nonetheless cherished an image of themselves as hardworking and middle-class. With no claims to land in the new state, they took over businesses and homes abandoned by the Hindu community in Karachi. But they found far more problems trying to fit in with their Muslim countrymen. "With the coming of Pakistan, a great deal of misapprehension seems to have been aroused in the hearts of many living in Pakistan," said Liaquat Ali Khan, Pakistan's first prime minister, three days after the Partition. The Sindhis, Pashtuns, Punjabis, Baluchis, and Bengalis all resisted the campaign to make Urdu, the language of the mohajirs, the official national language. Even today, less than 10 percent of Pakistanis speak Urdu at home. Khan added, "[Those living in Pakistan] seem to think in terms of Sindh for Sindhis and Bengal for Bengalis, but Pakistan is the very opposite of provincialism and racialism."

Resentment against the mohajirs began to manifest during the regime of General Ayub Khan, who staged a coup in October 1958. Soon after taking power, Ayub, a Pashtun from the North-West Frontier Province, moved the capital from Karachi to Islamabad, a planned city cut into lush, forested foothills near NWFP. The relocation put hundreds of miles between the new center of political power and the mohajir strongholds in Karachi and Hyderabad.

The Sindhis felt embittered toward the mohajirs, too, so when Zulfiqar Ali Bhutto, a feudal lord from northern Sindh, became president in 1971, he quickly set about tweaking the quota system. Quotas allotted government jobs and university enrollment on the basis of ethnicity and the relative size of one's home province. Punjabis received the most seats because they represented the largest chunk of the population, while Baluchis received the fewest. In Sindh, the presence of millions of mohajirs complicated things. According to Bhutto, native, ethnic Sindhis, who often lived in remote rural areas, were disadvantaged because they had to compete with mohajirs, who lived in cities and tended to be better educated. He decided to further divide the province into "rural" and "urban" Sindh, a euphemism for Sindhis and Mohajirs.

Bhutto wasn't done. He also wanted to call the mohajirs something different, and announced that, going forward, mohajirs should be referred to as New Sindhis, and native Sindhis would be called Old Sindhis. Mohajirs interpreted this as a deep insult, as the term "mohajir" harked back to the Prophet Mohammad, and those of his followers who made the *hijra*, or pilgrimage, from Mecca to Medina in 622. To deny the mohajirs their name was to deny them their central narrative — that of making the hijra to Pakistan. Riots frequently broke out during the 1970s between mohajirs and Sindhi nationalists.

In this environment, Sattar had applied to Karachi University's medical school but was denied admission. He blamed the quota system. Altaf, meanwhile, made it into the pharmacy department at Karachi University, where in 1978 he helped form the All Pakistan Mohajir Student Organization, or APMSO. Altaf was twenty-five years old at the time, with a coif of black hair and, according to one scholar, a preference for "shockingly tight trousers." At the APMSO's first meeting, he grabbed students' attention with his bombastic style and penchant for playing on feelings of victimization. "Two million Muhajirs gave their lives for the sake of Pakistan, a country which was achieved in the name of Allah. We left our homes and hearths for Pakistan, our entire cities were destroyed, but we are being killed for it," a founding member of the APMSO once said. The MQM eventually grew out of the APMSO.

While Altaf quickly gained a reputation on campus as a skilled orator, few people had heard of him outside the universities in Sindh. (Sattar attended a school a few hours north of Karachi, where he had also joined the APSMO.) Altaf and the APMSO believed that discrimination against the mohajirs had gone too far. Pakistan, in Altaf's mind, was a failed promise. On the morning of August 14, 1979, the anniversary of Pakistan's formation, Altaf scaled the steps leading to the mausoleum of Mohammad Ali Jinnah, the founder of Pakistan. Jinnah's body lay in a marble tomb inside. At the top of the steps, Altaf unfurled a Pakistani flag and lit it on fire.

The police immediately hauled Altaf away, and five days later they tried him in a military court, which convicted him of treason. Altaf served an abbreviated jail sentence — nine months and five lashes — then moved to the United States, where he drove taxis in Chicago. Sattar remembered him calling one day from the Windy City. "The time has come," Altaf said. "I am coming back." Sattar and the APMSO faithful flooded neighborhoods and universities, distributing literature and drumming up support for Altaf's return and the mohajir movement he planned to inspire. "We stayed up at all-night training sessions, studying different revolutions and different histories of freedom movements," Sattar told me.

I asked what revolutions they focused on.

"Lenin, Mao, Mandela, and the French Revolution," he said. In March 1984, the MQM was finally formed.

AFTER THE RASH of ethnic riots in Karachi in the mid- and late-1980s, usually pitting the MQM against the Pashtuns, the military establishment created the MQM-Haqiqi — The Real One — in an effort to break Altaf's hold over the city. The 1988 election of Sattar as mayor had solidified the MQM's control, and, with a nod to Al Capone, they fused politics and crime with brutal precision. The police began uncovering torture cells throughout Karachi, which were allegedly run by the MQM. Feeling the heat of impending arrest, Altaf departed for London in 1991, ostensibly to seek medical care for a failing kidney. He would never return to Pakistan. In June 1992, Pakistani security forces launched Operation Clean Up, with the goal of capturing or killing the MQM's leadership. Many of them had already fled.

But rather than eliminating the MQM, the military operation actually revived the party. According to Oskar Verkaaik, the author of two books about the MQM, the party looked to be on the verge of self-destruction in 1992. In his book *Migrants and Militants: Fun and Urban Violence in Pakistan*, Verkaaik argues that the army's campaign to brand the MQM as terrorists turned into a propaganda coup for Altaf, who could now play up his credentials as a martyr: "The appropriation and reversal of the terrorist stigma into a new... image of a self-sacrificing, persecuted freedom fighter was one of the techniques the MQM used to resist the state operation against the movement."

Knowing about the MQM's violent history, I had difficulty reconciling Sattar's erudite, mild-mannered personality with all the talk of torture cells and Kalashnikovs. I wanted to believe that Sattar was somehow different. Maybe Sattar just didn't know about the party's criminal side? But could a non-thug exist in a thuggish party? The longer I stayed in Pakistan and observed the endemic culture of violence in the country, the more I wondered if all the political parties perhaps insulated certain leaders from direct involvement with their militant activities, to give them plausible deniability. Perhaps I was being naive.

I thought Mahmood Sham, the editor of *Jang*, the largest Urdu-language daily newspaper in Pakistan, might know the answer. He agreed to meet me one night for dinner at the Pearl Continental Hotel in Karachi. While we dined on plates of sheep's brain, I asked him about Sattar. Sham smiled, and then began recalling stories of MQM-sponsored goon squads busting into his office during the 1990s. "Five or six people would show up with pistols and say, 'We are sending news. Keep a four-column space open,'" Sham told me. "They kept up this kind of pressure for years. Even though their news was being published correctly, they said that the other parties' violent acts were being overlooked."

Sham lifted his head from his plate of brains and caught my gaze. "Farooq Sattar knows about all these encounters. He was there."

* * *

SATTAR AND I had not been talking for more than five minutes in the room with the two clocks when an aide pushed open the door and pointed at his watch.

"Nicholas, I am afraid that I have to leave. An MNA"—member of the National Assembly—"of ours died this morning, and I have to go to Hyderabad for his funeral," Sattar explained. "But if you want, you can ride with me."

Soon after this, our Camry had taken the lead position in the motorcade as we barreled through Karachi.

We arrived in Hyderabad about two hours later. Mourners landed on Sattar like honeybees. Although the death of the MQM parliamentarian marked the occasion, Sattar, as the MQM's top guy in Pakistan, was the main attraction. He threaded through the crowd, shaking hands and expressing condolences. Young boys lunged forward to kiss his hand. Sattar turned to me to explain the royal reception he was receiving. "This is the people's only chance to meet their party leaders."

The funeral procession began with a thick jumble of men pushing and bumping against one another as they tried to hoist the parliamentarian's coffin onto their shoulders. The coffin was covered with a lacy black fabric, stitched with gold lettering that spelled out verses from the Quran. Rose petals had been sprinkled on top. I drifted along, swept up by the mass of people. Soon the procession outpaced Sattar. I wanted to drop back, but needed to extricate myself from the human tide; I eventually grabbed hold of a lamppost and held tight as mourners pushed past me.

Sattar, surrounded by ten senior MQM leaders, walked the vacated, winding roads of downtown Hyderabad, past rows and rows of shuttered storefronts, toward the graveyard. No one spoke. Sattar clasped his hands behind his back. The rubber tap of his shoes echoed down the empty streets.

In the graveyard, teenagers leapt over headstones and mounds of dirt to jostle for position around the pit. A couple hundred people crowded into a corner of the graveyard. A disagreement broke out over how the corpse should be lowered into the ground. The deceased's family members argued back and forth. A mullah stood by quietly, clutching a Quran and awaiting his turn to speak, while another debate ensued about how to unwrap the burial shroud. Anyone who said Islam was undemocratic had clearly never witnessed a Muslim burial.

Once the body lay in the ground and dirt had been packed on top, one of the family members nodded in the direction of the mullah, who opened his Quran. I watched him closely as he stood beside the mound of dirt, reciting verses. He began reading dispassionately, but soon grew more emotional. Dusk approached and low-flying bats swooped over our heads. The mullah halted mid-prayer, just as he was about to pronounce the dead man's name. He paused. Then someone in the scrum called out the name. And as if on cue, the mullah finished the prayer.

On the way back to Karachi from Hyderabad that night, Sattar, a handful of MQM leaders, and I stopped for dinner at a roadside restaurant, advertised as "BBQ."

"Can I ask something?" I said.

Everyone nodded.

"What happened with the mullah? Is that part of Islamic tradition, stopping and letting someone in the crowd fill in the name of the dead?"

They howled with laughter.

"No," Sattar said, smiling. "The mullah just forgot his name."

About a week after Sattar and I went to Hyderabad for the funeral, Altaf was scheduled to speak over the telephone to several thousand followers in a pink-walled park near Nine-Zero. The funeral and the rally both highlighted the profound importance of identity politics in Pakistan, where people normally voted based on their ethnic group or sectarian affiliation, regardless of a party's platform. Sattar had no qualms appealing to a single group's history and hardships. "Every strong party in Pakistan inherently carries an ethnic message," he told me. But lawyers, journalists, and rival politicians often characterized the MQM as a "fascist" party, and even compared Altaf-led rallies to ones Adolf Hitler led in Nuremberg. Curious to see what all the hype was about, I showed up early and combed the grounds.

A cinema-screen-sized poster faced the gathering, with lettering across the top that read, in English, STAND BY THE FLAG. It depicted a shadowed and featureless man holding the MQM's flag in an Iwo Jima–like pose; an industrial landscape loomed in the background with cranes, skyscrapers, skeletal oil derricks, and a couple of hourglass-shaped reactors. Speakers the size of New York City apartments stood on either side of the poster and around the park.

Altaf's face was ubiquitous on smaller posters positioned around the site. Some pictures were posed; others captured him in the middle of delivering a speech. In the action shots, he often clenched a fist or wagged a finger at the crowd. He wore different outfits in most of the posters, but in all of them he sported a thick mustache, slicked-back hair, jowls, and orange-tinted aviator sunglasses. He looked like a revolution-ary skeet shooter.

Some people brought handmade posters, too, odes to "Brother Altaf" and "The Great Leader." Bedsheets painted with slogans read: WE NEED A LEADER, NOT A DESTINATION, and HE WHO BETRAYS ALTAF DESERVES DEATH.

The evening air was cool, like most nights in Karachi after the sun had set and the sea breeze drifted across the city. Spectators sat quietly and spoke in hushed, church tones. Rows of uncovered lightbulbs hung over-head like phosphorescent popcorn. Karachi had never seemed so bucolic.

Sattar joined the other top leaders of the MQM sitting cross-legged on a strip of Astroturf laid in front of the "Stand by the Flag" poster. He held a microphone in his lap to amplify his chants. He gestured for the crowd to be silent. Altaf was ready.

Video cameras taped the rally, apparently for local news stations. I wondered if Altaf was watching a live feed, monitoring his deputies from afar. What a difference a week and a change of scene had made: in Hyderabad, MQM faithful had been swarming Sattar, kissing his hand and treating him like a saint; now he looked pitiful and timid. He nod-ded, shyly, in my direction. At that moment, he was just another parish-ioner in the church of Altaf.

ALTAF'S VOICE PUNCHED over the PA system: "Haaallllloooooo." He repeated it twice. "Can you hear me?" he asked in Urdu.

The mere sound of his voice—gravelly and phlegm-ridden—trans-formed the crowd.

I watched the mass intently as Altaf recited passages from the Quran.

When he spoke, everyone sat, docilely. But when he paused, someone invariably leapt up and screamed, "Long Live Altaf!" For a very brief moment, those people were sucked into Altaf's world. It must have been quite a rush. They would continue chanting until the sound of Altaf pushing the speakerphone button, gearing to resume, beeped over the PA system. Church voices returned.

Much of Altaf's address that night centered on the publication of several allegedly blasphemous cartoons in European newspapers, and the Pakistani response to those cartoons. The cartoons first appeared in the Danish newspaper *Jyllands-Posten* in late September 2005. For months, there was hardly any reaction. But word of mouth spread, and rumors of the West slandering Muslims reached Pakistan in early February 2006. Mobs torched Western fast-food joints and stoned Western banks. Most people who participated had never even seen the cartoons. They simply reacted to the exhortations by the Islamist parties, who tried to gain some political leverage out of the controversy. Altaf used any opportunity to attack the Islamists, who had organized the protests, and with whom the MQM had been feuding for decades.

"The opposition mullahs are using people in the name of the Prophet, peace be upon him," he said. "I am hugely upset. I ask myself and you: 'What is the difference between these mullahs and the blasphemers who have done these cartoons for their own agenda?'"

A party worker jumped from his seat and offered an answer: "We have a leader of huge stature, and that leader is you, Altaf!" The crowd roared with approval.

The rally lasted about an hour. Near the end of his long-winded rant, Altaf was growling, sounding both frenzied and exhausted. He finally hung up. I pictured him standing in his home studio in North London, his jowls and neck dripping with sweat.

As the crowd dispersed, I remained in my seat, transfixed by Altaf's explosive energy over the telephone, and by his followers' devotion to a man halfway around the world.

An MQM party worker stood next to me, grinning wide. I looked past him on one side and noticed the cameras still rolling. Behind me, Sattar answered questions from a local reporter. "You must think we are crazy about Altaf Hussein," the party worker said.

In the looming omnipresence of Altaf, I was not about to disagree.

CHAPTER 3

"DON'T SPEAK ENGLISH
IN PUBLIC"

TRIBESMEN FLOCKED FROM ALL OVER NORTH WAZIRISTAN AND GATHERED around the gallows. They shouldered rifles and wore floppy wool caps. Some of them were Taliban, experienced in fighting against the American military in Afghanistan, just a few dozen miles away. But many of them were simply local people, tired of robbers and thieves and punks creating problems. Someone should punish those people, they thought. And so, on a crisp winter day, tucked in a valley near the Afghanistan border, the Taliban hanged five alleged criminals in the main bazaar. Once the bodies went limp, the Taliban lowered the five men, cut their heads off, and then restrung them, decapitated and upside down, from the scaffold. I watched all this on a grainy, Taliban-made propaganda DVD, distributed in the winter of 2006. The video offered a rare peek into Pakistan's otherwise impenetrable tribal areas. But even more than that, its distribution announced that, from here on, the Taliban ruled Waziristan.

The Taliban's formal declaration of an "Islamic State of Waziristan" didn't come as a surprise. They had been in control for years. Following the American invasion of Afghanistan in October 2001, hundreds, if not thousands, of Taliban and al-Qaeda fighters fled to Pakistan. They soon transformed South and North Waziristan, two of the seven agencies that comprise the Federally Administered Tribal Areas (FATA), into their jihadi headquarters. From there, guerrillas equipped with guns and suicide bombers outfitted with explosive vests streamed, unfettered, across the border into Afghanistan. In 2007, an American staff sergeant based in Khost, Afghanistan, whose base was being hit by rocket and mortar fire at least once a week, told the *New York Times* that Taliban fighters based in Pakistan "cross the border on a regular basis."

But Pakistan was more than just a staging ground, and the Taliban began transforming their lawless sanctuaries into self-governed enclaves. They policed, adjudicated, and levied fines and taxes to supplement their military budget — all in the name of Islam. "We want to live an Islamic life, to live under an Islamic government," a young man from South Waziristan told me around the same time the DVD came out. "The Pakistani government has failed us; now we'll see what the Taliban can do," he said. "The Taliban's only problem is coercion. Otherwise, they are doing a good job."

THE PAKISTANI GOVERNMENT and the Taliban shared some history. When Mullah Omar lorded over Afghanistan, Islamabad relished its first working relationship with a government in Kabul, as the two countries had long been at odds with one another. Plus, most of the turbaned men who filled the ranks of Omar's government had graduated from Pakistani madrassas. (Omar did not, though he was later awarded an honorary degree from Darul Uloom Haqqania, a large madrassa outside of Peshawar.) Islamabad supported the fundamentalist militia, but for more than just religious and political reasons. There were economic ones, too. The Taliban ended years of civil war in Afghanistan and eliminated banditry on the main roads through the country which enabled Pakistani traders to transport and sell their goods in Iran and Central Asia.

September 11 complicated things. A few hours after terrorists hijacked four commercial airliners, Deputy Secretary of State Richard Armitage reportedly asked the director general of the ISI, in no uncertain terms: "Are you with us or against us?" (The ISI chief happened to be in Washington that day.) When the Pakistani spymaster balked, Armitage rephrased the question and warned that if Pakistan chose not to cooperate, it should prepare to be "bombed back to the Stone Age." The ISI chief relayed the conversation to Musharraf, who had heard something similar when speaking to Secretary of State Colin Powell earlier that day. Musharraf opted to side with the United States. His decision to ditch the Taliban didn't go over well back home. Several advisers urged him to reconsider. The Taliban were viable, long-term allies, whereas the United States, they argued, was an unreliable partner.

Sections of the political establishment in Washington, cognizant of the dissent surrounding Musharraf, constantly questioned his loyalties, mostly in private, but openly, too. To prove his mettle, Musharraf deployed more than eighty thousand soldiers into North and South Waziristan, the first time in Pakistan's history that regular troops crossed into FATA. But while the deployments were substantial in number, and casualties were also significant (more than seven hundred Pakistani troops died in the first five years), Taliban and al-Qaeda fighters continued to flow unchecked across the border into Afghanistan. Moreover, Pakistani troops were unfamiliar with counterinsurgency tactics, and the Taliban defeated them time and again. The militants' tactical victories gave them the time and space they and al-Qaeda needed to establish a new strategic headquarters—inside Pakistan. "[Al-Qaeda] has protected or regenerated key elements of its homeland attack capability," declared a 2007 National Intelligence Estimate, a periodic assessment by American intelligence agencies to assess security threats, "including a safe-haven in the Pakistan FATA."

How could the Taliban operate so freely in Pakistan? Where were they getting support? The more I looked around, the more I realized that everyone, everywhere in Pakistan, seemed to be offering some help. The military's intelligence agencies played a double game, taking money from the Americans and still aiding the Taliban. Pakistanis on the street praised the Taliban as humble, pious servants of Allah. "Ninety-nine point nine percent of Pakistanis, from their heart of hearts, are happy to see the Taliban creating problems for the Americans in Afghanistan and for Musharraf in Waziristan," Hamid Mir, a columnist and talk show host, told me in his Islamabad office one day. In the 2002 parliamentary elections, voters handed a coalition of Islamist parties, whose support for the Taliban had formed a central tenet of its election campaign, a larger share in the assembly than any Islamist party had received in the past.

Pakistanis loved the *idea* of the Taliban. As Mir pointed out, they just feared the actual guys with the turbans and the guns. "One hundred percent of people don't want the Taliban in Islamabad, Rawalpindi, or even Karachi," he added.

Support for the Taliban came in multiple ways, including financial, moral, and military backing. At the Red Mosque in Islamabad, all of these aspects gelled in one place. Before I traveled into the Taliban-affected areas near the border of North Waziristan, I visited the Red Mosque, hoping to learn more about how it fit into the cross-border jihadi puzzle. Two brothers ran the mosque, the older one, Maulana Abdul Aziz, who delivered the sermon every Friday, praised Osama bin Laden, raised donations for the Taliban, and encouraged parishioners to wage jihad, and the younger one, Abdul Rashid Ghazi, who held a master's degree in international relations, spoke fluent English and was a sharp observer of global politics. I had met Ghazi once before when I had been referred from Khalid Khawaja, the former pilot and intelligence officer.

In 2004, the brothers issued a fatwa declaring that Pakistani soldiers killed in South Waziristan should be denied a proper Muslim burial. The fatwa outraged Musharraf and his circle. But they could do little against the mosque. Some members of Musharraf's own cabinet regularly prayed there.

"The fight against the coalition in Afghanistan is definitely a jihad," Ghazi told me once while I was visiting him inside the Red Mosque. "The Afghans are not sufficient by themselves. Others should go. We say this all the time. America has done aggression against innocent people, and we should defend them.

"People used to say, 'The Taliban are finished. Just get 1, 2, or 3 people and it's done,'" he said. "But the Taliban idea involves a belief in certain things. They are a reaction. In Afghanistan, they were a reaction to lawlessness and the warlords fighting against one another."

"And in Waziristan today?"

"Like I said, the Taliban is a reaction to a chaotic situation. There were *dacoits* all over North Waziristan, and now local people are very happy that the Taliban have killed them," Ghazi said, referring to the bandits hanged on the DVD from North Waziristan that I had seen. "But there are dacoits all over the Punjab, too. So these Taliban will spread."

* * *

ON THE RIDE to Peshawar, we coasted over the Indus River, dividing Punjab and the North-West Frontier Province. The river, colored like cream of mushroom soup from churning silt, slices through a canyon midway between Islamabad and Peshawar. South Asia's irrigated plains fell off to one side, while the dry, rocky mountains of Central Asia rose on another. Throughout history, the river had always separated one civilization from another. But in the days after the MMA swept to victory and formed the provincial government in NWFP, crossing the Indus meant entering an Islamic state.

Street signs dotted the roadside from the Indus River onward to Peshawar, the capital of NWFP. They illustrated the extent and spread of the MMA's Islamization campaign. The more benign ones read: DON'T SAY "HELLO," SAY "ASALLAMU ALEIKUM," and SMILE, IT'S YOUR RELIGIOUS DUTY. Others, like JIHAD WILL CONTINUE UNTIL DOOMSDAY, were less welcoming. Women walked along the road cloaked in light blue, shuttlecock-style burqas. In Peshawar, vigilantes had painted over billboards picturing women's faces so that genderless models now advertised the latest shampoo product.

My travel companion was a thirty-year-old journalist from South Waziristan named Pir. Pir belonged to the Mehsud tribe, one of the two major Pashtun tribes in South Waziristan. (His fellow tribesman, Baitullah Mehsud, would be later accused of masterminding Benazir Bhutto's assassination.) More than twenty-five million Pashtuns live on either side of the Pakistan-Afghanistan border, where they harbor a reputation as ruthless fighters and have spent the last few thousand years repelling countless foreign armies, including that of Alexander the Great, the British Empire, and the Soviet Union. Of the many different Pashtun tribes, the Mehsuds were considered the fiercest. In 1947, shortly after Pakistan was formed, a militia of Mehsuds marched from the tribal areas to Kashmir, where they hoped to wrest control of Muslim-majority Kashmir from its Hindu and Sikh leaders. (They ultimately failed.) The Mehsuds were "tougher, [both] spiritually and physically" than any other Pashtuns, wrote one Englishman.

No formal government has ever existed in Waziristan. Even the border that demarcates Afghanistan from British India—and later, Pakistan—remains contentious. The border, known as the Durand Line, was drawn in 1893 as a way for the British to undermine the unruly tribes in Waziristan and areas north. Instead, it merely made the tribes resent the British authority even more. And they ignored the border. Today, tens of thousands of people cross the border daily, without passports or visas, for work, to visit family, or, increasingly, to fight against American and NATO forces in Afghanistan. Flabbergasted at the recalcitrance of the tribes in and around Waziristan, Lord Curzon, the former viceroy of India, once said: "No patchwork scheme—and all our present recent schemes, blockade, allowances, etc., are mere patchwork—will settle the Waziristan problem. Not until the military steamroller has passed over the country from end to end, will there be peace. But I do not want to be the person to start that machine."

PIR AND I had taken a bus to Peshawar, where we rented a car and then continued south to Bannu, a town on the border of North Waziristan. Like other towns in the so-called settled areas adjacent to FATA, Bannu was in serious jeopardy of falling to the Taliban. A week before we arrived, the uncle of the provincial chief minister was shot and killed in a nearby village; almost everyone suspected the Taliban were responsible. Around the same time, the *nazim*, or mayor, of Bannu had reportedly received an envelope containing 500 rupees (the equivalent of $83), along with a note, signed by the Taliban, suggesting he use the money to purchase a coffin for himself.

Politicians weren't the only ones targeted. The Taliban intimidated and threatened journalists, too. They called local newspapers and demanded to be referred to as "mujahideen," rather than "miscreants" or "militants." They showed little tact in managing the press, and they grew increasingly more paranoid. An editor in Peshawar told me that the Taliban blamed newspapers for focusing excessively on the presence of foreigners and beheadings, coverage that they believed compelled the Pakistani security forces to attack them. One of the editor's correspondents had fled his home in the tribal areas upon hearing that the Taliban were unhappy with his work. Shortly after that, the militants bombed the journalist's house. More and more, journalists filed their stories anonymously.

Reporters working in the border regions faced more problems than just the Taliban. Some suspected the Pakistani intelligence agents, masquerading as "militants," of planting roadside bombs and conducting kidnappings, both activities designed to keep reporters out. The fact that the

Taliban ran parts of Pakistan inevitably embarrassed Musharraf and jeopardized his cash flow from Washington; after 9/11, the United States was paying more than a $1 billion a year to Musharraf for his efforts in the War on Terror.

In December 2005, a journalist from North Waziristan named Hayatullah Khan had filed a story with *Ausaf*, an Urdu newspaper, accompanied by photographs that provided evidence of U.S. air strikes against Taliban- and al-Qaeda-linked targets inside Pakistani territory. Until then, the government in Islamabad had denied such strikes. On multiple occasions, when a house blew up, government spin doctors would blame it on a gas leak or a spontaneous explosion. In Khan's photos, he showed a piece of a U.S.-made Hellfire missile. The day after Khan's story and photos were published, gunmen ran his car off the road and kidnapped him. Six months later, his body turned up, with five gunshots in the back. Khan had written a will weeks earlier that said: "If I am kidnapped or get killed, the government agencies will be responsible."

Foreign journalists weren't spared either. Officially, we were barred from even entering the tribal areas, reminded by a sign at the entrance to most entrances into FATA: NO FOREIGNERS ALLOWED PAST THIS POINT. When a female American writer tried to sneak into South Waziristan disguised in a burqa, Pakistani intelligence agents detained—and then deported—her.

Heading down to Bannu, I sought some kind of anonymity, too. But standing more than six feet tall, blond, and fair-skinned, what were my choices? A periwinkle-colored burqa was never going to cut it.

"Is there anything I should do?" I asked Pir.

"Don't speak English in public," he said.

PAKISTANI LAWS DON'T apply in the tribal areas. Fifty years passed after the creation of Pakistan before residents of FATA even enjoyed voting rights. And still, their enfranchisement lacked substance: FATA representatives sat in the parliament, though none of the laws drafted there pertained to the tribal areas.

Like their English predecessors had done, Pakistani leaders had for years "governed" the tribal areas through proxy, relying on *maliks*, or tribal elders. The maliks intermediated between the political agent, who acted as the local government representative, and the tribesmen. Islamabad paid cash to the political agent with instructions to keep things under control, and the political agent, in turn, paid cash to the maliks, with similar orders. If tribesmen stepped out of line, the political agent could punish an entire tribe for the crimes of one man. This system, while draconian and often criticized by human rights organizations for its application of collective punishment, generally achieved its goal: the tribes remained, overall, obedient.

But the anti-Soviet jihad in Afghanistan had begun a process that damaged beyond repair the stability and sanctity of the Pashtun tribal system. In the late 1970s, anti-Communist countries, led by the United States, capitalized on the strategic value of Pakistan's tribal areas as a staging ground for military operations against the Red Army. The CIA worked closely with Saudi Arabian intelligence services to flood the tribal areas with weapons to enhance the operational capability of the mujahideen (the West referred to them as mujahideen back then, not "terrorists" or "jihadis") and built madrassas to strengthen their ideological commitment to jihad. An archipelago of madrassas and training camps provided an endless flow of eager martyrs.

But for a Mehsud tribesman, it made little difference whether his adversary was from London, Moscow, or Washington; any non-Pashtun who occupied Pashtun lands instantly became an adversary. "These people of Waziristan have been trained to fight for centuries," said Hamid Gul, a retired general in the Pakistani army and the former director of the ISI, told me one day at his home in Rawalpindi. "Their war horse starts snorting and they want to go muck it up with whatever force it is."

The jihad also effected a cultural transformation. Warlords and mujahideen commanders, not the maliks as in the past, soon began to wield increased authority over the tribes. The political agent, whose access to gold and guns had made him the ultimate kingmaker, became less relevant. The influx of weapons and money created a parallel, war economy. A professor at Peshawar University told me that "the presence of all these foreigners stopped the colonial structures from working." Having worked in the Afghan refugee camps during the early 1980s, the professor recalled watching Arabs, "with briefcases full of clean notes," wandering the camps, handing out money to budding insurgents.

After the American invasion of Afghanistan in 2001, another wave of foreigners arrived, this time Arab and Uzbek al-Qaeda affiliates. They resided in the tribal areas and urged the local Taliban to upend the existing system. The Taliban soon began murdering maliks by the hundreds. They threatened anyone who represented traditional authority. Khalid Aziz, a former political agent in North Waziristan, wrote in a 2008 column, "The British failed to end tribalism in a hundred years, and Pakistan failed to do so in sixty years. However, the militants have been successful in only seven years."

PIR AND I stopped at a roadside restaurant a couple of hours before we were scheduled to reach Bannu. Large trucks parked in a dirt lot to the side. The black-and-white-striped flag of Jamiat Ulema-e-Islam (JUI), the leading party in the MMA coalition, flew from the trucks' antennae. A white brick bathroom, with a hole in the floor for a toilet, stood in a thicket of grass. We lunched on a couple of bowls of greasy onions and okra, followed by a plate of marbled meat. Flies huddled around the rim of the water pitcher, like young kids eager to jump into the neighborhood pool.

The other patrons stared at us. I guess no one was fooled into mistaking me for a local by my beard and shalwar kameez. After eating, Pir and I reclined on wooden benches and each drank a cup of green tea. We spoke quietly, in Urdu. The mountains of Kurram Agency rose across the plain. Just beyond that loomed Tora Bora, Afghanistan, where top Taliban and al-Qaeda leaders escaped from the American military in late 2001. Most of them had ducked into Pakistan.

"You know, these Taliban are becoming so respected," Pir said casually. He told me how, a month earlier, bandits stole his family's car—and kidnapped the driver—from right outside their home in South Waziristan. "The first thing we did was call the political agent. He said, 'I can't do anything.' So then we called the local Talib commander. Within a few days, the Talibs raided a safe house, got the car, and freed the driver." Pir added, "Now they are being praised as heroes."

Even people like Pir, who didn't sympathize at all with the Taliban, had to admit that they were doing some good. Those hanged on the DVD were the most reviled characters in North Waziristan. Many considered their execution an act of justice. Ideology wasn't motivating people to support the Taliban as much as the lack of a rival authority.

The waiter, a bearded, burly man with the forearms of a lumberjack, asked us where we were going. The man spoke English and had icy blue

eyes. Pir was quick to answer; the closer we got to Bannu, the more anxious he had become. He told the waiter we were heading to another city,
an hour south of Bannu.

I stared at him, looking confused.

Pir waited until the lumberjack left, then leaned forward and whispered, "I don't tell people when I go to Bannu anymore. I don't want anyone there waiting for me to arrive. Now let's go."

A DUST STORM welcomed us to Bannu. Thick yellow clouds rolled
through the city, obscuring the tops of minarets. Scraps of trash raced
down the empty streets. Merchants hurriedly lowered their metal shutters, while groups of children who had been playing cricket in a grassless
field sprinted for the cover of nearby trees.

Mesh shades covered the back windows of our car. With the instability in North and South Waziristan having spilled into Bannu, it was
essential to keep a low profile. Earlier that week, two explosions had
rocked the cellular transmission towers, disturbing phone service for days.
Rockets and mortars occasionally landed in the army cantonment.

Very few Westerners wandered down to Bannu. Those who did, like
John Walker Lindh, had a mission. Lindh was "the American Taliban"
who spent six months in early 2001 at a madrassa in Bannu. After he
memorized the Quran, he joined the Taliban. I now showed up, five
years later, hoping to understand what fed the ranks of those attracted to
what Abdul Rashid Ghazi called "the Taliban idea."

We parked in an alleyway behind the Bannu Press Club and met a
newspaper reporter in his late forties with a long, gray beard, who asked
us not to use his name. The man was based in Bannu, but often shuttled
back and forth to Miramshah, the capital of North Waziristan. "Every
home in this area has at least one Talib in it," he said, sounding confident
of this fact and even a bit proud of it. "This is all because of the army
operation." He told me about a farmer in North Waziristan, who had
been tilling the fields when Pakistani helicopters strafed his village with
machine-gun fire. The farmer's sister was killed instantly while taking a
bath. "That farmer grabbed his gun and went to the mountains. Now he
is with the Taliban."

In such an environment, I wondered how the Taliban could ever be
defeated. Collateral damage fueled the insurgency as the culture's empha-

sis on honor and vengeance drove ordinary Pashtuns into the arms of the Taliban. American unmanned drones routinely tried to kill top al-Qaeda leaders, but, more often than not, missed the intended target and instead killed dozens of locals. In October 2006, a Predator drone fired missiles at a madrassa in Bajaur, the northernmost tribal agency, targeting al-Qaeda's number two, Ayman al-Zawahiri. (The Pakistani army acknowledged "sharing intelligence" with the United States, but said "to say that [the Americans] carried out the operation is totally wrong.") The attack failed to kill Zawahiri, but left more than forty madrassa students dead, and featured in countless propaganda speeches and leaflets distributed by Pakistani jihadi groups.

Rather than eliminating enemies, each missile strike only created more. "The government thinks it can persuade people to its side through development," the Bannu journalist said. "And you know what? The people might thank the government. But revenge will never leave their minds. No one will forget that the Pakistani army attacked them. The day you forget your revenge, you are not a proper Pashtun."

Pir spoke up and added, "People here are keeping score."

The journalist mentioned rumors of another large-scale military operation against the Taliban in and around Bannu, similar to the ones ongoing in North and South Waziristan. "I can feel it in the air that this is coming," he said.

"That what is coming?" I asked. "The army or the Taliban?"

"One leads to the other. If there is no operation, the Taliban won't grow. But it takes the death of only one man to cause an entire village to take up arms."

"What would happen if the Taliban truly came to Bannu?" I asked, pointing to the public executions, the morality laws, and the bans of television that the Taliban enacted in Afghanistan, and now in Waziristan.

"The Taliban are relatively harmless people," he answered. "Basically, the concept of the Taliban is projected wrongly. If they come to Bannu and don't hurt anyone, then there won't be any objections."

WHEN THE DUST storm subsided, Pir and I left the press club and drove to his friend's house. The friend, called Shams, was muscular and styled his thick mustache into the shape of a handlebar. We sat in the guest room, called a *hujra*, on jute beds. Giant ants scurried across the dirt floor.

Shams was active in the local branch of the Pakistan People's Party (PPP). He hated the Islamists and the Taliban. When I asked him if he worried about the Taliban moving into Bannu, he shrugged his shoulders and pointed to the corner, where an AK-47 leaned against the wall. "I have my own Kalashnikov," he said.

Pir, Shams, and I soon headed downtown to witness one of Bannu's famed traditions.

On the way, Pir asked me my age. When I said that I was twenty-seven, Pir recommended that I add another ten years, if anyone asked. "They love young boys down here," he said. They?

Apparently, burly tribesmen believed that their womenfolk should be kept at home, and so, every evening, a few hundred males congregated in the bazaar, draped in jasmine necklaces. In other words, despite their beards and guns and conservative tribal customs, these Pashtuns, especially those in Bannu, had a soft side, too. They processed from one end of the bazaar to the other, singing and beating on drums. According to custom, one man would spot an attractive boy (usually many years younger), sneak behind him, and loop his jasmine necklace around the boy's neck. Those wearing a necklace were considered "taken." "You know what they say about the pigeons in Bannu?" Pir asked me, grinning. "They fly over the city with just one wing...and use the other to cover their tail."

As we neared the bazaar, Shams twirled the ends of his mustache and insisted that we stay in the car. He said something to Pir in Pashto, and they both broke into giggles while glancing back at me.

"What's so funny?"

"They love blonds in Bannu," Pir said.

At the next intersection, Shams rolled down his window and called to a boy standing at the corner selling jasmine necklaces. He bought one for each of us. Smelling of jasmine—and, apparently, stuck with Shams for the night—we cruised down the road alongside a throng of drummers. Men walked beside the car on either side holding hands adorned with purple rhinestone rings. With all Bannu's women stashed away back home, flirtation remained an all-male activity. I wondered how long this tradition would survive if the Taliban ever moved in.

At dinner that night, I asked Shams what he had heard about foreign militants roaming around the city. After the Afghan jihad, many Arabs had stayed behind. Some were like Ayman al-Zawahiri, Osama bin

Laden's right-hand man, who learned Pashto and married a local girl in Mohmand, one of the northern tribal agencies. A top Arab al-Qaeda leader arrested outside of Peshawar in 2005 later confessed to having spent time in a village near Bannu. "They're everywhere. Yesterday I was at court and saw three people I didn't recognize. So I tried to speak to them," Shams said. "A Bannucchi interrupted, and said, 'Don't talk to them. They're got nothing to say to you.' They were Arabs."

A friend of Shams's joined us for dinner. The man had just left a meeting with several officials from the ISI. He rehashed parts of that conversation with Pir and Shams. They alternated between Pashto and Urdu. I understood enough to know that the ISI officials had been talking about the presence of foreigners in Bannu. I interrupted and asked, "Were they talking about Arabs?"

"No, man," Pir said, laughing. "They were talking about you." My eyes widened with alarm. "Don't worry. It's normal. These ISI guys are tracking people the moment they enter the city. I don't even think about it anymore."

It was just after midnight when we left Shams's house and stepped out onto the sidewalk. The roads were empty. Across the street, a yellow light shined on a playground with rusty chains dangling from a swing set. An old man with a whiskbroom beard walked along in our direction. He held a hunting rifle in one hand, and as he passed, he paused to stare.

"Asallamu Aleikum," Pir called out to the man, who returned the greeting and carried on.

On the drive to our guesthouse late that night, everyone else I saw on the road was carrying guns. Order was breaking down. Insecurity prevailed. The government was nonexistent. With vacuums made to be filled, the Taliban couldn't be far behind.

By 9 A.M. the next morning, the heat felt oppressive and Pir and I headed for the guesthouse pool. The pool sat in the middle of a grass lawn. Mesh netting formed a canopy over the top to keep out leaves and animals, and a fence surrounded it. Pir and I opened a gate where the owner had posted a list of rules in Urdu at the entrance. Rule #5 notified swimmers that shalwar kameez were prohibited in the water. Neither of us had a bathing suit. Then I saw the pile of communal trunks—a few dozen pairs of damp shorts hanging on a line of hooks.

Most of the shorts had elastic waistbands stretched wide enough to fit a middle-aged oak tree. I paused for a second and looked around. Was the pool just a ruse? Another chapter in the prior evening's jasmine-necklace tradition? Pir and I laughed at my paranoia; I had only been living in Pakistan a few months, but my attention to conspiracies was already well-tuned. Meanwhile Pir had rummaged through the pile of suits and pulled out a couple of pairs of khaki trunks. Both, thankfully, sported a drawstring. A crowd of teenage Bannucchis had gathered around the fence to watch the *gora* (literally: "white," or foreigner) swim. After knotting the waist and tugging on the shorts to assure I didn't give the young Bannucchis more than they bargained for, I dove into the pool.

While drip-drying after the swim, I noticed a stack of movie posters across the lawn, leaning against a building. The posters, hectic and colorful, featured mustachioed men holding guns, dripping with blood, their muscles flexed beneath ripped clothing. I asked Pir, "Is there a cinema nearby?"

"Right here at the guesthouse," he said. "There are three theaters in Bannu alone."

Pashto films provided a window into the culture clash raging in northwestern Pakistan. For decades, Pashto films had glorified gangsters and gore, but when the Islamist MMA rose to power in 2002, their twisted moral dictatorship immediately cramped the film industry. Producers continued making gory, violent films, but they saw their distribution curtailed. The MMA promoted an image of Pashtuns as pious Muslims, devoted to defending their coreligionists in Iraq, Afghanistan, and Kashmir against the tyranny of the infidels. They tried to monopolize every social, political, and religious debate. Political disputes quickly turned into religious ones, which quickly turned into anti-American ones.

"The MMA smells blood and they won't let go," Khalid Aziz, the former political agent in North Waziristan, told me. "The secular forces have been ousted."

THE BELEAGUERED Awami National Party best represented those "secular forces." Whereas the MMA tried to herald the mullah as the most powerful figure in society, the ANP regarded the tribal chiefs in that role. They were Pashtun nationalists, who lobbied hard for greater provincial autonomy (and renaming NWFP as Pashtunistan or Pakhtunkhwa—the

Pakhtun nation) and viewed most political debates through an ethnic lens. Like other ethnic nationalist parties in Pakistan, including those in Baluchistan and Sindh, the ANP grounded their ideology in revolutionary Marxism: they considered the Punjabi elite an imperial force and believed that "Talibanization" was a product of the Pakistani army's neocolonial attempts to dominate NWFP, and eventually Afghanistan, through religious proxies.

When Pir and I returned to Peshawar after a few days, we headed to the home of Latif Afridi, an ANP leader. Afridi's private army—five men nervously clutching Kalashnikovs—met us at the door. In the adjoining room, Afridi sat upright in a chair. Somewhere in his mid-fifties, Afridi slicked his white hair back and squinted as if he were staring in the sun.

AK-47s leaned against the back wall. I asked Afridi if the situation in the tribal areas could be remedied peacefully. He shook his head. The Taliban had ruined the whole tribal system, he said. The *jirga*, or tribal council, was becoming irrelevant, and the power of the traditional and secular politicians was in decline. Afridi seemed bitter, but also desperate, almost to the point of sounding defeated. "All of history for these people"—the Islamists—"revolves around twenty-nine years," Afridi said. "The time of Mohammad and the four caliphs. That's it."

I pointed out that both the ANP and the Taliban seemed to desire that the frontier regions exist independent of Pakistani rule. Did they agree on more than that?

"Yes, we are all Afghans. And eventually, we want to join Afghanistan," he replied. "There are five nations here, and three factors are keeping us together: economic interdependence, the bondage of Islam, and the army."

Pir mentioned that we had just returned from Bannu.

"Then you have seen for yourself," he said. "The only way that Punjab can enchain us is through Islam. Thousands of madrassas are being built in Bannu. The U.S. government has given hundreds of millions of dollars to the Pakistani army. For what? To 'Talibanize' the tribal areas?"

Afridi caught his breath. "When I think of the future, I see it bleak and dark." He ran his hand over his scalp, slicking down his hair and breathing a loud sigh. "The body politic in Pakistan has been poisoned forever."

CHAPTER 4

"LEFT ALONE IN
A CAVE OF TIME"

DR. SHAZIA, A MIDDLE-AGED WOMAN DRESSED LIKE A FIVE-FOOT PIECE of saltwater taffy—pink heels, pink purse, pink pants, pink tunic, and, of course, pink head scarf —stood at a podium facing two dozen extremely conservative mullahs. Fake roses tilted in small, ceramic vases placed along the U-shaped table where the mullahs sat. They hailed from Baluchistan, the arid, remote province bordering Afghanistan and Iran; some of them hadn't seen a city for years. They wore a variety of check-ered turbans and shawls. A few donned colorful, hand-stitched prayer caps studded with hundreds of tiny mirrors. They picked their noses, belched, and scratched their balls in public; sometimes they managed to do all three at once.

"How many of you have a credit card in your pocket?" Shazia asked.

Each of the clerics scanned the room to see if any of their peers car-ried plastic. None of them raised their hand.

"There's nothing un-Islamic about a credit card," said Shazia. "You all are missing out on the world."

Shazia brimmed with sass, but also knew a thing or two about Islam; she held a doctorate in Islamic jurisprudence from Karachi University, where she also taught in the Department of Quran and Sunnah. Her academic credentials—and her attitude—made her an ideal presenter for the ten-day workshop, titled "Madrassas and the Modern World," which brought together the mullahs who sat before her. The workshop organizers invited her to speak about the relationship between Islam and contemporary Western economic theory.

"Does anyone know about Adam Smith?" she asked.

Again, no hands.

"Adam Smith and the Prophet Mohammad had a lot in common," Shazia said, before expounding on the virtues of Smith's economic philosophy. The mullahs scribbled furiously in their notebooks, craned their necks to see the whiteboard, and peered over one another's shoulders to be sure they hadn't missed any salient points amid the deluge of unfamiliar names.

"What's the invisible hand?" one asked.

"She's going too fast," another one mumbled.

"The Prophet used to say that kings shouldn't be the ones setting prices in the market," Shazia said. "It should be the job of the merchants." Her point? The Prophet busted up monopolies in his own day, and Smith's notion of the free market was totally compatible with sharia, Islamic law. But Shazia wasn't done. She wanted to tie economics to education, since, after all, she faced a room full of teachers. "When Adam Smith talked about wealth, he wasn't only talking about money. How do you teach your students? The way you teach shows how you regard wealth."

For the ten days of the workshop, two dozen crotch-scratching, Taliban-supporting mullahs listened to lecturers like Shazia, with the hopes that what they learned could be used to improve their own teaching techniques back in Baluchistan. The workshop wasn't focused solely on pedagogy—it was also an immersion in modernity. Shocking the madrassa teachers seemed to be the unstated goal. In addition to the startling Shazia, the workshop took place at a gaudy hotel in Karachi, where neon palm trees decorated the lobby and mirrors lined the walls. In the downstairs restaurant, a clown wearing a wide-brimmed hat, frills around his wrists and ankles, and white paint over his face greeted diners. I found the hotel overwhelming, so I could only guess at its impact on the mullahs.

Midway through the workshop, one lecturer asked the mullahs if they had heard of Wal-Mart. "Did you know that Wal-Mart—one store!—makes more money than the entire country of Pakistan?"

A husky madrassa teacher from a village near the Afghanistan border wrinkled his brow and raised his hand. He didn't understand how it could be possible. One store? Better than all of Pakistan?

The lecturer admitted that Wal-Mart was a chain, not just a shop on the corner. But his point remained the same: the gap was growing between the modern, Western world and the one these mullahs dwelled in.

"How can we get out of this hole?" the husky one asked. "How have we left the guiding principles of Islam and created all these problems for ourselves?"

MADRASSAS HAVE EXISTED for more than a thousand years, typically as small classrooms attached to mosques where young men gathered to read the Quran with a local mullah. They were an integral part of Muslim society. No one called them "jihad universities" or "dens of terror," as many in the West do today.

The madrassas began to change, and become more politicized, in the middle of the nineteenth century. Following the Indian Mutiny of 1857, the British administration placed a disproportionate amount of blame for the uprising on the Muslim community, leading to both a spiritual revival and a growing resentment against the Raj. In 1867, a handful of leading *ulema* congregated in the Indian town of Deoband to create the Darul Uloom Deoband, or Deoband University. The madrassa in Deoband spawned the sect of Sunni Islam known as Deobandi. Of the roughly sixteen thousand madrassas in Pakistan today, more than ten thousand subscribe to the Deobandi sect. Most Indian, Bangladeshi, and Afghan madrassas also follow the basic curriculum taught in Deoband, called *dars-i-nizami* (the study system).

In the 1980s, to meet the challenge posed by the Soviet Union's invasion of Afghanistan in 1979, thousands of madrassas peddled the virtues of jihad to young boys. When the war in Afghanistan ended, those who had imbibed radical theology relocated to Indian-occupied Kashmir. In the mid-1990s, with Afghanistan paralyzed by civil war, lawlessness, and banditry, a movement led by madrassa students (and heavily backed by Pakistan's intelligence services) rolled out of the southern city of

Kandahar and swiftly conquered the country. "Let the students take over Afghanistan," one madrassa teacher reportedly told the ISI at the time. In 1996, a movement of turbaned students toting RPGs (rocket-propelled grenade launchers), known as the Taliban, indeed became the rulers of Afghanistan. They pledged their allegiance to the Quran, sharia, and jihad.

After 9/11, once the Taliban were accused accurately of harboring Osama bin Laden and al-Qaeda, the words "madrassa" — which means "school" in Arabic—and "Taliban"—which means "students"—took on radically new and dangerous definitions. Though I had left my career as an aspiring philosopher years before, suddenly at least one idea of Jacques Derrida, the French deconstructionist, seemed all too right: words such as "school" and "student" had no meaning in and of themselves; society shaped language's values and meanings.

In the ensuing years, the U.S. government spent tens of millions of dollars trying to reform the madrassas in Pakistan. In doing so, they relied on cooperation from Islamabad. But the Pakistani government wasn't so eager to cooperate. Insofar as many madrassas provided a pool of recruits for the ISI to use in waging jihad in Kashmir and Afghanistan, the madrassas had become an arm of Pakistan's foreign policy. They were understandably reluctant to implement wide-scale reforms that might counter their assumed strategic interests. President Musharraf told the United States that he was trying his best and that he needed more time. Musharraf promoted a plan to register each madrassa, expel foreign students, and force the schools to incorporate "modern" subjects like natural science, math, computer science, and English. Musharraf said that, one day, he hoped madrassa students would be able to go on to become doctors, scientists, and engineers.

The madrassa debate boiled down to questions about encountering modernity. Musharraf talked about "mainstreaming" and "modernizing" the seminaries, but what did that mean? In the absence of standardized tests to gauge student progress, the measure of "modernization" devolved into tallies of how many computers or teachers or air-conditioning units there were in each madrassa.

The Darul Uloom al-Muhammadia in Lahore, a city of roughly seven million people a short drive from the Indian border, pitched itself as the vanguard of reform. I went there to have a look. I walked in to find a couple hundred boys crouched over ankle-high bookstands in a bunker-like room made of crusty cinder blocks sprouting rebar. They were reciting the Quran, chapter by chapter, in its original text, even though none of them spoke or understood more than a few words of Arabic. Their collective voices filled the bunker and mimicked a Gregorian chant. In order to stay awake through the marathon memorization sessions, they swayed back and forth like the weighted arm of a metronome.

The principal of the school, meanwhile, waited for me in an air-conditioned office upstairs. He boasted about the ornaments of progressive education strung throughout his school. "We even have Coca-Cola," he said. More than a dozen new computers, outfitted with the latest version of Windows, hummed in the library. The school subscribed to a range of English- and Urdu-language newspapers. Even the ranking U.S. diplomat at the American consulate in Lahore had recently visited and signed the guest book. "You see," the principal said to me. "We are cooperating with the government. What more can they ask from us?"

After bingeing on Coke, we took a tour.

"You are lucky," the principal said. "The senior students are practicing their speaking skills at this hour." In two adjoining rooms at the end of a hallway—one where students spoke English and one where they spoke Urdu—a student stood at the head of the class, facing a room full of his peers. "We make them defend various positions, even of other sects," said the principal. They hoped to foster the oratorical skills of these budding mullahs. "Sometimes I even assign them the task of defending the U.S. government."

This must not have been one of the "defend America" days.

"America is full of liars!" said a peach-fuzzed boy in the Urdu room. He asked how George W. Bush could talk about democracy but still support Musharraf.

In the English room, a gangly teenager yelled out: "You must have jihad in your grip! If you have jihad in your grip, you cannot be defeated, not by the Jews or the Hindus or anyone else!"

"What's going on in there?" I asked the principal, who stood a few feet behind me.

He smiled awkwardly. "It's nothing. They are just practicing," he said, anxiously. "Come, there are other things to show you."

* * *

AMERICAN NATIONAL SECURITY strategists remained deeply concerned over the fact that the madrassas were actually growing in number. In the autumn of 2003, Secretary of Defense Donald Rumsfeld penned a memo in which he confessed that "we lack the metrics to know if we are winning or losing the global war on terror." Rumsfeld added, "Are we capturing, killing or deterring and dissuading more terrorists every day than the madrassas and the radical clerics are recruiting, training, and deploying against us?" At the time, I was interning at the Center for Emerging Threats and Opportunities, a think tank in Quantico, Virginia, conducting research on religion and violence around the world. Frankly, I didn't know much on the subject, though Rumsfeld's memo piqued my curiosity. Why were the madrassas growing in number? And were terrorists, like the ones involved in the 9/11 plot, prone to plan a sophisticated attack inside one of these backcountry schools?

Soon after arriving in Pakistan I embarked on a journey around the country to observe an array of madrassas—and to find out what compelled students to go there, and whether they showed any signs of the reforms Musharraf had promised to enact. I found that, in many cases, economic factors and the state's collapsed education system—rather than some obsession with radical ideology—offered a better explanation for why parents sent their students to madrassas. At the public schools teachers didn't show up for work, schools laid in disrepair, and the nation's literacy rate hovered around 50 percent. For parents, especially in the more desperate households, opting to pull their children out of public schools and put them in madrassas was an easy choice. In a 2004 essay, Dr. Tariq Rahman, author of *Denizens of Alien Worlds: A Study of Education, Inequality, and Polarization in Pakistan*, wrote that, of the madrassa students he surveyed in his research, "76.6 percent belonged to the poorer sections of society."

To serve the most destitute families, some madrassas even offered scholarships, according to Amir Rana, a terrorism analyst in Lahore. "For each child they send to a madrassa, a family could make another eight or ten dollars a month," he said. "A poor family with no chances for work could send five or six kids to madrassas, and use the money they get to feed the rest of the family." Plus, those who attended the madrassa received three meals a day, clean clothes, and a place to sleep. In the absence of a welfare state, or even a well-functioning state, madrassas

performed the double role of being a school and an NGO (nongovern-
mental organization).

"In the U.S., they say madrassas are a big problem in Pakistan. That's
not our problem," Dr. Ata-ur-Rahman, a sharp, impressive leader of
Jamaat-i-Islami, former member of parliament, and a principal of a
madrassa in the North-West Frontier Province, told me. "Our problem in
Pakistan is not madrassas. Our problem is clean drinking water. Our
problem is sanitation. Our problem is health care. These are our problems that you should highlight somewhere."

More than anything, the madrassas wanted to be left alone. "There is
no reason the madrassas should be reformed. We have been teaching Islam
for hundreds of years. We are teaching the religion that we believe to be
the true religion," said Dr. Abdul Razzak Sikander one morning at his seminary in Karachi. Sikander presided over the Binori Town madrassa, a
rose-colored structure facing a busy road in the center of town. In
October 2001, one of the teachers issued a fatwa declaring jihad against
the United States. There were unverified stories that militants hid Daniel
Pearl there and that Osama bin Laden received medical treatment at the
madrassa. A veritable Who's Who of Islamic radicals had graduated from
Binori Town, including both Abdul Rashid Ghazi's father and brother,
and the founders of Harakat ul-Jihadi Islami, Jaish-e-Mohammad, and
Harakat ul-Mujahideen. When I showed up, fruit carts and booksellers
fought for space on the sidewalk out front.

Sikander walked with a cane. He kept his beard long and died it red
with henna. As we spoke over cups of tea, Sikander's students gathered
around, listening. "These boys come to our madrassa because they want to
become experts in Islam," Sikander said. "Musharraf says he wants them
to become doctors. But they don't want to be doctors. If they wanted to do
that, they would have gone to medical school. This is no different. So why
is the government trying to tell students: 'If you want to specialize in medicine, that's o.k.' But if they want to specialize in Islamic studies, they are
supposed to diversify? Why are my students having their rights denied?
Why are we the center of your attention? Why not the Jewish institutes?
Or the Christian ones? Basically all this talk about madrassa reform just
shows that Western powers are trying to rule Muslims in every respect. In
the West, gays and lesbians have rights. Why don't my students have the
same rights?"

I asked Sikander about his madrassa's relationship with the Taliban, but he ignored my question and continued.

"You know, I recently had another American visitor. She was from the institute of peace... or something like that," he said, referring to the United States Institute of Peace, a think tank in Washington, D.C. "How can the United States have an institute of peace, and still be involved in so many wars?"

THE MADRASSAS' SKEPTICISM and suspicion rendered all government-supported reform efforts ineffective. But what about private ones? Many other services that should have been provided by the state—such as electricity, water, security—were handled by private generators, wells, and security guards. Why should madrassa reform be any different?

Owing to my own sense of despair after watching the Pakistani government pretend to implement reforms, I was cautiously optimistic when I first heard about the ten-day madrassa workshops organized by the International Center of Religion and Diplomacy, based in Washington, D.C.

ICRD's representative in Islamabad told me how they convinced Deobandi ulema from Baluchistan to attend. "We make it as clear as possible that we are not against the madrassas. We tell them, 'We want to see the madrassas flourish. We want to see them serve the social and religious needs that only they are capable of serving.' We ask the participants in the beginning: 'Do you want your students to be followers or leaders in society?' All of them say, 'Leaders.' So we ask them if they are giving their students the tools to do that. When we tell them that we will teach them new skills for better educating their students, that often makes up their mind."

But for this to work, ICRD needed someone trusted by both the mullahs and the Americans, with credibility in both worlds. Enter Hafez Khalil Ahmed. ("Hafez" meant that he had memorized the Quran.) Ahmed was a reformed firebrand from a prominent religious family in Quetta, where his madrassa housed the regional headquarters for Jamiat Ulema-e-Islami (JUI), a political party and outspoken supporter of the Taliban. Shortly after 9/11, Ahmed led a procession through the streets of Quetta, chanting, "Long Live Osama" and "Long Live Mullah Omar." He had solid hard-line credentials.

Ahmed's thoughts about the Taliban began to change, however, as Afghan refugees fled the fighting in their country for the relative security of Quetta. He soon realized that common Afghans didn't love the Taliban as much as the Taliban said they did. "We thought the people of Afghanistan supported them," he said. "But we were wrong." Ahmed soon embarked on a mission to convince anyone who would listen that the Taliban's ideas were backward and misleading. He told me that he wanted to correct "wrong perceptions" people had about the West and the United States. He targeted those he knew best: madrassa teachers.

Ahmed had the thick, square jaw of a bulldog. Each time we met, his post-9/11 progression from Taliban-loving mullah to peace-loving, Gucci-wearing ambassador of progressive Islamic education seemed more obvious. He clipped his beard shorter and found flashier sunglasses. A part of me wondered what—or who—was behind Ahmed's turn, but I left it alone. After all, juggling the expectations of an American NGO and his fellow mullahs was no easy task. If he appeared too close to the sensibilities of the hardened mullahs, he would lose the trust of the Americans. But if he appeared too close to the sensibilities of the Americans, he would lose the even more important trust of his peers.

I asked Ahmed how he convinced the mullahs to attend the workshops in the first place.

"Because of my background," he said, puffing his chest, "people don't refuse when I ask them to come."

THE INTERNATIONAL CENTER for Religion and Diplomacy eschewed quantifiable benchmarks for reform, like "number of madrassas registered" and "number of computers per madrassa." With a proven record of resolving otherwise intractable political disputes around the world through unconventional, faith-based means (they had brokered a tenuous peace between Christians and Muslims in Sudan), they seemed up to the task. "Our biggest hope is that we can change the focus from teacher-centered learning to student-centered learning," the ICRD representative in Islamabad told me. And in the process, they wanted to sell the mullahs on the merits of non-Islamic subjects.

Abbas Hussein, another guest lecturer who spoke at the workshop the day after Dr. Shazia, explained that, by focusing solely on Islam, the mullahs were neglecting parts of their students' brains. To illustrate this, Hussein sketched out Howard Gardner's theory of multiple intelligences on the whiteboard. Gardner's theory identified nine types of intelligence:

Conservative clerics from Baluchistan studying the new teaching methods in Karachi. PHOTO: NICHOLAS SCHMIDLE

verbal/linguistic, logical/mathematical, visual/spatial, bodily/kinesthetic, musical, naturalistic, interpersonal, intrapersonal, and existential. "Unfortunately," Hussein told them, "you are only using a few of these."

During a tea break that day, Hussein sounded a tone that bordered on pity as he described the participants. "These people have been left alone in a cave of time. Now they are being woken to this bizarre reality, where they can't be put on hold because there is music playing in the background"—Islamic fundamentalists consider music un-Islamic—"and where they can't even stand in an elevator because of the Muzak."

"How do you think the ulema are taking Gardner's theory?" I asked.

"Honestly, I expected more resistance," he said. "I have been to similar workshops in the past and been asked if Howard Gardner was a Jew."

On the third day of the workshop, a Shi'ite scholar named Mohsin Naqvi proposed a provocative and unorthodox way of reading the Quran, borrowing heavily from Jacques Derrida and deconstructionism. The Sunni mullahs looked suspicious even before he had begun speaking, on account of Naqvi being a Shia. Now, Naqvi used Derrida, a staunch athe-ist, to discuss how the meaning of texts were fluid, and subject to infinite readings. An interpretation of a text depended on the reader, their history, their present situation, the time, and a whole range of other factors hav-ing nothing to do with the text itself. The concept struck me as potentially blasphemous to this crowd.

"Every word of the Quran should be considered in the context of time, space and situation," Naqvi said. "Remember that you are teaching a fourteen-hundred-year-old book. Besides the *kalma* [procession of faith], everything in the Quran is moving."

The mullahs squinched their faces and eyed Naqvi even more skep-tically.

"Are you suggesting that the Quran is relative?" one of them asked. He looked ready to brand Naqvi as a heretic.

"The Quran says that we should go to Mecca on camels and by car-avan," Naqvi replied. "But we don't do that anymore, do we? Times have changed."

I WAS SNACKING on a tomato-and-mayonnaise breakfast sandwich on the last day of the workshop when a mullah reached over to hold my hand. He was a heavy man wearing a prayer cap and a cream-colored shalwar kameez. He had a long, black beard spotted with silver patches. Crumbs from an earlier tomato-and-mayo item sprinkled his beard. He patted my hand and said he had a question.

"Mr. Nicholas, last night I watched... what they call it?... WW some-thing... fighting, you know?" he said in Urdu, stumbling over words.

"You watched WWE professional wrestling last night?" I asked.

His eyes lit up as he nodded yes.

He had stayed up late the previous night in his hotel room, flipping through the channels on the TV. He didn't have a TV at home. He had also never met an American. "I have seen some foreigners in the market," he said, "but you are the first who I have shaken hands with and eaten with." Finally, he had the chance to pose some hard questions to a real American.

Then his face wrinkled into a quizzical, somewhat troubled, expres-sion. Still holding my hand, he leaned a little closer.

"What *is* it?" he asked, as if he couldn't decipher a piece of modern art. He made thrashing and punching movements, like wrestlers often do. He wondered why the guys in spandex didn't bleed when their opponents smacked them with a foldable chair. With a bright, mischievous glow in his eyes, he held both hands in front of him, as if he were pinning two basketballs against his chest. "And who are those women? Are they married?"

The American flags hanging from the rafters and decorating the wrestling ring gave him the impression that pro wrestling was the national sport. When I explained to him that I wasn't a fan, that WWE wrestling wasn't real, and that not all women in the United States paraded around in public wearing flag-printed bikini tops, he looked disappointed. He released my hand and shifted his attention to the guy standing at the front of the U-shaped table, lecturing about pedagogy.

That afternoon, we took a field trip to a nearby church, which doubled as a Protestant college. We walked there and had to duck through eight lanes of Karachi traffic—which meant closer to ten or twelve "lanes" of cars, motorcycles, rickshaws, and buses. The mullahs shuffled across the street, giggling as their turbans unraveled and their sandals flew off their feet. When we arrived at the church, a middle-aged, spectacled Christian greeted us and welcomed us into a classroom. The mullahs squatted in the kind of small chairs intended for children, at knee-high desks. Five choir men filed into the room and assembled behind a table covered with musical instruments. The instruments included a harmonium and a pair of tablas, a type of drum played in South Asia. They broke into a hymn.

So there we were: two dozen extremely conservative mullahs (most of whom deemed music un-Islamic and Christians as infidels) and me, in a church, listening to hymnals that repeated the chorus, "Badshah Aye, Badshah Aye," or "The King has come, the King has come." All but one or two of my bearded companions, those who couldn't bear to watch and fumbled with their phones to seem preoccupied, fixed their gaze on the singers.

After listening to a few songs, we headed back to the hotel, and on the way, I asked one of the madrassa teachers what he thought. He said he had never been in a church before, nor had he heard such a kind of music, but that he thought it was "pretty good."

At the closing session, Maulana Mohammad Amin, one of the most senior workshop participants and a squat man with a maroon henna-stained beard, stood on the same podium where Dr. Shazia had stood before. During a five-minute speech, Amin's voice rose and fell with the dramatic flair of a Baptist preacher. He goaded his fellow mullahs to act, to inspire a revival in Islamic education.

"This is now *our* responsibility," his voice boomed. "We have to ask ourselves: How can we better educate our children? In the future, we will go forward with new techniques and new thoughts." He said he would "always be lukewarm to the idea of 'modern' education," but that "we cannot bring good religious and social change until we accept these subjects."

Amin paused and then added: "This week, a lot of my misperceptions have melted away. We had a lot of bad information about our own political and religious leaders. I am angry I believed this."

The mullahs listened attentively. Some nodded. Some pulled at their beards. A few of them scratched their balls. One dug in his ears with the tip of a pencil. All of them mumbled *"al hamdulilla"*—Praise Allah—under their breath. Amin added, "Just as the West has bad information about us, we had bad information about the West."

CHAPTER 5

"IT JUST SOUNDS AWKWARD TO CALL MYSELF A PAKISTANI"

ABOUT A DOZEN PEOPLE SQUEEZED INTO MAJID SOHRABI'S OFFICE ONE hot October morning. We sat on black pleather chairs pushed up against the walls. Just outside the door, the air was sticky and salty; a sea breeze stirred periodically. Overhead, a ceiling fan whirled and wobbled on its axis.

Sohrabi looked overwhelmed. For the youthful *nazim*, or mayor, of Gwadar, a town with roughly eighty thousand people on the coast of Baluchistan, a province in southwestern Pakistan, politics were something new. Baluchistan is massive, underdeveloped, and sparsely populated. Before Sohrabi won an election in 2005, he had spent ten years working for various NGOs around Gwadar, implementing nutrition and education programs for women. Unlike many of his fellow politicians, scions of landed wealth who considered it their divine right to hold office, Sohrabi lacked pretense; he wore a plain gray shalwar kameez, and his front tooth was chipped in half and slightly blackened. A trickle of sweat inched down the side of his face.

Half of the people in the office were townsfolk, there to complain about shortcomings in drinking water, electricity, and schools. The others were political activists in their mid- to late-twenties, most of them former members of the Baluch Students Organization, or BSO. They served simultaneously as Sohrabi's couriers and his think tank, off running an errand one minute, proffering advice the next. But when an old man groaned that the water in his neighborhood ran for only a few hours a day, Sohrabi scanned the room for feedback and the others stared down in their laps. The ceiling fan speedily clicked away.

Eventually, Sohrabi released a long, puffy-cheeked sigh. "Gwadar is supposed to be a city for the future, but every day these people are crying about water and basic health facilities," he said, turning to me. "If the government can build a port, why can't they build a new school?"

A violent controversy surrounded Gwadar when I arrived there in autumn of 2006. An insurgency was simmering across Baluchistan. By most measures, you could have described it as a civil war, and yet, news of specific attacks or bombings hardly, if ever, made the international press. Even local journalists had a difficult time covering the conflict, primarily because the fighting occurred in the hardscrabble hills of eastern Baluchistan, a jeep trip that took days from Quetta, the provincial capital. Rebellious Baluchis had been fighting against the government on and off for decades; this particular phase of violence erupted in large part because of the Baluchi opposition to what they considered the Pakistani government's "colonization" of Gwadar.

Gwadar embodied one of contemporary Pakistan's most significant challenges: How do you reconcile the nostalgic appeal of age-old traditions with the curious tug of modernity? President Pervez Musharraf wanted to turn Gwadar, a sleepy fishing village, into a booming, neon-lit port city along the likes of Dubai and Shanghai. Musharraf, who modeled himself on Kemal Ataturk, the founder of modern Turkey, hoped to lead Pakistan into a progressive, secular future. Gwadar, in many ways, was the cornerstone of Musharraf's vision, and one that he hoped would project his legacy across the Arabian Sea. Musharraf claimed to envision "history being made" when he publicly announced his plan to build a deep-sea port in Gwadar in March 2002. "There is no doubt that Gwadar port, when operational, will play the role of a regional hub for trade and commercial activity. The people of Gwadar and Makran"—the coastal belt of Baluchistan—"will get ample job opportunities which will raise their standard of living."

According to the plan, Majid Sohrabi's town would become a seaside metropolis in thirty years with skyscrapers, fancy resorts, and docks big enough for the *Queen Mary* II. (Two weeks before I arrived, the first five-star hotel opened, showcasing two glass elevators.) In the 1920s, a team of visiting British engineers noted Gwadar's optimal natural layout for building a deep-sea port, though they never acted on their plans. For centuries, Gwadar's hammerhead-shaped harbor drew fishermen and traders shuttling between Africa, the Middle East, and Southeast Asia. But Musharraf and his advisers hoped to attract more than just fishermen and dockhands: the Gwadar Development Authority, the office tasked with preparing the town for the future, officially estimated that 1.7 million people would relocate to Gwadar within three decades. When I privately queried a representative from that same office, he told me that 4 million was a more reasonable guess—"and potentially in much less than thirty years." It seemed that the official booster didn't want to alarm locals of the massive impending migration.

This imminent population explosion seemed like it could be the dream of many Baluchis: waves of gullible tourists, delegations of investors armed with expense accounts, and a long list of big-money construction contracts. But that's not how some saw it unfolding. "Just look at our history," said Sohrabi. "The government has simply not been sincere with the people of Baluchistan."

BALUCHISTAN'S SOCIAL DEVELOPMENT indicators were terribly low, even compared to other provinces of Pakistan. Just 20 percent of people had access to safe drinking water, compared to 86 percent elsewhere in the country. Only 15 percent of women could read. Health care facilities were underequipped, understaffed, and unsanitary. Though the five-star Pearl Continental Hotel, perched atop a cliff, was meant to be seen as a beacon of Gwadar's future course, many residents viewed it with disdain, as a cruel reminder of their own penury. Locally owned hotels stocked their bathrooms with plastic pails of water so guests could bathe when the taps ran dry. Electricity and running water were scarce commodities throughout the province.

Meanwhile, in Islamabad, Musharraf and his technocrat prime minister, Shaukat Aziz, trumpeted economic indicators that reflected the *true* state of Pakistanis' well-being, or so they claimed. They often cited GDP data, which had increased more than 6 percent a year for several years in a row; or the fact that more than half the population owned a mobile phone; or the *BusinessWorld* magazine story that called the Karachi Stock Exchange the best-performing market in Asia. But pronouncements in Islamabad hardly, if ever, corroborated with realities on the ground, especially in far-flung parts of the country.

Baluchis were frustrated and angry. Some channeled these emotions into demands for the creation of an independent Baluchistan. But Majid Sohrabi wasn't one of them. His political party, the National Party, promoted Baluchi rights, such as being able to learn Baluchi in public schools (teachers in public and private schools were prohibited from teaching the Baluchi language), and encouraged the central government to cede more autonomy to Baluchistan and Pakistan's two smaller provinces (the North-West Frontier Province and Sindh). The National Party pledged to confine its struggle within the parameters of the Pakistani constitution.

Provincial autonomy, as the National Party conceived it, could be achieved primarily through a redistribution of wealth. The current system required each province to send its revenues to the central government in Islamabad, which then passed out proceeds to each province, based on its share of the population. While Baluchistan covered nearly half of Pakistan, its share of the population—and thus, of the total revenue— accounted for less than 10 percent. Getting that relatively small amount of money to remote villages, spread across a territory the size of Germany, was nearly impossible, which, in part, explained the abundance of mud huts and the shortage of electricity.

The National Party wanted to rejigger the system so that the income from Gwadar would be sent to Quetta, the provincial capital, rather than to Islamabad, the federal capital. Baluchi nationalists had been arguing this for decades, as they observed the natural gas-rich areas of eastern Baluchistan sink into depravation. With Gwadar expected to generate huge profits in the coming years, Sohrabi and his party were determined to get a better deal this time around. "We simply want what is legitimately ours," he said. "We Baluchis should be the owners of our mines, our seas, and our lands."

But not everyone sitting in Sohrabi's office that morning, and certainly not everyone in Baluchistan, agreed with his party's commitment to working within the system. Among the four major Baluchi national-ist parties, the National Party was undoubtedly the most moderate. The youth were growing impatient. Jabbar, a soft-spoken, twentysomething activist, sat beside me on one of the pleather chairs and explained why he had never considered himself to be a Pakistani, though he had lived his whole life in the country. Whenever he or his Baluchi friends went to Dubai or Muscat (from Gwadar, a boat trip to either city took less time than driving to Karachi), they always introduced themselves as Baluchis, not Pakistanis. "It just sounds awkward to call myself a Pakistani," Jabbar said. "People in other countries don't trust Pakistanis. We don't either."

But didn't Sohrabi and other senior members of the National Party repeatedly affirm their desire to be part of Pakistan?

"If our leaders in the National Party can demand and gain our full provincial rights, then, okay, we'll be happy."

"And if they can't?"

"Then we'll build up pressure...and achieve our target," he said.

"What is your target?"

"I want a Baluchistan of freedom."

In some parts of Baluchistan, the rebellion was already under way. The Baluchistan Liberation Army (BLA) operated in the mountains of Kohlu and Dera Bugti, two districts in eastern Baluchistan that sat on most of the province's natural gas deposits. Their insurgency kicked off in early 2005, when an army officer raped a female doctor at the Sui gas plant, the largest in Dera Bugti. Akbar Khan Bugti, chief of the Bugti tribe and commander of a militia numbering in the hundreds, perceived the rape as an insult to him and his tribesmen. Bugti and his men launched a heavy assault of rocket, mortar, and Kalashnikov fire on the Sui gas plant. (The army had already evacuated the victim from the plant and was keeping her under house arrest in Karachi to isolate her from the press.) The fighting interrupted the gas supply from Sui, which supplies around half the country's gas.

To counter Bugti's militia, Musharraf deployed another forty-five hundred soldiers, with tanks and helicopters. "They will not know what hit them," Musharraf said on a nationally televised warning. In the ensu-ing months, the BLA expanded their resistance from sabotaging railway tracks and gas pipelines, to attacking military installations and convoys.

The BLA sustained a low-level insurgency during most of 2005, 2006, and 2007. They confined their attacks primarily to the unpopulated canyonlands in and around Kohlu and Dera Bugti. The insurgency killed dozens of soldiers every month, and strained the resources and attention of the Pakistani army.

Perhaps even more damaging than loss of life and material, the rebellion threatened the cohesion and integrity of the state. Jabbar didn't belong to the BLA, as far as I knew, but he and many other Baluchis his age supported the BLA's cause. To borrow Mao's metaphor, the BLA could increasingly swim wherever they wished because the sea of people supporting them was deepening.

Shortly after I arrived in Pakistan, I dined with a Baluchi friend at a Chinese restaurant in Islamabad, and he had invited me to make a plan to visit Quetta. He encouraged me to come soon. The violence was growing worse by the day, and discerning the responsible parties became more and more difficult. The BLA, the Taliban, and even the Pakistani intelligence services were all suspect, my friend said. "Seriously, don't wait too long," he whispered. He scanned the restaurant, in an attempt to assure that no suspicious characters were eavesdropping on our conversation. Then he cracked a devilish smile and leaned across the table with his voice low. "If you wait, you might need a visa."

DESPITE THE BLA's limited reach, it quickly got wrapped up in geopolitical games. In July 2006, hardly six months after the insurgency began, the British government listed the BLA as a terrorist organization. The move legally obliged the United Kingdom to arrest any BLA activists on its soil and to freeze the bank accounts of any suspected members. Yet with its interests and activities confined to the hills of eastern Baluchistan, the BLA posed no threat to the U.K. or its citizens. But if the United States or Great Britain wanted Pakistani cooperation chasing down Taliban and al-Qaeda leaders hiding in Pakistan, well, then, Pakistan wanted its enemies eliminated, too.

By late 2006, it had become exceedingly difficult for the Pakistani government to determine which Baluchis posed a threat and which ones didn't. While the BLA's guerrilla struggle and sworn purpose of seceding from Pakistan made it easy to discern their goals, nationalist politicians often spoke out of both sides of their mouths. On paper, everyone demanded provincial autonomy. But some parties voiced their frustrations in sterner language than others.

Akhtar Mengal, the head of the Baluchistan National Party (a separate organization from the National Party), said that he felt like the Musharraf government had pushed him into a corner. In the late 1990s, Mengal had served as the chief minister of the Baluchistan assembly, a fixture of the establishment. And yet now, Mengal realized that any public reference to the parliament or rule of law meant political suicide for him in the eyes of his supporters, whose antistate feelings hardened day by day. It was a self-fulfilling prophesy: as the Musharraf government increasingly treated Baluchi nationalist leaders, including some who had been elected to the highest national offices, as rebels, the politicians increasingly acted like rebels. Mengal, by way of explaining his advocacy of violence and Baluchi independence, told me, "The Pakistani army has given us no choice."

I met Akhtar Mengal in Quetta. A tall, steel gate fronted his house, like all the others in the neighborhood. The night before our meeting, a bomb blast had ripped through a gas pipeline in the city, and just a few days earlier, gunmen shot and killed the brother of the district superintendent of police near a park in broad daylight.

Quetta sat in a desert valley, about a mile above sea level, surrounded by mountains the color of burlap. Because of its close proximity to the Afghan border and the Pashtun majority inside the city, Quetta had become a refuge for routed Taliban leaders as bombs fell on Kandahar and Kabul in late 2001. Men with long beards and hard, creased faces walked the streets of Quetta with their heads wrapped in bulbous turbans; those women who dared to venture out either cloaked themselves in blankets and scarves, or wore the head-to-toe burqa. Taliban roamed the markets and gathered every evening to watch young boys play soccer on a dusty field. None of this was a secret: after being driven out of Afghanistan, the Taliban's preeminent decision-making body was even renamed the Quetta Shura, after the city where it convened. Anyone in the city who could afford a tall steel gate had one.

The confluence of Taliban chiefs, Baluchi separatists, and Pakistani intelligence operatives made Quetta a tense place for journalists to work. The intelligence agencies were by far the most difficult to anticipate. While they often ignored the movement of Taliban kingpins here and there, they harried Baluchi leaders and activists by tapping their phones, trailing their movements, and, with growing frequency, snatching them off the sidewalk and throwing them into secret prisons. The intelligence agencies showed no tolerance for foreign reporters either. In 2005, freelance reporter Nir Rosen received a phone call in his hotel room, with someone saying: "I'm calling to inform you that people are after you. We know exactly what you are doing, and if you do not leave the area, the consequences will be like Daniel Pearl." Two months after my trip, intelligence agents barged into the hotel room of Carlotta Gall, a *New York Times* correspondent, punched her, and seized her computer and notebooks. She had been reporting a story about the nexus between the intelligence agencies and the top Taliban leadership.

I stood at Mengal's gate and rang the bell. Half a dozen bodyguards mingled on the inside, two of them clutching Kalashnikovs. One of them peered through a peephole and waved me in. He led me across the interior courtyard to Mengal's office. Mengal sat behind a large, executive-style desk. A gun catalog rested atop a stack of magazines on his coffee table.

Mengal struck me as an unlikely leader of the swelling nationalist movement; he was short, in his mid-forties, with a clipped beard and thinning hair. He was not especially charismatic. But through his message and open resistance to the central government, he hoped he could fashion himself as the political leader of the movement. Just a month earlier, he and his fellow party members had resigned from their Senate, National Assembly, and Provincial Assembly seats to protest against the military's continuing operation in Baluchistan and the killing of a revered tribal chief, Nawab Akbar Khan Bugti. Outraged by the military operations, Mengal said, "During two hundred years of British rule, they never did the kind of things to Baluchis that Pakistan has done to us."

POLITICS AND CULTURE in Baluchistan revolved around the tribe. So even though Akhtar Mengal presided over the Baluchistan National Party, had previously served as the chief minister of Baluchistan, and had been elected to the National Assembly in 2002 (a position he held until a few weeks before our meeting in October 2006), he derived the bulk of his authority from being the *sardar*, or chief, of the Mengal tribe. The

Mengals numbered approximately one hundred thousand people in southern Baluchistan. As the sardar, Mengal managed private courts, jails, and militias. "Our tribal system, if not misused, is the quickest and easiest justice that people can receive," explained Akhtar Mengal's father, Ataullah Mengal, one day at his home in Karachi. Tribesmen resolved their disputes through a *jirga*, or tribal council, which ruled on everything from adultery to robbery to murder.

Although the jirga was a long-standing tradition, the sardars were not. In the course of colonizing the subcontinent, the British had empowered local chiefs along the restive frontier regions to handle daily matters. When Pakistan assumed control of the Baluchi areas, it continued with this ruling scheme. A 1968 ordinance declared 95 percent of Baluchistan under tribal law, maintained through jirgas, tribal militias, and sardars. (The remaining 5 percent was to be governed according to Pakistan's legal code.) The arrangement benefited both Pakistan's new government and the sardars. The sheer expanse of Baluchistan rendered futile any pretensions of administering it from far away, but the sardars could act as surrogates, or so figured the central government. In turn, the sardars enjoyed the freedom to rule their lands according to their own personal whims, accountable to no one. But it would only be a matter of time before Islamabad felt compelled to cut the sardars down to size.

In the 1970 elections, Zulfiqar Ali Bhutto, father of Benazir and founder of the Pakistan People's Party, won the most votes in West Pakistan, while a party of Baluchi nationalists emerged with the most votes in the Baluchistan provincial assembly. The Baluchi nationalists formed a government and named Ataullah Mengal chief minister. Mengal's government provided the nationalists with a political platform; they could now voice their grievances according to the laws of the constitution. It also offered an opportunity to enfranchise millions of Baluchis who had always seen themselves more as Baluchis than as Pakistanis.

But in February 1973, Bhutto dissolved the Baluchistan Provincial Assembly. His justification? An alleged discovery of a weapons stash, totaling some three hundred Kalashnikovs and forty-eight thousand rounds of ammunition, in the Iraqi embassy in Islamabad. Bhutto claimed that the weapons were destined for Baluchistan. The Iraqis, he argued, hoped to kick-start a transnational rebellion among the Baluchi tribes in Pakistan that would spill over into the Baluchi-populated areas of Iraq's archenemy, Iran. "The whole thing was such a cock-and-bull story," Ataullah Mengal told me one day at his home in Karachi. "Bhutto was a victim of a severe inferiority complex. He just wanted to prove to himself that he was the most powerful." To display his intolerance for dissent, Bhutto threw Ataullah Mengal and two other leading nationalists into jail.

When the news reached tribesmen that Bhutto had thrown their beloved sardars into prison, bands of guerrillas grabbed their weapons and, for years afterward, they battled the Pakistani army. The shah of Iran, fearing now that the insurgency would indeed inspire his Baluchi population, donated $200 million and thirty Huey helicopters to buttress the eighty thousand Pakistani soldiers already deployed in Baluchistan.

The Baluchis never stood a chance, armed with only Lee Enfield .303 bolt-action rifles, a World War I–era weapon. "Back then, if you had 50 rounds of ammunition, you were a rich man," the elder Mengal said. "Then, after five or six shots, the gun would get all hot and stuck." More than five thousand Baluchi fighters and three thousand Pakistani military personnel died in the four-year insurgency; while the Pakistani army struggled and was ineffective in any fights against India, it has displayed a penchant for ruthlessly crushing domestic rivals.

Peacemakers often come from what seem to be the most unlikely of corners. General Zia ul Haq, shortly after his 1977 coup in which he overthrew Bhutto, ended the war in Baluchistan. He promptly dismantled the tribunal Bhutto had established to try Mengal and the other top sardars on treason charges. Once freed, Mengal set off for London. He stayed there for almost twenty years.

PERVEZ MUSHARRAF DETESTED the aristocratic, feudal mind-set of the sardars, personified by Ataullah Mengal. While the average Mengal tribesman couldn't read or write his own name and lived in filth, Ataullah received guests in the gilded drawing room of his Karachi mansion. His clothes were finely pressed and—as I can attest, we shared a couch—he smelled like baby powder. Bald, with a thin mustache twisted at the ends, he reminded me a bit of Vladimir Lenin.

Besides Mengal's physical likeness to the Bolshevik leader, his ideas—and those of most Baluchi nationalists—were grounded in Marxism. During the 1980s, while the American and Pakistani governments joined hands to equip the mujahideen fighting Afghanistan's Soviet-backed government, the KGB paid Mengal and Marri tribesmen, two of the most antigovernment tribes in Balchistan, to spy on jihadi training camps. Ataullah Mengal, still recovering from his imprisonment and trial, had remained in London throughout this period. By 1995, however, London's long, overcast days had become "suffocating and sickening." Mengal decided to come home. Besides the weather, he also thought that "things had changed." During the civilian governments of Benazir Bhutto and Nawaz Sharif, the two-time former prime minister, Mengal recalled that "there was some political juggling going on. But when there is a military dictator like Musharraf, you can't do any political juggling. Either you leave the country, sit in the corner and forget about politics, or wait for the worst. Right now, we are waiting for the worst."

In 2005, another wave of agitation and insurgency swept across Baluchistan. This time, however, the guerrillas replaced their antique Lee Enfield rifles with Kalashnikovs, mortars, and rocket-propelled grenade launchers. Musharraf blamed the violence on three tribes and their "anti-development sardars"; he accused them of inciting violence in Gwadar and the gas-rich districts so that they could preserve their dying, tribal traditions—and specifically their individual claims to power. The "anti-development sardars" were Ataullah Mengal and his son Akhtar, Khair Baksh Marri and his son Balach, and Nawab Akbar Khan Bugti. "The sardars have been pampered in the past," Musharraf said. "But no more. The writ of the state will be established in Baluchistan."

Musharraf envisioned that Gwadar would create thousands of jobs and improve the livelihood of poor people. As a result, he believed, people's devotion to the sardars would crumble, and Baluchis would soon feel they had a greater stake in the future of Pakistan. The process, Musharraf imagined, would eventually render the sardars obsolete. "Musharraf is right about us being his political enemies. We will not allow him to use the port in Gwadar or to continue taking our gas," Ataullah Mengal explained to me. "The people of Baluchistan have the right to use that port and to use the natural gas on their lands for their own good. If there is a surplus, then Musharraf can have some."

Ataullah Mengal, despite his seventy-six years, fostered a reputation as a firebrand, calling newspapers to demand independence for

Baluchistan and to question the validity of Pakistan. He boasted that he had never once set foot in Punjab, a claim that other Baluchi dissidents considered a badge of honor.

His son, Akhtar, was even more combative. Sitting in the office of his high-walled Quetta home, Akhtar didn't mention a word about sharing any part of Baluchistan's wealth with the rest of Pakistan, surplus or not. "We have been demanding provincial autonomy for decades," he told me. "But every time we ask for it, the military launches another operation. The youth don't believe that asking for autonomy will bring any change. They feel like they are banging their heads against the wall. If we are going to face the army's wrath either way, why not demand separation?"

In the summer of 2006, *Armed Forces Journal*, a monthly magazine published in the United States with a readership composed mostly of military officers, ran an article, titled "Blood Borders," that proposed a radically redrawn map of the Middle East and Central Asia. The map carved the present conglomeration of postcolonial states along ethnic and sectarian lines. With Iraq embroiled in a civil war that pitted Shia against Sunni against Kurd, American military thinkers had begun to reexamine the cause of conflict in postcolonial Asia. Some believed that part of the problem was a failure to recognize ethnic identities. The map in *Armed Forces Journal* showed a "Free Baluchistan," spreading across Pakistan, Iran, and Afghanistan. I asked Akhtar Mengal if he knew about the article.

"We weren't aware of that map until it came under discussion in the National Assembly," he said. According to Mengal, a member of one of the Islamist parties initially mentioned the *Armed Forces Journal* map, which, the mullah argued, evinced American designs to divide and conquer Pakistan. It created an uproar. Conspiracy-hawking newspaper columnists wrote that the CIA's plan to dismember Pakistan had finally been exposed.

AKHTAR MENGAL INSPIRED fear in the Pakistani intelligence agencies. As a fluent English speaker, he could articulate the problems of Baluchistan to foreign diplomats and reporters. And increasingly he seemed to illustrate what the agencies thought could be a wider phenomenon, of politicians leaving their seats in parliament to wage, or at least openly advocate, guerrilla war. By 2006, the agencies were "practically ruling Baluchistan," in the words of a senior journalist in Quetta. A report by the Human Rights Commission of Pakistan discussed how young men suspected of sympathizing with the nationalist movement and the BLA were snatched off the streets and taken to "private torture cells run by the intelligence agencies." They were "blindfolded and handcuffed and tortured through various means, including injection of unknown chemicals, humiliation, and stripping." At the peak of the state-sponsored kidnapping policy, more than five hundred Baluchi men were listed as "missing." In Quetta alone, there were at least five secret prisoners; I knew about them from someone who had been shackled there.

The agencies used a variety of techniques to break people like Mengal. They kept Mengal, his family, and anyone they interacted with under heavy surveillance. In April 2006, agents from Military Intelligence (MI) tried to kidnap Mengal's kids. Mengal's two daughters attended Karachi's Bay View Academy. One morning, the principal there received a phone call from a man who said the girls had been abducted. The girls hadn't yet arrived at school, though, so the principal rang Mengal's wife, who then called Mengal, who was in Quetta. "Don't let the kids leave the house," Mengal said. He dropped the phone, jumped into his car, and sped across the desert, from Quetta to Karachi.

Two days later, Mengal drove the children to school himself. On the road, he noticed a pair of Honda motorcycles, both of which carried two passengers, trailing him. When he dropped his daughters off at Bay View, which had guards of its own, the bikes were idling in his rearview mirror. Returning to his house, the bikers followed him. Mengal was prepared for something like this and had ordered his own bodyguards to trail in another car. Mengal called his bodyguards on their mobile phone and told them to close ranks. Then Mengal stopped in the middle of the road. His bodyguards' car did the same, trapping the two bikes. One duo dropped their bike and escaped. Mengal and his guards dragged the other two into his house nearby. Mengal recalled slapping them a few times, he told me, but "not enough to draw blood."

"Who are you?" he screamed. "Why are you following me?"

Mengal suspected that they worked for the agencies, though the two men—one in his twenties and the other in his early thirties—looked "like any other ordinary mobile-phone snatcher, car-jacker, or kidnapper." Their ID cards proved that they worked for MI.

"We are on duty," one said.

"What duty do you have trying to kidnap my kids?" Mengal asked.

The men denied that they were trying to kidnap the children and said that any kidnappers "belonged to another agency." Unsatisfied with their answers, Mengal kept them tied up his living room.

Meanwhile, the two motorcyclists who escaped on foot had reached MI headquarters and relayed news of their colleagues' capture. Thirty minutes later, a major from MI, not in uniform, showed up at Mengal's front door. "You have my guys," said the major.

"Yes, your men are with me," Mengal said. "I will hand them over to the police." The police soon arrived to demand the release of the two men. In exchange, they handed Mengal an official notification canceling the licenses on all of his personal weapons. Mengal told his guards to retrieve two AK-47s, and Mengal removed his pistol from its holster. Meanwhile, as he looked over the policemen's shoulders, he saw law-enforcement authorities besieging his house. Police vans parked at skewed angles out front and snipers perched behind walls and on neighboring roofs. As night fell, floodlights illuminated the block around Mengal's home. Nearby, the police parked passenger buses across the main road to prevent Mengal's supporters from reaching the house to protest. Authorities cut the water supply, telephone lines, and electricity.

The floodlights stayed on for a week, with no one allowed to enter or leave the house. Mengal's father, Ataullah, shuttled food to the front door, which the police inspected beforehand to guarantee that handguns weren't being smuggled in with the dal. By the end of the week, with Mengal and the others trapped inside running short on water, several hundred supporters commandeered a water tanker, pushed past the police cordon, and parked in Mengal's front yard. This broke the stalemate. I drove through Mengal's neighborhood in Karachi six weeks after the standoff; a handful of policemen were still there, sitting beneath a makeshift lean-to pitched against a telephone pole, watching the street.

As Mengal finished telling me the story at his home in Quetta, he shook his head back and forth. "There is simply no space for us anymore under the umbrella of Pakistan," he said. Resources weren't Mengal's biggest concern; the Baluchis' identity was at stake. "When your history is denied, when your culture is in danger, and when your language disappears, how can you say, 'I have a future'?"

"What does that mean for you as a political leader?" I asked.

"They say that all is fair in love and war," Mengal replied. "When the matter comes to war, everyone has the right to destabilize the government. When will the world see what the Pakistani regime has been doing to us for the last sixty years? Why does the world keep neglecting our screams?"

HOURS AFTER MY interview with Mengal, the intelligence agencies came looking for me. I had opted to stay in a lesser-known hotel while in Quetta, hoping to get in and out before the agencies noticed. But a visit to the Mengal household put me on their radar in a hurry.

The hotel was a single-story place, with all the rooms facing a semi-circular driveway in front. That afternoon, during some downtime, I opened the front door and noticed a white, two-door hatchback pulling into the driveway. Eight people had crammed into a car meant to seat four. An arm poked out of one window, a head from another. I watched the car out of pure curiosity as it parked by the reception desk. Two men emerged from the tangle of limbs in the backseat and approached the desk. I stood roughly one hundred feet away and couldn't hear their conversation, but the manager pointed at my room. The two men nodded, thanked him, and headed toward me—just a couple of intelligence goons out for an afternoon stroll.

I had to give them some credit: heading out on duty with what seemed like their extended family in a backfiring jalopy showed a marked indifference to being inconspicuous. When I was sure that the two agents were coming for me, I met them outside my door.

"Are you Mr. Schmidle?" the shorter of the two men asked in Urdu.

"Yes. Who are you?" I answered in Urdu. Both men smiled.

"We are from Special Branch," the short one said. Special Branch, secret police who report to the Interior Ministry, were one of the many intelligence outfits. "Do you have an NOC"—a Non-Objection Certificate—"that allows you to be in Quetta?"

"I don't need an NOC to visit Quetta," I said, switching to English. They well knew that foreigners didn't need special permission for Quetta, and they conceded the point. I handed them my business card, which introduced me as a Visiting Scholar at the Institute of Strategic Studies in Islamabad, and added, "If you have any problems, you can call my office in Islamabad." The agents took my business card and went away. They would come around—or at least their friends would—again.

A MONTH LATER, as Akhtar Mengal was preparing to lead a "Long March" from Gwadar to Quetta in protest against Musharraf's military operation in Baluchistan, police placed him under house arrest. The government filed a charge sheet stemming from the incident involving his detention of the two MI agents, and announced their plan to try him in Pakistan's Antiterrorism Courts. He was detained for almost two years. When the judge called him to testify in court midway through his detention, Mengal was wheeled into the courtroom in a metal cage. "The BNP leader is being humiliated because he resisted illegal action of intelligence agency personnel," the Human Rights Commission of Pakistan declared in a statement.

But Baluchistan remained, for the most part, a black hole of media coverage. While a story about top Taliban leaders roaming the streets of Quetta occasionally sparked some interest, the Baluchi nationalists' struggle for autonomy and recognition garnered little. Mengal was right. The world was neglecting his screams.

MORE THAN A thousand years before the creation of Pakistan, the Baluch people parted from their Kurdish brethren in the mountains of modern-day Syria, Turkey, and Iran and migrated to modern-day Baluchistan. Like the Kurds, the Baluchis lived beyond the borders of today's nation-states.

Baluchi nationalism emerged in the middle of the eighteenth century when Naseer Khan, the sixth Khan of Kalat, expanded his unified control over the Baluchi-speaking regions of modern-day Iran, Afghanistan, and Pakistan, and ended three hundred years of tribal feuding. The map of "Free Baluchistan" pictured in the *Armed Forces Journal* article corresponded, more or less, with the borders of Kalat during the reign of Naseer Khan. Naseer Khan had raised an army of thirty thousand men. This both shored up his authority and crushed any of the lower khans' ambitions to gain power. Naseer Khan was once described as "a most extraordinary combination of all the virtues attached to soldier, statesman or prince" by Sir Henry Pottinger, an English spy who journeyed through Baluchistan disguised as a Tatar horse trader. When Naseer Khan died in

1794, the Baluch kingdom had reached its zenith; the "Great Game," pitting Russia and England against each other for control of Central Asia, was just heating up, and both countries considered Baluchistan a prize piece of real estate.

By the middle of the nineteenth century, the Russian Empire was growing by an average of fifty-five square miles a day. The British, wanting nothing more than to protect their "jewel" in India against Russian invasion, looked for any opportunity to push their orbit of influence farther and farther west. After two failed military expeditions in Afghanistan, the British redoubled efforts to secure allegiance from the Khan of Kalat. If successful, the Khan's territory would create a buffer along the western frontier of the Raj's sprawling colony in the subcontinent. Eager to gauge the Khan's inclinations, the British sent a seasoned political officer named Robert Sandeman to meet Khodadad Khan, the serving Khan of Kalat and Naseer Khan's successor, in the summer of 1876.

The meeting between Sandeman and Khodadad Khan changed Baluchistan forever. "He was the last sovereign ruler of Baluchistan," Noori Naseer Khan, an eighty-seven-year-old historian in Quetta, told me. By the time Sandeman parted from Khodadad's company, he had been named the first governor-general of Baluchistan. This diplomatic coup, by which British political control extended into Baluchistan, also pushed the frontier of the Raj to the border of Afghanistan and Persia. Noori Naseer Khan told me that it signaled the foreign occupation of Baluchistan. "When the British conquered India, they conquered two other independent countries: Burma in the east, and Baluchistan in the west."

Over the next seventy years, the British ruled Baluchistan from New Delhi. They recognized, early on, that controlling the hinterlands would be problematic, so they propped up a few sardars who could keep their respective areas under control. To institutionalize this policy, the British divided Baluchistan into two parts: "British Baluchistan" and "Baluchistan." British Baluchistan encompassed the region bordering Afghanistan, populated almost entirely by Pashtuns; Baluchistan consisted of the remote, sparsely populated areas populated by Baluchis.

By early 1947, the British were trying to figure out how they could leave the subcontinent without inciting a civil war. One of the challenges was determining what to do with the more than seven hundred "princely states" scattered throughout India. Like the arrangement hammered out between Sandeman and Khodadad Khan, the British government had wrestled land concessions from hundreds of other khans, princes, and maharajas. Now, with independence looming, the royals wanted assurances that they wouldn't be swallowed by another colonial power: Pakistan or India. Ten days before the Partition of India, the British viceroy notified the reigning Khan of Kalat that Kalat would gain full independence. (Burma had proclaimed its independence a decade earlier.) On August 11, the Khan of Kalat announced the formation of his new state, called Kalat; the *New York Times* printed a story with an accompanying map the following day. Soon thereafter, the Khan went to work, forming a bicameral government in Kalat, with one house formed from elected representatives, and the other from sardars.

But Baluchistan fell apart before long, a throwback to the era of feuds and fractures that prevailed before Naseer Khan arrived in 1749. By 1948, three swaths of territory—including the coastal region of Makran—had already seceded from Kalat and joined Pakistan. During a long discussion one night at his home in Quetta, Noori Naseer Khan, the historian, showed me a cutout from a political cartoon published in March 1948. The cartoon showed the Khan of Kalat with his legs and arms hacked off, squirming around on the floor. The severed limbs symbolized Makran and the other two defected regions. Dreams of a unified, independent Baluchistan, the picture suggested, were in their death throes even then.

Once Makran peeled off to join Pakistan, the Khan of Kalat convened a council of seven members to decide the fate of Baluchistan. The historian Noori Naseer Khan, who was a member of the Khan's family, attended that meeting. He was twenty-nine years old. He argued that, on the heels of Partition and the radical reeducation about Islam that preceded it, the Baluchis were in great danger if they insisted on their independence. Baluchis are also Muslims, but they consider themselves Baluchis first. And during this phase of history, as Pakistan marshaled the forces of religious identity to forge a new state, expressions of separate, ethnic-based identities were discouraged. "The Muslims of India—Pashtuns, Bengalis, Punjabis, Sindhis and Mohajirs—have been pumped up, and are full of Islam," he told the council. "In the name of Pakistan, they will massacre all of us. Therefore, under duress, I accede to Pakistan." By the end of that month, the council had heeded his advice;

the Khan of Kalat folded his empire into Pakistan. Losing Makran isolated Kalat from its access to the Arabian Sea and eventually forced the Khan of Kalat to integrate into Pakistan.

BALUCHISTAN HARDLY SEEMED a prize. Its long coastline was a great asset for trade, but otherwise, the climate was unbearably harsh. Temperatures in the summer often exceeded 120 degrees, and in the winter they dropped well below freezing. A water expert in Quetta once told me that there had been no substantial rainfall for almost eight years, and the water table, already one hundred feet below the surface, was falling between three and four feet annually. A U.S. Geological Survey once described Baluchistan as the closest thing on earth to Mars.

In 1953, Baluchistan's fortune looked like it might change when the Pakistan Petroleum Company discovered natural gas in Sui, a town in eastern Baluchistan. Residents in major Pakistani cities soon enjoyed gas stovetops and furnaces. But the gas flow only exacerbated Baluchis' perception of being treated as colonial subjects, as it took thirty-three years for piped gas to reach Quetta. Residents in Sui still haven't received piped gas.

Sui is located in Dera Bugti district, where Nawab Akbar Khan Bugti lorded over the Bugti tribe. Bearded and bespectacled, Bugti had become the face of the insurgency; from early 2005, Bugti fought the Pakistani army with a private militia of some five thousand loyal tribesmen, who claimed to be fighting for *"Sahil, wa Saheil, Haqiqiane,"* or "Coast, Resources, and Control for the People." Seeing that Bugti, a onetime governor and chief minister of Baluchistan, had taken up arms against the state, Baluchi youth raised him to mythical, Che Guevara–like status. The few foreign correspondents brave enough to drive across the desert all night, without any headlights for fear of giving away the car's position and inviting rocket fire from a Pakistani helicopter, tended to idolize him, too. When one reporter reached Bugti's mountain redoubt, he found the seventy-nine-year-old tribal chief reading a recent copy of *The Economist.* Bugti got a kick out of peddling myths, such as the one about him attending Oxford, or the other about him killing his first man at age eleven. Both stories were untrue but found their way into Bugti's self-made canon.

Bugti gave Baluchi insurgents what Ahmed Shah Masood, the

famous, floppy-hat-wearing mujahideen commander who spoke fluent French and recited poetry, had once given the Afghan mujahideen: someone for the West to relate to, a heroic and human face among anonymous guerrillas.

When Pakistani security forces bombed Bugti's cave and killed him in August 2006, Baluchistan burned for days. Thousands of rioters spilled into the streets of Quetta, chanting "Death to Pakistan" and stomping on portraits of Mohammad Ali Jinnah, the founding father of Pakistan. Dozens died and hundreds were arrested. Authorities blocked roads and canceled air and rail service to and from Quetta. In Gwadar, protesters burned the office of Pakistan International Airlines, ransacked the office of the pro-Musharraf party, Pakistan Muslim League, and torched a life-size effigy of Musharraf. To heap further insult on Musharraf, demonstrators soaked the effigy's crotch with water before they set it on fire, suggesting he had lost control of both his country and his bladder.

Enraged Baluchis attacked Punjabis, prompting many to flee Quetta, leaving their homes unguarded and their businesses to be vandalized. The BLA established checkpoints around the province, stopping motorists to ask them their ethnicity. Those who answered "Punjabi" were often killed. Earlier in the year, gunmen shot and killed three picnickers at a serene camping spot an hour outside of Quetta after learning that they were Punjabis. When I asked Akhtar Mengal about the BLA, he quipped, "Our BLA is an organization to stand against the PLA—the Punjab Liberation Army. The Pakistani Army is the PLA."

Moyheddin Baluch, the chairman of a radical wing of the Baluch Students Organization, also pitched the guerrilla struggle in ethnic terms. "We are fighting the Punjabi establishment, its policies, and its terrorism," he said. On the day of Bugti's death, Moyheddin issued a statement calling for civil disobedience across the province. "We don't accept any law of the state," he told me.

I asked him if he belonged to the BLA himself.

"Ideologically, we support the insurgents. But they are struggling with their arms and our ideology is only political. We agree in our demand for a free Baluch state."

I personally never met Bugti, but he represented one of the most difficult challenges to assessing the situation in Baluchistan: deciding who was right. Bugti was a warlord, accused of killing his own people as well as Pakistani soldiers. "He and the other sardars are enemies of this country," a colonel in Quetta once told me. And yet, his argument for taking up arms—fighting for the rights of Baluchis—was convincing to many. The world over, rebels enjoyed an unwarranted amount of prestige just for being underdogs. But who was fighting the good fight here? The Pakistani army battled to keep the country united, while their actions further galvanized the Baluchis to break away. Bugti's death seemed like the final blow.

Jamil, Bugti's son, told me that his father's death was "a very clear signal to everyone that Baluchis should form their own nation." I met Jamil twice. Our first conversation took place at French Beach, about an hour's drive from Karachi, where we spent an afternoon eating BBQ and taking tequila shots. Our second occurred in Quetta, hardly a month after helicopter gunships pounded his dad's cave. The government had placed Jamil on an exit control list and frozen his bank accounts. By the end of 2006, nearly every nationalist leader in Baluchistan had been killed, arrested, or placed under house arrest. Jamil understood the government's message—and threat—well. But he chose to ignore it and continued calling for an independent Baluchistan. "I don't see any progress coming from the Gwadar port," he explained when I mentioned Musharraf's stated plan to crush the insurgency and improve the lives of ordinary Baluchis. "Baluchis will only become minorities in their own land. After all these mega-roads are built, the Baluch will still be there with their donkey carts. This is a business venture of the colonial power— 'either you submit or we will treat you like we treated Akbar Khan Bugti.'"

On the political front, arguably the most significant result of Bugti's death was the reemergence of the Khan of Kalat, whose role had been marginalized by that of the Bugtis, the Mengals, and the most militant of the tribes, the Marris. Throughout the fall of 2006, Aga Suleiman Dawood, the fortysomething descendant of the Naseer Khan the Great, called a jirga of all the Baluchi sardars from Iran, Afghanistan, and Pakistan. "We have to sort out our home," he told me at his residence in Quetta one evening. "We have been like a herd of sheep without a shepherd." The jirga decided to present a case before the International Court of Justice in The Hague, arguing that Pakistan had robbed the Baluchis of their own state.

"We were never supposed to be part and parcel of Pakistan," said

Dawood after taking a drag on the cigarette he held between his meaty fingers. He contended that the treaty of accession signed in March 1948 between Mohammad Ali Jinnah and Ahmed Yar Khan, Dawood's grandfather and the serving Khan of Kalat, might have spelled out Kalat's merging into Pakistan, but said nothing about the Khan of Kalat being subservient to Pakistani rulers. "We are sitting on gold and anytime we speak up and ask for due compensation, we get a bloody spanking. We didn't come to Pakistan for this," he said. The jirgas were intended to measure the "strength of the Baluchi nation." He added, "We are eyeball to eyeball with the state."

A few months later, Dawood flew to The Hague to file his case. While he was out of the country, the intelligence agencies contacted him and told him not to come home. He has been in exile, his exact location unknown, since early 2007.

Before leaving Dawood, I asked which, of all of Baluchistan's problems, worried him most.

He took a final drag from his cigarette, smashed the butt into the ashtray, and said, without pause, "Gwadar."

I WANTED TO drive from Quetta to Gwadar, but was discouraged against it, as the road passed through some remote, dodgy areas, where bandits controlled the highway after dark. So I planned to fly to Karachi, and then drive from Karachi to Gwadar. Before I did any of that, though, I needed special clearance in the form of a Non-Objection Certificate, a kind of permission slip required to travel to areas deemed dangerous or politically sensitive. On my last day in Quetta, I went to the Home and Tribal Affairs Department, which issued NOCs. I waited a couple hours outside an official's door, who chitchatted and laughed with some friends. He eventually called me in and dictated a letter to a scribe, who ran it upstairs to the typist, who pulled the dustcover off his typewriter, wrote the letter, handed it back to me so I could bring it back downstairs to the official, who signed it and sent me off.

An NOC served several functions. The explicit, stated one is that it guarantees a foreigner's own protection, since most of the regions that necessitate the NOC are dangerous and the authorities often assign a policeman or gunman for protection. The unstated functions are to either keep foreigners out of certain areas, or to alert the intelligence agencies that an inquisitive foreigner is on the way. For instance, two weeks before my trip, a Norwegian journalist had flown to Gwadar without the document; when he couldn't produce the NOC upon disembarking from the plane, he was put on the next flight out.

At the bottom of my single-page letter was a list of all the parties who would receive a copy of the same letter. They included: District Police Officer, Gwadar; Sector Commander, ISI (Inter-Services Intelligence); Sector Commander, Military Intelligence; Chief of Staff, Headquarters 12 Corps; Joint Director General, Intelligence Bureau; DIG Police (Special Branch); Personal Secretary to the Home Secretary. I marveled at the impressive lineup. It seemed that I wouldn't be able to slip in and out of Gwadar quietly.

In Karachi the next day, I went to the office of the Gwadar Port Implementation Authority, where I met a well-dressed, slightly anxious, senior representative. The man refused to be identified by name, claiming that he was not supposed to be speaking with journalists. His apprehensiveness illustrated one of the paradoxes of Gwadar: How can a state attempt to build a multimillion-dollar seaport and advertise it to foreign investors, yet be cagey about sharing information? The reason for their tension traced back to the political sensitivity of the project, as it both exacerbated the grievances of the Baluchi nationalists and offered a potential glimpse at the struggle between China and the United States for influence around the world.

After the unnamed GPIA rep gave what sounded like a memorized PowerPoint presentation, I asked him whether he also predicted that Gwadar could be the "next Dubai"—that desert oasis of free trade in the United Arab Emirates tricked out with mega-malls, man-made island resorts, indoor ski slopes, and Russian prostitutes. His answer began optimistically—"of course, of course"—before cautioning, "This will take some time. Dubai took thirty years to build, and they had oil money and no political pressure."

Chinese investment supplanted Pakistan's lack of oil wealth; Beijing covered the bulk of Gwadar's start-up costs. Besides providing most of the initial $250 million needed to dredge the harbor and build two berths, the Chinese had also sent six hundred engineers to Gwadar. "Their role has been comprehensive," said Mohammad Rajpar, a Karachi-based shipping magnate who also advised government ministers on Gwadar.

"The Chinese brought all their own labor—from engineers to bathroom scrubbers. They aren't even letting the Baluch sweep the floors, citing 'security concerns.'"

Ordinarily, the Chinese prefer to stay abreast and out of other countries' domestic squabbles, but in Baluchistan, they were thrust into the center of an insurgency. Hard-core Baluchi nationalists blamed China for cooperating with Islamabad's "colonial project" in Gwadar. In May 2004, a massive car bombing in Gwadar killed three Chinese engineers as they were traveling from their hotel to the worksite. Terrorists had killed and wounded Chinese engineers in Baluchistan in 2003, 2006, and 2007.

China's activity also concerned the United States, since a functional port in Gwadar would further expand China's economic profile and access to markets, particularly oil ones in the Middle East. "[China is] adopting a 'string of pearls' strategy of bases and diplomatic ties stretching from the Middle East to southern China that includes a new naval base under construction at the Pakistani port of Gwadar," reported the *Washington Times* in January 2005, citing a document sponsored by Net Assessment, the Pentagon's office of future-oriented strategy. By establishing a listening post and a naval presence in the Indian Ocean, the article continued to say, "many Pentagon analysts believe…that China will use its power to project force and undermine U.S. and regional security."

I asked the GPIA representative to what extent the insurgency and protestations from Baluchi nationalists had slowed the pace of construction in Gwadar.

"Not at all," he said. "Yes, many things are still lacking; there are no hospitals, clinics, or schools, for instance. But people of this area seem to be very happy. The price of their land has gone up, job opportunities have increased, and business has improved for merchants. They know this will be good for them."

"But aren't the tribal leaders telling them something different?"

A naval officer entered the room and the rep in the suit suddenly looked relieved. The officer answered my question without introducing himself. "The locals want this port very much," he said. "Gwadar is a different ball game from the rest of Baluchistan. The tribal system in the coastal areas is weak and the sardars have less power in Gwadar than they do in other places. The trouble in Baluchistan is because of an international dimension." The officer narrowed his eyes and spoke in short, stern sentences. "There are outside hands"—the oft-heard euphemism meaning either the CIA, Mossad, or RAW [Research and Analysis Wing], India's intelligence agency—"helping these rebels. Why are you people fighting your proxy wars in my country?"

The officer, the suit, and I sat around the table for a long, quiet minute. I had no other questions for them, and they showed no desire to keep chatting, so I thanked them and excused myself. I needed to pack. I was leaving for Gwadar in the morning.

A MOUND OF snack bags covered the backseat of the white Toyota Land Cruiser. As if the road from Karachi to Gwadar was not already desolate enough, our trip fell in the middle of Ramadan, the month of fasting, which meant that anything resembling a restaurant or rest stop was sure to be closed. Three men I had never met picked me up from my hotel at the request of Hasil Bizenjo, the secretary general of the National Party. One of the guys in the backseat was Bizenjo's nephew. He spoke good English and said he had nothing else to do, so he had decided to take a few days showing me around Gwadar.

The journey took a little more than eight hours, including the hour we spent parked on the outskirts of Karachi when our antitheft tracking device automatically seized the engine. Due to the high rate of carjacking in the city, almost anyone with a decent car equipped it with a satellite navigation system so that if the car was stolen, the team of employees back at the main office could pinpoint—and recover—the vehicle anywhere in the city. Carjackers often tried to take cars to Baluchistan, and then to Afghanistan. To prevent that from happening, the company automatically killed the engine as the car reached the city limits. So there we were, in a shabby, industrial neighborhood on the outskirts of Karachi, sitting in a luxury Land Cruiser with soft leather seats and a disabled engine. We waited for almost an hour until we reached the teenage son of the Land Cruiser's owner on the phone and told him to call the navigation company and disarm the service. A few minutes later, the engine hummed back to life and we pulled away.

We rode along the newly paved Makran Coastal Highway. Knee-high scrub brush and a smattering of palm trees turned into sand dunes and steamrolled desolation as we ventured deeper into Baluchistan. Far off on the horizon, mountains looked like drip castles.

About every hour, we saw what passed for a gas station: stacks of fifty-five-gallon drums of petrol lined up behind a bucket-and-hose contraption used to strain crud from the dirty gasoline. When we stopped to fill up, the wind hissed across the desert and seeped into my shirt, shoes, and ears. A motorcycle transporting three men, each of them wrapped like mummies, pulled into the pump as we were leaving. We didn't see another vehicle for almost an hour. A street sign that read SLOW DOWN DURING DUST STORMS had caught my attention earlier in the trip. When we finally ran into one, I experienced a bout of vertigo. The dust storm raced across the flat expanse to our left, at an angle, like a cheetah heading off its prey. The road disappeared in front of us and the desert melted against the windows, while the sun burned a pinhole through the clouds. The whole onslaught lasted hardly more than a minute and coated the fronds of the palm trees in ashlike sand.

Billboards popped up on either side of the road as we approached Gwadar. Shorn pieces of plastic shopping bags decorated the branches of tumbleweeds. The billboards' juxtaposition of color and scale against the drab desert reminded me of Las Vegas. They advertised neighborhoods with names like Golden Palms and White Pearl City. One showed a large arrow pointing to the new international airport under construction. Another pointed to a desalination plant. "The desalination plant is a lie," Majid Sohrabi, the mayor with the chipped tooth, told me later. "They aren't building any plant and they are slowly killing us with this disease-filled water."

The drive closer into Gwadar made me think less of Las Vegas and more of a deserted industrial wasteland, perhaps the site of a nuclear test or a chemical spill in the former Soviet Union. Behind all the hype and all the billboards, there were very few people, and even fewer businesses and shopping malls. As for construction, a handful of giant, arachnid-looking cranes loomed up ahead. Other than that, goats rooted through piles of garbage littering the roadsides and graffiti marked up the wall of a building, spelling out "BLA." Bleached from the sun and battered by sandstorms, the once-bright billboards made for a drab welcome.

* * *

SHORTLY AFTER CHECKING into a hotel in Gwadar, Hasil Bizenjo's friends showed up to take me to Koh-i-Batel, which means "small fishing boat mountain" in Baluchi, the hammerhead-shaped plateau that juts out into the Arabian Sea and forms Gwadar's natural harbor. Bizenjo's National Party enjoyed widespread popular support—far more than Akhtar Mengal's party, for instance—throughout the Makran coastal region, and particularly in Gwadar. I asked Shakeel Ahmed Baluch, Bizenjo's deputy, why the National Party, unlike the other, more radical, Baluchi nationalist parties, maintained such popularity. We stood on the top of Koh-i-batel, and looked west to Iran. The wind blew hard across this exposed highland; my pants drew tight around my legs and whipped against themselves. "Gwadar is just different," said Shakeel. "It's always been."

During the eighteenth and nineteenth centuries, when the Great Game was raging across Central Asia, an Arab prince from Muscat, the capital of Oman, ruled Gwadar. His brother, who was king of Muscat at the time, had exiled the prince. Feeling magnanimous, the Khan of Kalat offered to host the brother, and even gifted him with a protectorate of his own: Gwadar. According to the deal, once the Omani prince was cleared to return home, he would give back Gwadar. But decades passed, and successive Khans of Kalat were too preoccupied with maintaining their own power to worry much about Gwadar. Long after the Omani prince moved back home and took over the kingdom, he still held on to Gwadar. Finally, in 1958, Pakistan paid Oman a reported three million pounds for the city.

Shakeel took me through the Gwadar bazaar. The bazaar was a crooked alleyway covered with ripped sides of cardboard boxes, yellowed and fibrous pieces of plastic, and plywood to shield against the harsh sun. Near the entrance, the market buzzed with people and flies, which congregated near the young boys selling sweet bread and rosewater-soaked desserts. A few hundred yards farther down, however, the alley lay exposed and uncovered, the stores boarded up and bleached from the sun. Shakeel described the phenomenon of change in Gwadar: every day, the abandoned portion of the bazaar crept a little bit closer to the one with the shops and the boys and the flies.

We met a man selling donkey paraphernalia. His inventory of ropes, bits, and horseshoes looked old and stained; hard times were evident, the man said, because he had to sell fishing line now to make a profit. The abandoned side of the bazaar started just two or three shops from his own. "The new money is settling across town," he said. "That's where everyone else went. I'll probably have to go soon." The donkey salesman sounded doubtful that he or his colleagues in the market would benefit from the development in Gwadar.

Shakeel and I walked farther up and into the oldest part of the bazaar. The "old city," as he called it, was one locked-and-boarded-up store after another. Small alcoves beside the doors once held candles, which residents had burned at night to guide the fishermen home. At the time when Pakistan purchased Gwadar from Oman, Hindus and Ismaelis, a small sect of Shia Muslims, owned most of the businesses. The Ismaelis were primarily fishermen and the Hindus managed the businesses. Fifty years ago, Hindus comprised almost half of Gwadar's population. But as sectarian pressures began to weigh on the Hindu community, many of them fled to India, Muscat, and Dubai. In the oldest section of the bazaar, a neighborhood child pointed out the crumbling, demolished ruins of a Hindu temple.

In the offices of the Gwadar Development Authority down the road, a city planner spread a map on a table and showed me how things would look in ten years. Just outside his window, the skeletons of several unfinished fishing boats lay on the beach. What did the developers plan to do with the fishermen and the shipbuilders when the expected millions of outsiders started arriving? "The fishing harbors will be moved. Specific locations have already been appointed for them," he explained, tracing his finger across the map and pointing to the newly designated harbor across town. He added, "Luckily, the fishermen are happy."

Shakur, a career fisherman, didn't sound happy when I talked to him later. "Nobody likes the idea of moving," he said. "The market is here in town. Why would we want to go across the bay?" While such distances hurt small fisherman, who didn't have access to refrigeration trucks or speedboats, big fishing enterprises would flourish. Many were already expanding their operations from Karachi and crowding out smaller, local businesses. "Generations of fishermen are being forced to sever their roots," he said. "Many of us are leaving to seek new work." Shakur had recently started a construction business, but that, too, was slow. "There are a lot of contracts, but they are going to outsiders. We didn't even know that a 'Master Plan' existed for Gwadar until recently. Punjabis have been studying it for years, though, and they know the value of the land better than we do. Some people have already earned billions of rupees here," Shakur said. "Few of them have been Baluchis."

The flight of Hindus and their capital in the late 1950s marked the first seismic shift in Gwadar's demographics. With the imminent completion of the port, locals were preparing for the second. Every day, the animosity Baluchis, and especially the youth, felt toward the Punjabi establishment grew more acute. I saw it firsthand when I tried to pass a checkpoint, manned by a handful of young soldiers, erected between the town and my hotel. The soldiers looked barely twenty years old; two of them carried machine guns and another held a clipboard.

"Names?" the one with the clipboard asked when we stopped.

"We are taking him to his hotel," the driver said, pointing to me in the front seat. Hardly twenty cars drove this road daily, and, for the past three days, our white Land Cruiser had picked me up and dropped me off half a dozen times. The soldiers knew who we were, yet the same handful of them insisted on quizzing us each time. On my last day, as we drove to the airport and the soldiers stopped us once more, one of the Baluchis in the backseat snapped as we pulled away. "Fucking Punjabis! Who are they to ask me where I am going? I am Baluch. This is my city!"

FOLLOWING MY TRIP in October, Musharraf's regime continued to crack down on the Baluchi nationalists. When the Khan of Kalat left the country to file his case at the International Criminal Court in The Hague, the intelligence agencies called him and warned him not to come back. Akhtar Mengal, who had detained the MI agents in his house, was arrested. Shakeel Ahmed Baluch, my guide in Gwadar, called me one morning from his jail cell during a short stint in prison. Hasil Bizenjo, who had arranged my trip to Gwadar, went missing for several days, abducted by the agencies.

I should have known better than to think that I would make it in and out of Gwadar, untouched by the agencies. Later, for weeks after I returned to Islamabad, ISI goons visited my house on a regular basis. They typically stopped by during the daytime, and would inquire from my guard who I was, what I was doing in Pakistan, and what I had been doing in Baluchistan. For foreign journalists, traveling to Baluchistan was radioactive: go once, and you were affected forever. The night before I was planning to make a return trip in late November to meet Aga Suleiman Dawood, the Khan of Kalat, in Kalat, I received a rash of phone calls from an unlisted number, with someone on the other end calling himself *churro*, or "dagger," and repeatedly expressing his need to meet me in person. The calls, I suspected, were mere harassment by the intelligence agencies, intended to deter me from going to meet Dawood. They worked. The next day, I called Dawood and told him that something just didn't feel right about making this trip. I hated caving in to such fears but on the empty, remote road from Quetta to Kalat, too many possibilities existed for a car "accident" or a random, hostile checkpoint.

ON MY LAST morning in Gwadar, while I was waiting outside of the ramshackle building that doubled as the Gwadar International Airport, a major in the army noticed me standing beside the Land Cruiser along with two of my Baluchi friends.

"Are you a foreigner?" he asked.

I nodded.

"Show me your NOC."

"Sir, with all due respect, I am a guest to this beautiful city. Should you be asking politely for my NOC?" I knew that I was both legal and leaving, so my response came out sounding a bit more cocksure than may have been required.

Now he nodded. "Okay, *can* I see your NOC?"

I pulled it out of my bag and showed it to him.

"Where is your armed escort?"

I wrinkled my brow. Armed escort?

He pointed midway down the single-page NOC. "It says right here that you 'may be provided with an armed escort' upon arriving." In my understanding of the word, "may" implied a possibility, not a certitude. But according to the major, "may" meant "should."

"This is a very dangerous area to be wandering around by yourself," the major said. He hashed out several scenarios that might befall what he called an "unsupervised" visit. "What if someone wanted to damage this mega-project by attacking an American? You'll either be in heaven or the hospital. But I will have to answer to your embassy and my seniors as to why you were traveling alone." The major turned to my two Baluchi friends and said, "How can you take these risks? Your future depends on this project." My friends looked as if they might either gag or laugh in the major's face.

I told the major that I appreciated his concern, but that I thought I would be even more of a target if I was driving through the streets of Gwadar with a uniformed soldier sitting in the backseat. After all, I was in the company of local Baluchi politicians. The BLA, wherever they existed and whoever they were, weren't interested in killing fellow Baluchis. They targeted soldiers.

"The armed escort is not a matter of preference, but of protocol," the major said.

"Sir, I have just spent several days here in Gwadar, and have thoroughly enjoyed my visit. It is a great city, with great people and great food. I plan to write about it, and I hope to come back soon. And I am leaving right now. Literally, I am getting on the next plane," I said, pointing to the pickup trucks ferrying luggage from the recently arrived flight to the one-room terminal.

Over the course of our conversation, his tone had softened a bit. As I leaned over to pick up my suitcases and head into the terminal, he requested that I forget our conversation had ever happened. "Don't mention anything about it in your story," he said. "Only write the good things."

CHAPTER 6

"WHAT WAS WRONG WITH PAKISTAN?"

THE HEAD OFFICE OF AL-MARKAZUL ISLAMI—A SINGLE TOWER WITH frosted, emerald-green windows—rose several stories above the coconut trees and rooftops in a residential neighborhood of central Dhaka. In the streets of the capital city of seven million down below, an urban orchestra sounded. Bicycle rickshaws, decked out with handlebar tassels, tin wheel covers, and carriages painted with faces of Bengali film stars, *ding-ding-ding*ed along. Car, dump truck, and bus horns blasted multinote jingles, while ambulance sirens wailed, seemingly unnoticed. Yet none of the commotion reached Mufti Shahidul Islam through the thick windows of his fifth-story office.

Shahidul founded and directed Al-Markazul Islami, an NGO providing free health care and ambulance services. Many Bangladeshis suspected that the NGO was just a cover, and that Shahidul's real business was jihad. "Mufti Shahidul is a very dangerous man," the owner of my Dhaka guesthouse me cautioned the morning I headed off to interview him. Shahidul's party, Khelafat Majlish, pledged to transform Bangladesh, a country about the size of Minnesota, tucked between India and Myanmar, into an Islamic state. In 1999, police charged him with masterminding a bomb blast that killed eight Ahmadiyyas, a minority sect that fundamentalists often branded as heretics. When I asked Shahidul about the charges, he rolled his eyes, laughed, and swatted his hand, as if dismissing an embarrassing childhood caper.

It's always important to consider the source of an introduction. In this case, Abdul Rashid Ghazi, who ran the Red Mosque in Islamabad, had referred me. Ghazi boasted about his adventures fighting the Soviet Union in Afghanistan, his relationship with myriad jihadi organizations, and his friendship with Osama bin Laden. Before I headed to Bangladesh, I had asked Ghazi if he knew anyone in Dhaka and he scribbled down Shahidul's name on a business card. A week later, clutching the business card, I walked into the downstairs reception area of Al-Markazul Islami. Barefoot men conversed over cups of tea as custom ring tones and landlines clattered away in the background. I took the elevator to the fifth floor where Shahidul, who was in his forties, sat behind a large desk, surrounded by assistants and relatives. His aging father-in-law looked on proudly.

"Asallamu aleikum," Shahidul exclaimed as I entered the room. A scraggly, henna-died beard framed his face, and a puffy, nickel-size *mehrab*, the bruise that pious Muslims acquire from intense and regular prayer, stood out on his forehead. He wore a white dishdasha and a diamond wristwatch. We exchanged greetings and made small talk in Urdu. Shahidul flashed a wide, comic-book grin the whole time.

Local newspapers described Shahidul as a former mujahideen who warred against the Soviet Union in Afghanistan. So I asked him if he had run into Abdul Rashid Ghazi in Afghanistan, perhaps a rendezvous on the front lines or a shared experience in a training camp?

"No, no, no. I *never* went to Afghanistan," he fired back, sounding defensive. He recited his life story, which included a stint at the infamous Binori Town madrassa in Karachi, and later, a short trip to Saudi Arabia to raise funds for Al-Markazul Islami. No stops in Afghanistan. "I started Al-Markazul Islami in 1988, how could I have the time for jihad?" he asked rhetorically. Later, during a lunch of french fries, cheeseburgers, and pizza, he told me, "My main business is driving ambulances and carrying dead bodies."

Shahidul had sparked a nationwide furor and reinvigorated a long-standing debate just a few weeks before I had arrived in Bangladesh. In

December 2006, four weeks before the parliamentary elections scheduled for January 22 (though later postponed), I had gone there to cover, his party signed a "memorandum of understanding" with the Awami League, one of the country's two mainstream political parties. Traditionally, the Awami League was considered a bastion of secularism. The agreement stipulated that Shahidul's Khelafat Majlish would team up with the Awami League for the elections. The Awami League would benefit from Shahidul's vote bank, and if they won, the Awami League promised to pay Shahidul back by enacting a blasphemy law, pushing legislation to brand Ahmadiyyas as non-Muslims, and officially recognizing the binding nature of fatwas issued by local clerics, including Shahidul.

The deal outraged secularists across the country. "Khelafat Majlish is a radical Islamist militant group which is against the spirit of the Liberation War," said the Anti-Fundamentalism and Anti-Militant Conscious Citizens' Society in a written statement. "By ascending to power through a deal with a section of fundamentalist militants, the Awami League . . . will never be able to create a secular Bangladesh."

For years, the Western media had designated Bangladesh as an "international basket case," citing Henry Kissinger's notorious description of the Muslim-majority nation of more than 170 million. Development indices routinely ranked Bangladesh in the company of destitute African countries; the UN Human Development Index placed Bangladesh between the Democratic Republic of Congo and Swaziland.

The country had developed in an environment of catastrophic violence, which some historians have gone so far as to define as a genocide. Chaudhry Rahmat Ali, in his 1933 treatise "Now or Never; Are We to Live or Perish For Ever?" proposed that present-day Bangladesh become an independent Muslim state called Bangistan. But when Pakistan formed in 1947, rather than enjoying independence, the region integrated into Pakistan, referred to as East Pakistan or the East Wing.

Twenty-four years later, Bangladesh split. The rulers of united Pakistan, all of them hailing from "West Pakistan," refused to acknowledge the results of the 1970 elections. In those polls, the Bengali nationalist party Awami League triumphed. Its vote count should have allowed it to form a majority in the parliament, and its leader, Sheikh Mujibur Rahman, should have been made prime minister. When the West Pakistani elite stalled the formation of the parliament, the East Pakistanis agitated for autonomy, if not all-out independence. In March 1971, the Pakistani army, clinging to the idea of a "greater Pakistan" and determined to suppress Mujib and his followers, launched a military operation in East Pakistan. The army failed. Within a year, an independent Bangladesh had formed.

During Bangladesh's independence struggle, the United States sided firmly with West Pakistan. At the time, the military government in Islamabad was negotiating a rapprochement between the United States and China. Former president Richard Nixon would soon travel to Peking to meet with Mao Tse-tung, solidifying the so-called Sino-Soviet split in the Communist World. India and the Soviet Union, meanwhile, backed the Bangladesh independence movement. The conflict, in other words, quickly boiled down to cold war politics, irrespective of democratic considerations or gross human rights violations. In April 1971, as the West Pakistani government used Islamists as shock troops against Bengali citizens, Kissinger sent a cable to West Pakistan's serving military dictator, thanking him for his "delicacy and tact" in handling the situation. Washington feared that Leftist and Communist extremists would overrun Bangladesh. Here we were, thirty years later, with Washington and the Western media worried that the same country was exceedingly vulnerable to its opposing ideological current: radical Islamism.

Alarming stories increasingly appeared in the press about Bangladesh's slide toward extremism. After September 11, every Muslim country fell under renewed scrutiny over its indigenous extremist movements and lawless territories that could be exploited by terrorists. Bangladesh is the second-largest Muslim-majority nation, after Indonesia. (India's Muslim population exceeds Bangladesh's, but Hindus form the majority there.) Since Islamist parties, and personalities like Shahidul, seemed relatively close to seizing state power in Bangladesh, Western countries worried even more. In 2005, the *New York Times Magazine* ran a piece about Bangladesh headlined, "The Next Islamic Revolution?" And while I was in the country, a story appeared in *The New Republic* predicting that, "left unchecked, Bangladesh could become another Afghanistan—a base for regional terrorism."

I went to Bangladesh in January 2006 with two purposes: to cover the parliamentary elections and to discern the viability of fears over an Islamist takeover there. I found that the prospects for the country were not nearly as certain—or dreary—as suggested. While Islamists parties had multiplied over the past decade and public support for them had grown, society remained overwhelmingly secular—even militantly so. The Islamists might have been grabbing the headlines, but the secularists were holding their own in an intense power struggle. Bangladesh had a long history of civil activism, and people were passionate and eager to voice their opinions in the streets. The secularists perhaps did not have the finances and weapons that the Islamist groups had access to. But the same leaders who fought against the imposition of Islamic politics during the Liberation War in 1971, in which Bangladesh seceded from Pakistan, were not about to hand the country over to men like Mufti Shahidul Islam. And he knew it. Whereas in Pakistan, a politician's jihadi credentials often impressed voters, in Bangladesh such affiliations constituted a political liability, which is why Shahidul hurried to change the subject whenever I brought his up.

I asked Shahidul several times how he knew Abdul Rashid Ghazi, but he dodged my questions. Finally, he asked one of his colleagues to find Ghazi's phone number. He called Ghazi. Ghazi picked up. Shahidul introduced himself, and said he was sitting with an American journalist who was asking a lot of questions about Afghanistan and jihad. Shahidul asked Ghazi if he knew me. Ghazi said yes. He wanted to talk to me. Shahidul handed me the phone.

"Nicholas?" he asked.

"Yeah, it's me."

"What's going on there?"

I rehashed the situation: how I showed up at Al-Markazul Islami, used Ghazi's name to get in with Shahidul, asked a few questions, watched Shahidul dial Ghazi's number, and now was talking to him. It was an awfully odd few minutes.

After hanging up the phone, Shahidul wanted to talk about other things. Take his constituency of Narail, a city in the western part of the country, for example. "There is no corruption there," he said. "And it is a big Hindu area." Before the partition of India in 1947, more than half of Narail's population was Hindu. Shahidul boasted that, because of his work, "Hindu people now say, 'Islam is a nice religion.'"

Three days after our meeting, I went to a village near Narail. The Bengali countryside was a bright, nourished green, almost the color of a traffic light. Much of it sat at the edge, or just below, sea level. Villagers built their huts in concentrated clusters on patches of dry land. Rice patties splayed out in every direction. The slightest fluctuation in tides had wiped out entire villages in the past. In November 1970, a massive cyclone stirred a tidal wave that flooded parts of what was then East Pakistan, killing hundreds of thousands of Bengalis. George Harrison and Ravi Shankar later played a benefit concert in Central Park for the victims.

In Narail, I met a teacher at a local girls' school and asked him if Shahidul's claims checked out. "Mufti Shahidul Islam has helped *a lot* of poor people — Muslims and Hindus," the teacher said. "He's not only built mosques. He has also drilled a lot of tube wells and distributed a lot of money. So everyone will vote for him again." A local journalist said that Shahidul had funded at least forty mosques, thirteen madrassas, and 350 wells.

Stories of Islamist parties gaining support by providing public services were not exclusive to Bangladesh, of course. Hezbollah had done it in Lebanon; Hamas in Gaza; the Muslim Brotherhood in Egypt. After the October 2005 earthquake in Pakistan, Jamaat-i-Islami and many other groups, some participating in the jihad across the border in Indian-held Kashmir, had provided unflagging relief and reconstruction aid. The Islamists in Bangladesh were pursuing a similar strategy. And many Bangladeshis didn't have any clue.

I asked the teacher if local people supported Shahidul's vision of an Islamic state.

"Most people don't understand what he really wants. They think, 'Mufti gave us so much money,'" he said. "That's why he is so popular."

BIMAN AIRLINES, Bangladesh's national carrier, maintained a dilapidated fleet of jets and a reputation for hardly, if ever, being on time. So imagine my surprise when, thirty minutes before the scheduled 3:40 A.M. Dhaka-bound flight from Karachi, an articulate, extremely presentable steward approached the counter, tapped the microphone, and prepared to make what I assumed would be an announcement that we were now welcome to board the aircraft. Scores of bleary-eyed passengers, sprawled across benches, their legs propped and twisted over armrests, straightened up and zippered their luggage.

"Attention: All passengers going to Dhaka," the steward said. "We will be departing two hours late due to fog in Dhaka."

Two hours later, the steward came on again.

"Attention: All passengers going to Dhaka. We will be departing two hours late due to fog in Dhaka."

Our plane eventually touched down, rattling like a tin can being kicked down the road; we were four hours late. Fat-fronded banana trees lined the runway. The stewardess's phone dangled from its wall mount, dislodged in the trauma of landing. After clearing customs, I waited almost two hours for my suitcase to spit out onto the carousel. Fortunately, I wasn't in a hurry. I had nothing to do for the coming month except to roam around Bangladesh. The elections I had come to cover had just been canceled after three months of protests and riots compelled the president, Iajuddin Ahmed, to declare a state of emergency. Army and police units poured into the streets.

The agitation stemmed from the Awami League's refusal to accept the caretaker government, who was to oversee the polls. The Awami League's political rival, the Bangladesh Nationalist Party, had appointed many of the "neutral" caretakers before it left power. The whole run-up seemed fraught with peril, particularly if one looked at how the Islamists had inserted themselves in both political camps: Khelafat Majlish teamed up alongside the Awami League, and Jamaat-i-Islami allied with the Bangladesh Nationalist Party. Perhaps that's why, when the army took over, no one seemed to care. Liberals supported the army, but urged cautious restraint. Western embassies followed suit. If Muhammad Yunus — the microcredit guru, recently anointed Nobel Peace Prize winner, and Bangladeshi native — hadn't flirted with the idea of entering electoral politics, as he had, the story might have slipped past the world's media altogether.

In the days and weeks after the declaration of emergency, the army locked up scores of crooked politicians. At first, they targeted low- and mid-level ones, but as time wore on, the net widened. Just about every politician was dirty; the question was over how high the army would go. (Shortly after I left the country, Sheikh Hasina, the head of the Awami League, and Khaleda Zia, the head of the Bangladesh Nationalist Party, were both thrown in jail.) It became increasingly difficult to schedule an interview with leading politicians because many of them had either switched off their mobile phones or were sleeping somewhere different each night to avoid arrest.

As the police paraded luxury cars—seized from corrupt cabinet members—before local TV crews, I took a rickshaw ride across town one mild evening to the home of Shahriar Kabir, an outspoken critic of the Islamists. Street kids swarmed my idling rickshaw at busy intersections, hawking bags of popcorn, peeled-and-spiced cucumbers, and copies of President Musharraf's autobiography, *In the Line of Fire*. Kabir lived in a one-story home, ensconced in thick vegetation, tucked at the end of an alley. He greeted me and led me into a sitting room decorated with tribal masks. Sandalwood incense burned in the corner. Kabir, a squat man in his late fifties with a hand-broom mustache, shouldered a hemp tote bag. He didn't strike me as the kind of freedom fighter that one might expect.

Kabir had become a cultural icon of the Left, and sworn enemy of the Right. During Bangladesh's struggle for independence in early 1971, Kabir joined hundreds of thousands of other nationalist freedom fighters, known as the *mukhti bahini*, in order to drive out the Pakistani army. He recalled, with some hint of nostalgia, "It was total guerrilla warfare in those days."

Kabir and I sat talking for hours. He reminded me throughout our conversation that sure, Bengalis were predominantly Muslim, but that Bengali culture wasn't excessively Islamic. According to Kabir, language defined Bengali identity, not religion. The author of the national anthem, Rabindranath Tagore, was a Bengali-speaking Hindu. Tagore, who also wrote poetry, won the Nobel Prize for Literature in 1913, and went on to write the national anthem for India, too. Kabir even attributed Bangladesh's secession from Pakistan to a mass reaction against Pakistan's attempts to impose Islamic fundamentalism on Bengalis.

In 1971, as the mukhti bahini mobilized against more than one hundred thousand Pakistani army troops stationed in East Pakistan, a ruthless, homegrown opponent lurked in places where uniformed soldiers could never go. Volunteer brigades of Bangladeshi Islamists collaborated with the army to try to crush the rebels. Supporters of Jamaat-i-Islami, a fundamentalist party founded in 1941, filled the ranks of the brigades, known as *razakars*. "They were a killing squad," Kabir said, "like the Gestapo in Nazi Germany." In the final days of the war, in December 1971, the razakars murdered hundreds of prominent doctors, engineers, journalists, and lawyers. They considered intellectuals, in Kabir's words, "the root of all evil for promoting the ideas of Bengali nationalism and identity."

On December 16, 1971, the Pakistani army surrendered at Dhaka's Ramna Racecourse. Bangladesh emerged from the war an independent—and fiercely secular—state. The 1972 constitution declared the four pillars of Bangladesh: "Nationalism, Socialism, Secularism, and Democracy." The constitution also banned Jamaat-i-Islami and all religious-based parties.

Bangladesh lasted just five years as an officially secular state. In November 1975, one of the heroes of the independence movement, a general named Ziaur Rahman (the husband of Khaleda Zia, head of the Bangladesh Nationalist Party), seized power after a rapid succession of military coups and countercoups, prompted by the assassination of Sheikh Mujibur Rahman, the father of the nation, in August 1975. Ziaur Rahman—no relation to Shiekh Mujibur—needed political allies. So in 1977, he scratched "Secularism" as one of the country's pillars, lifted the ban on religious-based parties, and welcomed Jamaat-i-Islami back into the mainstream.

The party had been gradually amassing power since. In the National Assembly, which sat from 2001 through 2006, Jamaat-i-Islami occupied seventeen out of three hundred seats, as well as two ministries. Most of the party's top leaders, Kabir told me, were former razakars and "enemies of Bangladesh." Fifteen years ago, Kabir formed a civil society group known as the Nirmul Committee with two objectives: to try former razakars as war criminals and to reinstitute the 1972 constitution's ban on religious-based parties. Kabir believes that the rise of Jamaat-i-Islami and Khelafat Majlish contradict everything he had fought for in 1971. "Three million people were killed during the liberation war," he said. "If we now have to accept Islam as the basis of politics to run the country, then what was wrong with Pakistan?"

MUHAMMAD KAMARUZZAMAN, the assistant secretary general of Jamaat-i-Islami, is an accused war criminal. Kabir and the Nirmul Committee described Kamaruzzaman as "the principal organizer of the Al-Badr force," one of the ruthless razakar brigades, and alleged that Kamaruzzaman once dragged a professor, naked, through the streets of

Sherpur, a city in central Bangladesh, while beating him with leather whips. They claimed that Kamaruzzaman also ordered numerous killings and supervised torture cells. I met Kamaruzzaman one morning at his office in Dhaka and asked him about the charges. He scowled. "Is there any evidence? Not a single piece! I was only a sixteen-year-old college boy. How could I lead such a political force?"

Kamaruzzaman wore a suit and gold-framed glasses. His mustache and goatee appeared to be stenciled onto his face. Critics and opponents sneered at him for being "all suited and booted." They said his Western attire dovetailed with Jamaat-i-Islami's program to dupe the masses. Kamaruzzaman and I snacked on plates piled with potato chips. He ate each one with his pinky askance.

The army had just taken over and delayed the elections indefinitely, while hundreds of politicians were already behind bars. Jamaat-i-Islami, meanwhile, remained unsullied by corruption charges, and its spokesmen repeatedly demanded elections at the earliest possible date. "Every devil has its pluses and minuses," a general in the Bangladeshi army told me. "At least Jamaat is relatively honest." In his office that morning, Kamaruzzaman repeated his democratic-sounding mantra: "Our idea is to bring change through a constitutional and democratic process."

Bangladeshi voters were facing a convoluted political scene: the army ran the show and civilian politicians were running scared. What constituted democracy? Elections? Liberalism? Jamaat-i-Islami was certainly more democratic than the klepto-dictatorships of the Awami League or the Bangladesh Nationalist Party. But who was a liberal, democratic Bangladeshi to support?

Kamaruzzaman admitted that many barriers still existed for his party. Jamaat-i-Islami's role in the 1971 war, he said, "can be an obstacle, but we are addressing it. We have accepted reality and are now working for Bangladesh."

"You didn't accept Bangladesh in the beginning," I said.

"In 1971, the leaders of Jamaat-i-Islami didn't want to see our Muslim state separated. We wanted the country to be united," he said. "But the game is over. The countries are independent. We made a politically wrong calculation."

Were there other obstacles that stood in the way of Jamaat-i-Islami and its vision?

"Poverty," he replied. "People in the villages don't want to hear you talk on and on about religion if you can't provide food to them."

I told Kamaruzzaman that I had just returned from Shatkira, a district in the western part of the country that bordered India and was considered a Jamaat-i-Islami stronghold. But on the way to meeting a local Jamaat leader in one of the border towns, I watched a crowd of Hindus celebrate a goddess's birthday with candles, music, and dancing. Hindu and Muslim cultures had cross-pollinated for centuries in Bangladesh; did Jamaat think it could ever win the culture war?

"At the moment, we are neither winning or losing," he said. "But one day, people will realize the effects of this so-called openness. Pornography and nudity in these types of Western and Indian films are encouraging violence and terrorist activities. Children shouldn't be distraught by such things. Society cannot be a boundless sky."

And what did Jamaat-i-Islami propose doing about it?

"We don't want to impose anything," Kamaruzzaman answered. "Of course, there should be a law that, in public places, someone should not be ill-dressed or undressed. But sense should prevail." He paused a moment, before reaching in my direction, palm upturned as if to present his next idea on a silver platter. "You know, like self-censorship."

I DIDN'T FIND Jamaat-i-Islami's high-brow Islamism all that threatening, especially when hard-core militant groups operated throughout the country. On the morning of August 17, 2005, Jamaatul Mujahideen Bangladesh (The Bangladesh Mujahideen Party) exploded 459 bombs in sixty-three out of the country's sixty-four districts. Several people died in the attacks, and leaflets sprinkled around the blast sites, printed in Bangla and Arabic, announced: "It is time to implement Islamic law in Bangladesh. There is no future with man-made law." I saw Jamaat-i-Islami and Jamaatul Mujahideen Bangladesh as distinct entities, but Shahriar Kabir, the former freedom fighter with the hand-broom mustache, and his peers considered Jamaat-i-Islami to be an umbrella organization for dozens of smaller militant outfits. Jamaat-i-Islami, he explained, comprised a "global jihad network." Kabir added, "They receive enormous amounts of money from the Middle East and enormous amounts of arms from Pakistan."

Kabir believed the Islamists' appeal stemmed mostly from a lack of education. And to challenge them, he had constructed dozens of private libraries around the country, each one doubling as a museum for the Liberation War of 1971. While Jamaat-i-Islami was trying to put 1971 behind them, Kabir was keeping the narrative alive.

At a library branch in the port city of Chittagong, 105 members— mostly teenage boys—paid an annual fee of 5 taka, or about 14 cents, for borrowing privileges. The shelves contained some of Kabir's own work (including more than seventy fiction and nonfiction books), classics by Tagore (the national poet), Bengali translations of *The Old Man and the Sea* and *Harry Potter*, and a section reserved for heroic tales about the mukhti bahini. Arif, a boy in his early teens with a spiky hairstyle, told me that he had just finished reading a Bengali translation of *Hamlet*.

"Did you like Shakespeare?" I asked.

"Not my favorite," Arif replied. "It was too much all about kings."

Afterward, I spoke with the president of the Nirmul Committee's Chittagong chapter of libraries. We sat on a bench in front of a hip book- store, where poets gathered each night to sip tea and swap verses. The president told me that, especially outside of the cities, secular education was tough to find. Madrassas were proliferating.

What did he hope to achieve with the libraries?

"We want to start a debate about what kind of secularism is best for Bangladesh," he said, adding that the top priority of a secular state should be to protect the rights of religious minorities. "When Hindus and the Ahmadiyyas were attacked by the Islamists in the past, our government didn't do anything. It must ensure the safety of minorities." (In late 2001, Kabir was arrested and charged with treason for filming a documentary that exposed organized violence against Bangladesh's Hindu community.)

But as the night wore on, I sensed that the principal directed his ani- mosity toward anyone who wore a head scarf or a beard. In his mind, sym- bols of religious revivalism and expressions of hard-line ideas were one and the same. "We are against anyone who capitalizes on religion for political gains," he said.

I left the bookstore and stepped into the frenetic streets of downtown Chittagong. I thought about Kabir, the principal, and the other militant secularists I had met over the preceding weeks. Most of them were root- ed in intellectual traditions grounded in Marxism. They romanticized the downtrodden. But it also seemed that, in trying to protect tens of thousands of poor and vulnerable Hindus from aggressive, proselytizing Islamists, they were neglecting tens of millions of equally poor and vulnerable Muslims.

AFTER OUR INITIAL meeting at Al-Markazul Islami, the diamond-watch-wearing, ambulance-driving Mufti Shahidul Islam and I stayed in frequent contact. He called me every few days to ask where I was and what local people thought about him. "They like me there, don't they?" he often asked. My Bengali journalist friends called him deceptive. It seemed that he liked having an American friend, like a stage prop, to shield him against damning allegations of being pro-Taliban.

In early February, Shahidul didn't show up for our meeting at Al-Markazul Islami one Friday morning. We had planned to rendezvous at the office and go to the Bishwa Ijtema together. The *ijtema*, or gathering, was an annual event hosted by Tablighi Jamaat that regularly attracted crowds exceeding two million people. Tablighi Jamaat espoused a conservative, yet nonpolitical, interpretation of Islam, and believed missionary work was the best method through which to purify contemporary Islam. Tablighis, as followers were known, eschewed bristle toothbrushes to clean their teeth with *miswak*, an aromatic stick used by the Prophet Mohammad, and drank a glass of water in three sips, apparently the same way the Prophet did. They convened each year on a 160-acre campground north of Dhaka to hear sermons and plan missionary outings for the coming year. Shahidul was to be running a booth handing out sample packs of free medicine. If I wanted to go, he said, I should show up at his office at 10 A.M.

That morning, I asked one of his colleagues, "Where's Mufti sahib?"

"He's in bed," the man responded. "High blood pressure."

Shahidul originally thought we might camp at the ijtema, so I carried a backpack, with some water and a change of clothes. Now, with no Mufti in sight, I had second thoughts. "You can still come with us," Shahidul's colleague said. I hesitated a second, but decided to pile into the back of a Land Cruiser, squeezed between two large vats of porridge.

A RIVER PARALLELED the road leading to the campground. Hordes of men (no women allowed) walked for miles, some with a sleeping bag under

Tens of thousands of worshippers prostrate at the Bishwa Ijtema in Dhaka.
PHOTO: NICHOLAS SCHMIDLE

their arm, others empty-handed. River skiffs ferried people to the site. Because we were carrying medicine, our car displayed a special sticker on the windshield that allowed us to drive right up to the Al-Markazul Islami booth. The campground stretched on and on and consisted of bamboo shafts stuck into the ground, each one holding up part of a long piece of canvas, draped like Gulliver-sized bands of ribbon overhead. A few tin-sided barns posted signs welcoming foreigners. Foreign attendees who registered in advance received sheltered accommodations, a special section of Porta-Johns, and three meals a day.

I headed to the tent reserved for Americans and spent the afternoon with a white artist from Boston named Abdul. Abdul wore a beard, with his upper lip shaved, apparently in the tradition of the Prophet. He told me that he had converted to Islam "back in the sixties." "I was a faithful worshipper of earthly beauty," he said, in a thick, Boston accent. "But I reached a plateau of consciousness." Tired of endlessly chasing skirts, Badi searched for some spiritual calling, which he found in a stethoscope.

"People say if you listen to your own heartbeat, it makes the sound: 'LOVE, dove, LOVE, dove.' One day, I took a stethoscope and placed it on my heart. You know what it said? 'AL-lah, AL-lah.'" While reliving this experience, he pursed his lips, nodded his head, and added, matter-of-factly, "You don't need to formally convert if you can hear the sound of your own heart."

When the evening's last sermon ended at around 10 P.M., I joined Abdul and his friends for dinner. We sat on the ground and plunged our hands into mounds of meat, rice, and salad. An African-American boxing coach from New York City asked me if I was a new convert.

"No," I said. "I am just a journalist."

The coach stared at me. "But I can tell something," he said in a gravelly voice. He held out his greasy upturned palm, opening and closing it as if he were kneading dough. "Your heart is gettin' softa' and softa'."

Abdul, who had already invited me to share tent space with him and his teenage son, watched as a handful of American Muslims worked their preferred missionary angles on me. Between the spicy food and the coach symbolically kneading the dough of my heart, my face broke out in a sweat. I wondered how I was going to make it through the night with this crew. Then, one of the doctors manning the Al-Markazul Islami booth called to say that he was heading back to Dhaka. Of all the calls I received from Mufti Shahidul Islam or his people over the preceding weeks, this one might have been the most welcome.

I thanked Abdul for his hospitality. And after bidding him and the coach farewell, I hurried to find the Land Cruiser idling beside the medical booth. I squeezed against the vats, now empty of porridge, and an hour later we were back in the center of Dhaka.

I NEVER SPOKE to Mufti Shahidul Islam again. Four days after the ijtema and his apparent bout with high blood pressure, local newspapers reported that he had surrendered to the police on terrorism charges. Almost two years later, he remained in police custody.

The morning after Shahidul's arrest, I visited Kamal Hossain, a former law minister and the author of the 1972 constitution. I met him at his house, in a room with vaulted ceilings, glass coffee tables, and Turkmen carpets laid on the floors and hanging on the walls. Hossain, a man of medium height, had a deep voice and modest bulges of fat around his cheeks, knuckles, and thighs. He headed a political party known as Gano, or the People's Forum. Gano belonged to the coalition led by the Awami League, which, by extension, made him Shahidul's running mate.

"I saw that the army arrested a political ally of yours yesterday," I said.

Hossain looked sincerely puzzled. "Mine? No, no, no." When I mentioned Shahidul, he glared at me. "I feel insulted and offended and outraged that I should be called an ally of this man," he said. "The signing of the deal with Khelafat Majlish was about rank opportunism and totally unprincipled politics." Spittle collected on Hossain's lips. "Some of us are still guided by principle."

Hossain described himself as a faithful, practicing Muslim. But like Shahriar Kabir, he said he believed that the rise of groups like Shahidul's Khelafat Majlish and Kamaruzzaman's Jamaat-i-Islami contradicted everything that Bangladesh originally stood for.

Hossain, after all, had been a close associate of Sheik Mujibur Rahman, the founder of the Awami League—and Bangladesh. I asked him if he ever imagined he would see the day when the Awami League would be signing memorandums of understanding with Islamist parties.

"Absolutely not," Hossain said. "I often ask myself, 'What have we done to deserve this?'"

Still, Hossain struggled to determine the best way forward. He worried that the Islamists had "psychologically blackmailed" society. People didn't know how to react.

But inaction seemed just one possibility. Overreaction was another.

ON ONE OF my last nights in Bangladesh, I sat on a flatbed trolley pulled by a bicycle in the far northwest corner of the country with Swapan, an activist and a former freedom fighter. "If I had the money, I would train a brigade of people in India and return to kill all the Islamic fundamentalists in Bangladesh," he told me. Swapan's statement floored me; he was otherwise a gentle man.

We passed a single-room madrassa standing on a dry patch in the middle of a rice patty. Banana and coconut trees leaned over the ramshackle building. "They are training terrorists in there," he said.

The madrassa sign was written in Bangla and Urdu, and I could read that the seminary was a place for females, most likely teenage girls, to memorize the Quran. "Swapan, it's just a girls madrassa," I said, chuckling. "Not every mosque or madrassa is training terrorists."

Swapan exhibited a nervous twitch, something he said he acquired during a spell in prison during the 1970s, and he jerked his head from side to side. "There is a Bengali proverb," he said. "One day, a cow gets burned by fire. And the rest of that cow's life, he is so traumatized that he cannot even look at the sun setting in the western sky."

Swapan took a deep breath. An early, dusk moon rose from behind the tropical canopy. "We are now thinking like that," he said. "When we hear about a new madrassa, we get frightened."

CHAPTER 7

"WE HAVE ACCEPTED THE CHALLENGE"

Our plane bumped and skidded down the runway a few minutes before 2 A.M. I had slept most of the flight from Islamabad to Karachi; I hoped to be sleeping again soon. Taxiing into the gate, I called the reception desk at the Embassy Inn hotel to confirm that their driver was waiting outside.

"I am sorry, Mr. Schmidle, but the driver was stuck in traffic," the receptionist said. "The whole city is shut down. Just take a taxi, and we will pay you back."

Hoping to beat the cabin full of passengers to the taxi stand, I hurried out of the airplane, through the terminal, and past the baggage claim. But when the automatic doors slid open, beyond which I expected to see a row of white cabs lined up along the curb, there were hundreds of stranded passengers. They had no way of getting home. Babies screamed. Food supplies were dwindling. The airport was under siege. Still half-asleep, I slapped both of my cheeks to perk up.

Ten hours from now, Iftikhar Mohammad Chaudhry, the suspended Chief Justice of Pakistan and President Musharraf's newfound nemesis, was due to arrive in Karachi. Musharraf had asked the Muttahida Quami

Movement (MQM)—the party led by Farooq Sattar and Altaf Hussein, and Musharraf's only ally with street muscle—to prevent Chaudhry from leaving the airport. The MQM agreed. They had blockaded the place. MQM party workers had hijacked hundreds of buses and trucks earlier in the day, and had now parked them across major roads to block traffic. In some cases, they drained the tires of air to assure the vehicles couldn't be easily moved.

I didn't want to be stuck at the airport when Chaudhry arrived. Even though I had planned my trip to Karachi to coincide with his visit, I was less interested in Chaudhry himself and more interested in witnessing the imminent street battles. A former prime minister had warned that tensions in the port city could escalate into a "civil-war-like situation," pitting the MQM and Musharraf's thugs against the nascent opposition forces (who favored Chaudhry). I wouldn't be able to see any of that at the airport. So, as wealthier families bought floor space in the lobby of the airport hotel (all the rooms had been taken by the first wave of stranded passengers), and poorer families unrolled blankets in the terminal, I shouldered my luggage and started to walk. Perhaps I could find a taxi somewhere. The sound of gunfire popped off in the distance.

Karachi is not the kind of city you would want to walk around, even on a good day. It is sprawling, with no pedestrian-friendly accoutrements like crosswalks. Mobile phone snatchers menace the streets. The prospect of navigating—on foot—an obstacle course of roadblocks manned by armed MQM activists didn't fill me with gladness. A policeman warned me that the MQM were burning tires to sow fear and keep the public off the streets. I usually preferred to travel and work alone, but at that moment I had never desired a travel companion more.

I wasn't the only one walking, though. "Excuse me," I called out to the man a few yards ahead of me. He spun around. He was of medium height, slender, and mustachioed. "Can I walk with you?" I asked.

He nodded. "Where are you going?"

"Actually, anywhere within a mile or so of the Embassy Inn would be great," I said. I tried to sound reluctant to accept his invitation, per what I felt were good manners. But looking back, I probably sounded pretty desperate.

"No problem. I can drop you off. My jeep and guard are waiting just around the corner," he said. As it turned out, luck was on my side; my new friend's name was Ahmed, and he headed Karachi's Anti-Violent Crime Cell. He had been vacationing with his family in Islamabad when his superiors called him back.

We reached Ahmed's jeep a few minutes later. He drove, and I sat in the front seat. Ahmed's guard crouched in the back. Ahmed attached a red, swirling police light to the roof, and we zipped away—initially in the direction of the Embassy Inn. The trip from the airport to the hotel typically took about fifteen minutes. But after fifteen minutes, we had barely left the airport, deterred by the passenger buses clustered cockeyed across intersections. The MQM's tricolor flag fluttered from the buses' antennae. For two more hours, we traversed the most circuitous route possible from the airport to the Embassy Inn. Ahmed ran over curbs to get around water tankers and dodged dump trucks as they emptied loads of sand onto bridges. We drove for miles down some roads, only to find them totally impassible. We would then turn around and seek another way. Vehicles littered the road, but we may have been one of the only cars actually trying to reach a destination. The city seemed to have fallen under a senseless, horrific spell.

I had been wary at first of talking politics with Ahmed, assuming that he would parrot the government's position and support Musharraf. But as our journey stretched on, Ahmed began cursing under his breath. "This is shameful," he said. "You are a guest of Pakistan. I am so sorry you have to deal with this." Neither he nor his guard sounded too keen on Musharraf.

"It's time for Benazir to come back," the guard said.

"This is Musharraf's last chance," said Ahmed. "I really don't know what is happening in this country right now."

Ahmed dropped me in front of the Embassy Inn a few minutes after 4 a.m. He had to be at work in three hours. I wouldn't be getting much more sleep myself. Rumors flew about a possible assassination attempt on Chaudhry the next day. Karachi's hospitals went on high alert.

JUST A FEW hours earlier, I had been in the company of good friends at a splendid dinner party in Islamabad. There were no bars in Pakistan, as alcohol was officially banned, and only those one or two restaurants catering to foreigners allowed customers to bring their own booze. Thus, nightlife in Islamabad consisted mostly of private parties, and this one may have been the best I had seen in months. Wine and good conversation flowed. A guitarist played in the garden. Plates full of shrimp kebabs had just been brought out when I ruefully bid folks farewell and took a taxi to the airport. With Karachi braced for another round of violence, and if the projections of riots turned out to be true, the midnight flight seemed like it could be the last plane into the port city for a day or two. I wanted to get there before the airport shut down.

For two months, Pakistan's lawyers had been marching in protest against Musharraf's suspension of Chaudhry, the chief justice. The protests represented a momentous turn. Until then, Musharraf had sailed along, without any major bumps, for eight years. When previous challenges to his rule emerged, the intelligence agencies quickly defanged them and moved on. The opposition leadership languished in exile. But now, the lawyers poured into the street, undeterred by Musharraf's massive security apparatus. They downloaded anti-Musharraf slogans as ring tones for their cell phones, and organized through bar associations. They weren't acting at the whims of a single leader, but on this shared belief in a cause. Chaudhry, in their minds, personified that cause: the rule of law.

While plenty of other top judges had been forcibly retired in the past, Chaudhry was the first one who refused to cower. He had challenged the ruling establishment vigorously over the preceding months with probes of high-level corruption. His court even questioned some of the central tenets of Pakistan's cooperation with the United States in the War on Terror, such as the hundreds of missing persons suspected to be in the custody of the intelligence agencies over allegations of terrorism. In his autobiography, Musharraf admitted receiving bounties from the United States for detaining and handing over certain suspects. Chaudhry had ordered the agencies to either release or formally try these men.

As Musharraf's reelection bid approached, some advisers believed that Chaudhry planned to rule against Musharraf's eligibility to stand for another term. That would have pushed Musharraf against a wall, leaving with him the unlikely option of stepping down, or the unpopular one of declaring martial law. Hoping to preempt the situation, Musharraf's team hastily filed a case against Chaudhry. They charged him with nepotism and abuse of power. Wasn't every Pakistani official engaged in nepotism and abuse of power? I asked this question to one of Musharraf's senior lawyers. What made Chaudhry's case different? "A judge stands on a different pedestal from the rest of society," said the lawyer, Sharifuddin Pirzada. "They aren't supposed to do things like this."

The United States played a role, too. The White House clearly didn't want to see Musharraf, its prime ally in the War on Terror, ousted from power, even though his credibility was dissipating in Pakistan. Pakistani newspaper columnists and TV talk shows railed against his ham-fisted ways. Yet despite protests against Musharraf raging across the country, Washington stuck to its position: "President Musharraf has made a commitment to change Pakistan, and we think that that is a positive thing."

Chaudhry made an unlikely hero. He was uncharismatic, something of a frump. He had a short, pear-shaped, and hunched physique. Heavy eyelids and natural circles under his eyes made him look perpetually stoned. But his unassuming presence suited the opposition fine. He symbolized the resistance to Musharraf, but neither Benazir Bhutto, Nawaz Sharif, nor any of the other opposition leaders felt threatened by him.

On the first Friday after his suspension, hundreds of activists and opposition leaders converged in the center of Islamabad to rally in solidarity with Chaudhry. The chanting soon turned into people chucking rocks at the police. The police wore helmets and padding for protection, and after they threw the rocks back from where they came, they then charged at the protesters with long bamboo sticks, called *latthis*. When the bamboo thatches didn't suffice to disperse the rioters, they fired rubber bullets and tear gas. Pitched battles between the police and the protesters went on for hours.

All day long, television cameras captured and broadcast the clashes. Coincidentally, the offices of Geo TV, Pakistan's largest private network, looked over the war scene. When the police realized that their suppression of the protesters was being caught on tape, they schemed a way to terminate the live broadcast. Before long, they had lobbed a few tear gas shells into the Geo building, barged through the front door, and ransacked the office. Cameramen filmed and broadcast the whole thing. "They wanted to destroy this newsroom," a Geo reporter later told the *Washington Post*. "They were trying to send a message to the whole media by attacking Geo TV."

I showed up at the Geo office the same day, about an hour after the police assault. Chunks of brick, shattered panes of car windows, and spent tear gas shells laid in the street. Government spokesmen had already apologized for the raid, but the damage was done. Footage of police in riot gear rummaging through the gas-clouded halls of Geo now streamed around the world. And on the front steps of the Geo office, lawyers, journalists, Islamists, and myriad other opposition activists called for the freedom of judiciary, freedom of the media, and the ouster of Musharraf. While I stood there, my eyes and nostrils stinging from the tear gas lingering in the air, a man approached me. He was shaking his head in disbelief. "In only a week, Musharraf has alienated two pillars of society: first the lawyers, and now the media," he said. "What is he thinking?"

Chaudhry took his show on the road. He and his chief counsel, Aitzaz Ahsan, a senior member of the Pakistan People's Party and leader of the burgeoning lawyers' movement, drove from Islamabad to Lahore. A gathering of lawyers waited for Chaudhry at the Lahore High Court. Chaudhry's admirers lined the road along the way, tossing rose petals on his car, beating drums, and chanting, "Musharraf is a dog!" The sacked chief justice sat with his head pasted against the headrest, looking overwhelmed. The journey, which normally took less than five hours, took almost twenty-four. It embarrassed Musharraf. Speaking to the state-run press agency, he called the judicial crisis a "temporary irritant." "We must stop taking this issue on to the streets and making it into a political issue," Musharraf said. He sounded determined not to allow another rose petal reception for Chaudhry. So when Chaudhry announced his intent to travel to Karachi on May 12 to address the bar association there, Musharraf had asked his most powerful political ally, the MQM, to help out.

The MQM promptly announced a counterrally on May 12 to demonstrate the people's support for Musharraf in Karachi. This set up a showdown between the two rival factions. Farooq Sattar, the MQM's most senior leader in Pakistan, told a British newspaper, "The opposition wants to show that Karachi does not belong to the MQM. We have accepted the challenge."

"We have accepted the challenge." What did that even mean? As I lay in bed at the Embassy Inn, shortly after Ahmed dropped me off, I watched the dawn sky lighten through the curtains, unable to sleep. I opened Ryszard Kapuściński's Another Day of Life and read about his description of landing in Angola just as the civil war there seemed primed to spin out of control. "People escaped as if from an infectious disease, as if from pestilential air that can't be seen but still inflicts death," he wrote.

Karachi felt choked by some pestilential air as we wondered how the MQM would react to this perceived challenge.

ON THE MORNING of May 12, after a few hours of sleep, I walked onto the roof of the Embassy Inn to have a look down over the city. Shahra-e-Faisal, the main road connecting the downtown area to the airport, was empty. Hawks circled above, buoyed by thermals radiating off the asphalt. Gas stations had switched off the pumps and closed so that rioters couldn't burn them down. Convenience stores, office buildings, and even the lobby of the Embassy Inn had draped thick curtains over the windows to prevent bricks from crashing through. But the absence of traffic made you wonder if all the preparations may have been for naught; how could there be riots with no people?

I heard the horns first. Down the road, a caravan consisting of more than forty trucks, buses, and motorcycles inched around a bend, heading in my direction. Men crowded on the tops of the buses, waving the plain red flags of the Awami National Party. The ANP belonged to the opposition and headed to the airport to welcome Chaudhry. Alliances were constantly shifting in Pakistan, and particularly in Karachi. Ethnic groups, political parties, and religious sects could be teamed up one day and fighting each other the next. On May 12, Musharraf, the mohajirs, the MQM, and the Pakistan Muslim League (Q) took one side, while the Pashtuns, Sindhis, Baluchis, ANP, Pakistan People's Party, and the Pakistan Muslim League (N) took the other. The day was a reminder of why some called Karachi the Beirut of South Asia.

The ANP is a Pashtun nationalist party, and the Pashtuns and the MQM had been fighting in Karachi for decades. Ethnic grievances between the two groups far eclipsed any short-term political disagreements about Musharraf or Chaudhry. The ANP caravan resembled a flotilla of warships heading to battle. Buried somewhere in the mass of vehicles and red flags, an amplified voice barked commands. The distortion on the speaker made it tough for me to understand what he was saying, but I gathered, from watching the activists, that it had something to do with violent disobedience. Men put down their red flags, leapt off the bus, and began throwing rocks at parked cars and homes. Others snapped branches off the trees that decorated the median and swung them at low-hanging telephone wires. I heard the deep-throated *chuck-chuck-chuck* of shotguns being fired into the air. The roof struck me as a bad place to be standing during aerial firing, so I headed inside.

Shortly thereafter, a journalist named Saleem rang me up. I had been waiting for his call. "We'll be by in a few minutes," he said.

He showed up with a local leader of Nawaz Sharif's faction of the Pakistan Muslim League named Hafeez. The three of us piled into Hafeez's hatchback and motored up Shahra-e-Faisal. We soon caught up with the boisterous ANP caravan; it had stopped at a cloverleaf, clogged with MQM-flagged vehicles. MQM activists soon surrounded the ANP and prowled the overpass carrying handguns. We got out of the car. I eyed the rival sides like a tennis spectator following the ball back and forth across the net. The phrase "powder keg" flashed in my mind. A television cameraman walked over to us. "Big, big clashes are coming here soon," he predicted. Hafeez went back to the car. He revved the engine to prepare for a speedy getaway. Saleem urged us to move on and we did. Gunfire soon erupted between the two camps, killing several people and initiating days of violence.

On the other side of town, the PPP information secretary drove her Lexus SUV with gunmen hanging off the running boards. MQM militants targeted them, and the gunmen, in turn, fired away down the road. Hafeez drove us toward the airport. As we sped the wrong way down a one-way road, I sat in the backseat, asking questions to Saleem and Hafeez.

"Have you guys ever seen something like this?"

"It used to be way worse than this all the time."

"Yeah, you should have been here during the eighties and nineties."

"Nawaz Sharif would never let this happen," said Hafeez, spouting the party line.

"Why not? What would he do different?"

"He has the support of the people. That's the main difference," Hafeez said.

Meanwhile, it was as though the police forgot to show up to work on the busiest day of the year. As we drove around to different parts of the city that afternoon, I saw only ten Rangers, an elite paramilitary unit designed to guard the border with India, but who were often recalled to quell urban violence in Karachi. Five of them guarded a Kentucky Fried Chicken and five guarded a girls' Montessori school. In both instances, rival groups

The ANP-supporting flotilla of buses and trucks in Karachi, heading toward the airport, about an hour before fighting broke out, May 12, 2007. Photo: Nicholas Schmidle

were clashing just down the street. When a private TV channel came under fire from MQM thugs, it took the police six hours to reach it. The channel, Aaj TV, continued broadcasting while technicians in the newsroom crouched under their desks to avoid being shot. Just outside the windows, MQM gunmen paced the parking lot, looking for targets.

As we cruised past a lean-to protecting several policemen from the harsh sun, Hafeez threw the car into park and we all jumped out. The officers were drinking tea and wearing aviator sunglasses. A few hundred yards away, the singed carcasses of two passenger buses smoldered in black, oily smoke.

"What's going on here?" Hafeez asked, his tone wavering between accusatory and genuinely curious.

The officers, as if choreographed, shrugged their collective shoulders and took loud slurps of tea. Days later, when I asked the provincial president of the ANP for Sindh why the police had acted so haplessly on May 12, he told me, "It's simple. The government wanted all this to happen."

More than forty people died on May 12. Most perished during the span of a few hours, between the time when Chaudhry landed in Karachi, sat marooned at the airport, and then eventually decided to fly back to Islamabad. He never spoke to any of the bar associations. Musharraf and the MQM blamed Chaudhry for the carnage.

That same afternoon, the MQM held a rally in downtown Karachi and patched in Altaf Hussein, live from London. They closed roads in the heart of the city, and tens of thousands of MQM faithful squatted in the streets. Altaf growled over the speakers: "Chief Justice Iftikhar Mohammad Chaudhry, the Sindh Home Secretary requested you to postpone your visit, but you didn't listen.... You stuck to your decision of coming here, and because of you, a number of people were killed. Are you satisfied now?"

In Islamabad on the same night, Musharraf led his own rally. The government paid some attendees small amounts of cash (less than ten dollars), waived the tolls on all the highways connecting Islamabad to nearby cities, and distributed complimentary snacks and drinks at the venue to guarantee that folks would show up. Despite predictions earlier in the week that half a million people would attend, most estimates put the actual number at no more than fifty thousand. Musharraf's prominent cronies took turns lauding his vision, purpose, and determination. The scene was joyous and celebratory. Generators pumped extra voltage into the lighting and speaker systems, even as electricity shortages and rolling blackouts crippled other parts of the country for several hours at a time. "Today is a historic date," said one federal minister. Most Pakistanis agreed. But it was the mobs that had rampaged Karachi and transformed the seaside metropolis into an urban apocalypse that would remain etched in their minds, not Musharraf's state-sponsored publicity stunt.

"My heart was bleeding when I watched the television today," Musharraf said as he stood atop the twenty-foot-high stage behind a podium encased with bulletproof glass. He wore a plain white shalwar kameez, doing his best to appear humble. "The people of Pakistan are with me," he added. At one point, he stood at the edge of the stage with his arms pointing at the sky and stretched in the shape of a V—a classic dictator pose. Some speculated that Musharraf would cite the violence in Karachi as a reason to declare a state of emergency, thereby allowing him to dissolve the parliament and the judiciary and to consolidate all power in the office of the president. He addressed the rumors: "I do not see any justification whatsoever to impose emergency.... What has happened today in Karachi is because of the chief justice who went there ignoring the advice of the government over the issue."

He saved a word for the opposition. "And if they think they are powerful, they should know that the people's power is with us!"

The whole escapade was sad and depressing. Pakistani pundits and foreign diplomats generally assumed that Musharraf was a clumsy politician with a good heart. But the longer he stayed in power, dodging crises and showing a cunning side that few people had anticipated, the more he looked like a delusional callous dictator on the wane. On May 12, he crossed a line. He showed that he was willing to subvert law and order to keep power. It was a point of no return.

ON THE MORNING of May 13, Rangers patrolled the main roads and certain neighborhoods in Karachi. The authorities had carted away the shipping containers, water tankers, and buses, cleared the piles of sand off the bridges, and even the police trickled in for work. Gas station owners opened tentatively, and motorists filed into long lines after a day and a half without fuel. Having totally run out, some pushed their cars up to the pump. Yet by the afternoon, restless youths had climbed out of bed and began another round of fresh looting and riots. Gas stations immediately closed. The provincial government issued orders to police and Rangers to "shoot on sight" anyone out past the curfew.

But while stores could lower their metal shutters, and forklifts could clear roads within minutes, once ethnic tensions were inflamed they are not so easily switched off. In Quetta, a mostly Baluchi and Pashtun city near the Afghan border, 415 miles from Karachi, arsonists torched the MQM office in retaliation for Saturday's state-sponsored brutality. And the Pashtun-dominated areas of Karachi turned into battlegrounds between mobs and the police. The ANP contended that more Pashtuns died on May 12, trying to welcome Chaudhry, than people from any other group. (Both the Pakistan People's Party and the MQM claimed the same, though, from what I saw, the ANP had a much stronger case.) And if you knew anything about Pashtuns, it was that their civilization had thrived on taking revenge. "If the MQM accepts their mistakes and apologizes, then there is no problem for my people and our culture," the ranking ANP leader in Karachi told me. "But if they don't, then there will be problems."

The violence on May 12 had transformed the opposition from an unsteady coalition of parties, groups, and sects into a large group with a more shared and purposeful cause. By lunchtime on May 13 in Lyari, a run-down, multiethnic slum on the coast, pitched battles were already raging between mobs and the police; kids swarmed into abandoned intersections around Lyari, stoning anyone who tried to pass. That morning, I had wandered down to a nearby gas station and met a dark-skinned man named Moeen. Moeen was filling his motorcycle. As it turned out, he came from Lyari.

"Interesting. I want to go over there sometime today," I said.

"Really? Have you been there before?" Moeen looked surprised.

"Many times."

Municipal services didn't exist in Lyari, so the roads were rutted with holes the size of bathtubs filled with sewage water, telephone and electricity wires were bunched like tangled yarn, and piles of trash laid along either side of the road. People simply leaned out of their apartment windows and chucked their filth below. Lyari's proximity to the sea gave it little respite in the way of a clean breeze; the neighborhood smelled like low tide and spoiled fish.

"Well, if you ever want to go, I can take you. My family lives there. I know Lyari like this," Moeen said, flipping his right hand back and forth to show me the back of his hand.

"How about today?"

"Okay. I will come to your hotel in one hour."

An hour later, Moeen pulled in front of the glass doors of the lobby. He chewed on a wad of pan, a locally grown tobacco-like product, some of which dribbled out of his lips. I jumped on the back of his bike and we took off.

As we neared the edge of Lyari, the stone-throwing kids were waiting. Moeen had ripped two ANP stickers from a streetlamp pole and stuck one on each of our shirts. A press pass didn't mean much to rioters, but if they saw the red flags on the breast of your shirt, you had a greater chance of passing without incident. Or at least that's what Moeen said. He opened the throttle and we sped past the rock-toting thugs. Luckily, most of them had weak arms or didn't know how to lead a moving target. Their rocks fell pitifully short, like a luckless golfer's ball plopping into a pond.

We cruised past a market doing brisk business and soon arrived at our destination, Aat Chowk. "Aat" means "eight" in Urdu, and eight roads connected to the *chowk*, or circle, like spokes on a wagon wheel. Vandals had destroyed a brick police post overnight, running the police out of the area. But the police returned with the Rangers. Together, they now occupied the center of the chowk. Shards of glass, chipped pieces of brick, and spent bullet casings littered the road. The glass and stones crackled and popped under their tires as the Rangers and police moved their trucks into position.

Lyari had inherited a mix of ethnicities as one of Karachi's oldest neighborhoods. Baluchis, Sindhis, Pashtuns, and even some small numbers of Punjabis and mohajirs lived there. Antigovernment protesters waited down five out of the eight roads connecting to the chowk, occasionally surging forward to throw stones or fire guns at the police. Down each road, the groups were waving a different colored flag, representing a different political party and ethnic group. The longer these battles raged, the more they became about ethnicity, and less about Musharraf and Chaudhry.

Moeen stashed his bike behind one of the police trucks, and we ducked behind another for cover. Rocks rained down and banged off the side of the trucks.

"You still like Lyari?" Moeen said, smiling.

A policeman crouched next to us. He held a tear gas gun. He rose, fired a charge, and then slipped back behind the truck. The gun made a sound like a match being lit, followed by a *thwack!* that propelled the gas canister into the air. Once, he misfired and the gas canister bounced off a telephone wire and fell woefully short. He didn't realize that the wind had turned and now blew in our face. A massive cloud of tear gas engulfed us.

After an hour of dodging rocks and inhaling untold amounts of gas, I retreated back to speak with the ranking police officer, a barrel-chested man who had just arrived in a white Toyota Land Cruiser.

"Who are you? What are you doing here?" he asked me in English.

"Nice to meet you, sir. My name is Nicholas," I said in Urdu, handing him a business card. "I am a writer, working on a book about Pakistan."

"Is your book going to be against Pakistan, like all the others written by Americans?"

I smiled and continued speaking to him in Urdu. "Sir, Pakistan is my home. I live here and love it here. Why would I write against it?" He reacted favorably, and within a few minutes we were talking about one another's family, wives, and (his) kids. Amid the siegelike circumstances, our polite and wandering conversation seemed all the more surreal. "Sir, can I ask you something? What happened yesterday? All day long, I didn't see any police. Now today, you all are everywhere. Did you receive some kind of instructions yesterday to stay at home and turn the city over to the MQM?"

The officer's glance shifted from my eyes, and he looked down at his shoes. "No comment," he mumbled.

Neither of us spoke for a minute, and then he broke the silence. "You are a journalist, so maybe you know better than me. What's happening in this country now?"

He answered his own question, shaking his head in disgust and rehashing the weekend, from the arrival of Chaudhry on Saturday, to the twelve hours of anarchy that pitched ethnic-based political parties against one another in bloody street battles, to the present, where the police and Rangers were expected to face the wrath of the opposition and to quell angry street demonstrators.

"This began as a judicial problem," he said. "Then it became a political one." He lifted his head and looked at the center of the chowk, at the myriad political flags and the police post, laying in a pile of bricks. "Now, it's an ethnic problem. They are always the most difficult to contain."

CHAPTER 8

"THE BLOOD OF OUR MARTYRS WILL NOT GO TO WASTE"

IN LATE JANUARY 2007, SEVERAL HUNDRED SCHOOL-AGE GIRLS, CLOAKED in black and wielding staffs, conquered a children's library in Islamabad, the capital city in the northern part of the country. They declared it to be ruled under sharia. When they posed for pictures later— standing in tight, single-file lines, all of them wearing a strip of white cloth tied around their heads that read SHARIA OR MARTYRDOM—they looked more like a team of ninjas than a class of boarding school girls. All of them studied at Jamia Hafsa, an all-female madrassa adjacent to the Pepto Bismol–colored Lal Masjid, or the Red Mosque, in Islamabad. They answered to Abdul Rashid Ghazi. Ghazi touted Jamia Hafsa as being the largest madrassa for women in the entire Islamic world. "Teach a man, and you teach one," he told me. "But if you teach a woman, you teach a whole family." Ghazi referred to the girls fondly as his "female commandos." When asked about them, he giggled and looked as shocked by their brazen activism—he called it "spontaneous"—as the rest of the country.

Despite his feigned surprise, Ghazi believed the takeover of the library was long overdue. President Pervez Musharraf's government had destroyed a number of mosques in Islamabad. By doing this, Ghazi said Musharraf "challenged the writ of Allah." His girls simply responded by "challenging the writ of the state." Always ready to dabble in rhetorical flair, Ghazi asked: "Whose writ is greater: Musharraf's or Allah's?"

A week after the "Talibat" (the feminine form of "Taliban") swept into the library, which was sandwiched between Jamia Hafsa and the Red Mosque and therefore unlikely in these times to be a place prone to uninterrupted, shushed reading and reflection, police and paramilitary units surrounded the mosque compound and postured like they were going to punish Ghazi and his female commandos. But the authorities balked. Ghazi took note. And throughout the coming spring, he and his followers — which grew in number, reaching more than four thousand women and one thousand men at a point — launched a Taliban-inspired campaign, ostensibly promoting virtue and preventing vice, in the middle of the capital.

They began by establishing sharia courts inside the mosque. One of the first "cases" involved a female federal minister accused of loose morals. The primary evidence against her? A photograph that showed her hugging a Frenchman who wasn't her husband. She and the Frenchman — who had helped deliver aid to the earthquake-ravaged parts of Pakistan in October 2005 — had just completed a tandem skydiving jump. Caving in to Taliban pressure, the government soon sacked the minister.

Then the Talibat kidnapped a brothel owner named "Aunty Shamim" and forced her to don an *abaya*, a black head-to-toe covering, and repent in public. DVD shop owners complained that squads of vigilantes had made personal visits and ordered them to close. One Friday after prayers, Ghazi's supporters packed the road beside the Red Mosque and lit a massive bonfire, using thousands of "un-Islamic" CDs and DVDs as kindling. Policemen who strayed too close to the mosque were snatched by militants, held on suspicions of spying, and then turned out after a couple days. Ghazi and his brother ruled a mini-Islamic state that covered a few acres in the heart of Islamabad.

ISLAMABAD GENERALLY LACKED what any Westerner would consider normal urban excitement. A friend dubbed it Lowselfesteemabad. It was a town full of bureaucrats, where a night out meant going to an ice cream parlor or a bookstore. Natural beauty — lush gardens and forests along the main roads, rolling hills in the background, and stalks of cannabis growing wild in the center of town—provided the capital with its greatest assets, but even that appeal soon wore off. We welcomed any flash of unpredictability. But Ghazi went too far. The expat community grew edgy. With many of us relying on DVD shops for entertainment, concerns that they might be closed—or bombed—sent shock waves through the foreign community.

"Ghazi, what's the story? We are worried that your boys are pressuring the DVD stores to close," I asked him one day.

"These boys are acting so polite," he said. "They go and they hand the owner a printed letter. Most of the time, they are just requesting that he stop selling the porno and vulgar material."

A rumor started that Ghazi's brother warned "sportswomen" to dress modestly or prepare to have acid thrown on them, a tactic used widely in Iran in the years after the revolution. My wife, Rikki, stopped exercising outside. (She had previously gone jogging around town in long pants and long sleeves, even in the height of summer.) "This is just propaganda by the intelligence agencies to be used against us," Ghazi said. "My brother would never say that."

"Some say your students are manning intersections around town and telling women that they can't drive," I said.

"I have said, again and again, *my wife* drives a car. She goes to the market and takes the children here and there. How is it possible that I should ask my students to stop women from driving? They would ask me first, 'Ghazi, tell your wife not to drive!'"

I used to wonder if, like some people who had an answer for everything, Ghazi had an answer for everyone. He had a way of connecting with people, of tailoring his conversations with different content and idiom for different people. (Some call it pandering.) When a Western reporter once asked Ghazi if his anti-vice activities signaled the "Talibanization" of Pakistan, he replied, "Rudy Giuliani, when he became mayor of New York, closed the brothels. Was that also Talibanization? You would never say that."

Besides being the spokesman, Ghazi was also the strategist and brains behind the movement. When he glimpsed opportunities, he seized on his opponents' weaknesses. Throughout the spring of 2007, Musharraf looked terribly distracted. The Baluchi nationalists continued their struggle against the state, a tribal uprising engulfed the region bordering

Afghanistan, and the threat persisted of the Taliban and al-Qaeda using bombs to destabilize Pakistani cities. Perhaps most significant was the emergence of a broad-based, middle-class movement, led by lawyers but supported by the rest of the country. They demanded the restoration of Iftikhar Mohammad Chaudhry, the chief justice whom Musharraf had sacked in early March.

Cynics parading as realists said Musharraf had everything under control. That his intelligence agencies allowed the various crises to fester and create the impression in Washington that Pakistan was beleaguered with threats—and that Musharraf was the only one who could manage them all. But judging from his public appearances (he looked pallid and pasty), reports that his circle of advisers was growing smaller and smaller (the classic trajectory of dictators in their final days), and his decisions (such as allowing mobs to take over Karachi on May 12), I was skeptical that he had much under control.

Ghazi recognized this vulnerability and took to taunting Musharraf. One morning, Ghazi stopped long enough between relaying messages on his walkie-talkie to articulate the two options facing Musharraf. "We want an Islamic revolution," he said. "Now, either the government does it, or the people do it themselves. If the government does it, it will be peaceful. If the people have to do it, it will be bloody. We are demanding a peaceful revolution, but it depends on the government's attitude. Time and again they have threatened to launch a military operation on Lal Masjid. We are ready for this," he said, as a young fighter, with a wispy beard and a Kalashnikov, ran into the room and whispered something into Ghazi's ear. "We are armed."

Everyone, according to Ghazi, was fed up with Musharraf, with the army, and with the entire existing system. "If we are killed, it will only give more momentum to our movement. The government knows this. And that's why they aren't coming."

Located on a quiet, leafy street in one of Islamabad's most expensive neighborhoods, the Red Mosque seemed an unlikely hub for an Islamic revolution. The compound was walking distance from the National Assembly building, the U.S. embassy, the ISI headquarters, and, incidentally, my house. But it looked more like a fortress every day. Hooded "female commandos" roamed the grounds. Young men brandishing sharp-pointed garden tools paced the sidewalks in front. Banners hung off the mosque's pink walls, with messages that read: JIHAD, JIHAD, and SHARIA OR MARTYRDOM. Dozens of black flags, showing two crossed swords and inscribed with Islam's procession of faith, *La illaha illa Allah* (There is no God but Allah) flew over the mosque and on lampposts at nearby intersections. When I asked Ghazi what the flags stood for, he smirked and said, "It is our own flag and our own design. But some people are saying it is like the al-Qaeda flag."

While Ghazi relished his al-Qaeda connections and the confidence such friends might have lent, I still found him to be surprisingly sensible and pragmatic. His eyes didn't burn with fervor. Nor did his rhetoric emanate hatred. He calmly explained the rise of anti-Americanism around the world as a product of the United States' "missed opportunity" to act as a benevolent, global leader. "After the Soviet Union finished, America could have been a big brother to the world, and we would have been happy to listen. But you chose a different path."

Over time, however, I got the impression that Ghazi was getting bad advice. Kidnapping policemen on patrol? He was pushing his luck. The decision by his band of vigilantes to take nine people hostage, six of them Chinese women, from a massage parlor across town seemed plain mad. Ghazi and his boys claimed that the women were providing massages to men (a jihadi no-no) and performing other "un-Islamic activities." Ghazi's bearded shock troops overpowered three guards at the parlor, took the ladies from inside, and brought them back to the Red Mosque. The women were released the next day, albeit significantly more clothed than when they had arrived. But the Chinese government wasn't willing to overlook the kidnapping so easily. Beijing had recently invested hundreds of million of dollars in the port city of Gwadar, as well as having built the Karakorum Highway that connected northern Pakistan to western China. The Chinese pressured Musharraf to do something against the mosque. They wanted some assurance their citizens wouldn't be kidnapped again.

A few days after the masseuses' release, police and paramilitary Rangers encircled the mosque once again. A crackdown finally felt imminent. On July 3, Rangers laying concertina wire at the end of the street facing the Red Mosque came under fire from militants hiding inside. One Ranger died. Police and Rangers fired back and chucked tear gas over the mosque's walls. Militants wearing ammunition vests, holding

Kalashnikovs, and sporting gas masks, soon emerged from the pink walls and ran into the surrounding roads. Some took up positions behind sandbag bunkers. Others walked boldly in the streets, waving their weapons and firing at anyone within sight.

Mosque leaders used the loudspeakers to egg on the militants. They beckoned them to wage jihad, threatened the government, and instructed the Taliban to be brave. They also encouraged anyone who would listen to join them in fighting. Across the street from the mosque, militants overran an office and torched the complex housing the Ministry of Environment. The building, along with all the cars in the parking lot, burned for days.

That afternoon, I headed in the direction of the thick plume of black smoke rising from the Ministry of Environment. On the way, I passed two hospitals, where crowds were gathering in front hoping for news about relatives who had suffered injuries around the mosque. Ten people, including the Ranger and a news cameraman, died by the end of the day. Dozens of others were wounded. "The army is shooting the girls of Pakistan!" an elderly man in the neighborhood exclaimed, referring to three female madrassa students reported killed.

I parked my car about half a mile away from the mosque and began to walk. I passed a market and a gas station, both of which had locked up hours earlier. Residents of the neighborhood frantically pushed suitcases into the trunks of their cars and hurried to get out. I hadn't gone a hundred yards when I saw a mass of people up ahead turn and begin sprinting my way. Their arms flailed wildly. Then I heard the *clink* and *fizz* of a metal tear gas canister hitting the pavement and spraying its contents. I joined the group sprint, wondering how running from tear gas in Islamabad compared to running with the bulls in Pamplona.

The gas filled my head and made me cry. I stopped to catch my breath and couldn't stop coughing. Eventually I moved on, hoping to get a closer look at the mosque. For more than an hour, I ran through the alleys and back roads of the adjoining residential neighborhood. I tried to coordinate with a few other journalist friends who were nearby, but anytime I got close to them, another cloud of tear gas appeared, or a round of gunshots echoed out in the smoky air. My body was dripping with sweat from the crushing July heat and my heart pounded from the surge of adrenaline.

On July 3, Ghazi's militants wore gas masks as they battled state security forces in the streets. PHOTO: AAMIR QURESHI/AFP/GETTY IMAGES

That evening, as the sun set and gunfire pierced the sky, the government's resolve hardened and they shut off the power to the whole area around the Red Mosque. Musharraf and his advisers sat in a meeting, hashing out the details for the impending military operation. By dawn, armored personnel carriers rolled down the streets of Islamabad and elite commandos moved into positions nearby. The government imposed a strict curfew. The standoff had begun.

Packs of gun-toting militants, meanwhile, roamed the streets in front of the mosque in the pitch black, guarding it from attack. The PA system crackled to life: "We are ready for suicide attacks. The blood of our martyrs will not go to waste."

GHAZI AND I used to talk frequently, often for two or three hours at a time. He never left the Red Mosque, a kind of homebody jihadi, so I went to him. He had his reasons for not venturing out. In 2004, the government accused him and an Egyptian terrorist of masterminding a plot to bomb the U.S. embassy, the National Assembly, the prime minister's house, general headquarters, and several other high-level offices and residencies.

Ghazi went into hiding for months; the government finally dropped the charges and dismissed the episode as a "misunderstanding." "The script of that drama had a lot of loopholes and lacunas, since it was not written by a good writer," Ghazi told me later. "They should have gotten it written by the FBI." Nonetheless, ever since then Ghazi, who denied any knowledge of the plot but admitted knowing the Egyptian terrorist "very well," believed that Musharraf wanted him dead. So he stayed home.

Pakistani intelligence agents constantly loitered around the mosque. On Fridays, when I would wander over there to hear Ghazi and his brother's take on events during the weekly sermon, agents often stopped me and copied down my personal information. I suspected that my file must have been getting thick. I also imagined that every phone line in and out of the mosque was being tapped, so I bought an additional SIM card, an unregistered one without any connection to my name, to use solely for calls with Ghazi. If I left my car in front of the mosque for more than a few minutes, I took a quick look under the chassis to check for bombs. Stay in Pakistan long enough, and you automatically became paranoid.

Ghazi and his brother, Abdul Aziz, ran the mosque together. But they couldn't have been more different. Ghazi was, by far, the more worldly of the two. He had jumped from one English-medium school to another, acquiring his command of flawless, idiomatic English, and a master's degree in international relations. Abdul Aziz graduated from the Binori Town madrassa in Karachi. Their father, Maulana Abdullah, had groomed Aziz to eventually succeed him.

Aziz was reclusive. He normally emerged once a week to deliver the Friday sermon. He wore thick, cloudy eyeglasses that hid his small, beady eyes. I only spoke with him once, shortly after the November 2006 congressional elections in the United States. He suggested at the time that, since Americans had reelected George W. Bush for a second term in 2004, they obviously supported Bush's policies in Iraq and Afghanistan. Therefore, ordinary Americans were equally responsible for killing Muslims, or so he believed. I disagreed, not only because I wanted to save my own skin, but also because the election results clearly indicated otherwise.

"Those elections showed that most Americans *don't* support Bush," I explained, speaking in Urdu. "It was really a strong vote against Bush and the Republicans. The war in Iraq is very unpopular in America."

Aziz looked slightly puzzled. If the vote went against Bush, he asked, then why was he still the president?

"The presidential election isn't until 2008," I said. "So we have to wait another two years for a new president."

"But if most Americans don't like him now, why don't they just go into the streets and overthrow him?"

Aziz and I leaned on wide pillows, propped against the walls. Ghazi sat across the room and smiled at me. Unlike his brother, Ghazi understood the foreign media and the West. He had enough of a foot in both worlds—the jihadi one and the Western one—to know how certain quotes would sound on the radio or look in print. He paid due deference to his older brother, and yet was willing to express quiet amusement at his naïveté and zeal.

The next Friday, Ghazi invited me inside the mosque to listen to his brother's sermon, rather than sitting outside on the curb as I normally did. I arrived early, and Ghazi, who wore his trademark maroon stitched cap, introduced me to a young man who had recently returned from fighting alongside the Taliban in Afghanistan. The man, in his late twenties, was lanky and bucktoothed. Although he passed his spare time inside the Red Mosque, he had graduated from a local university, not a madrassa. I saw this trend more and more; while the first-generation Taliban had been products of the Islamic seminaries, the new generation of fighters and Islamic guerrillas were often less studied in such subjects, yet still more emotional, youths. Ghazi and Aziz crafted and channeled those emotions.

While Ghazi, the young fighter, and I conversed in the courtyard between Ghazi's home and the Red Mosque, Aziz approached wearing a long robe and clutching a Quran against his chest. Three guards pointing AK-47s in the air surrounded him. Aziz, whose hair and beard was a light, sandy color, stared straight ahead. He clenched his face in an intense expression. He nodded once at us and continued inside of the mosque.

In his *khutba*, or sermon, he told the parable of Abraham destroying stone idols. The parable illustrated the need to smash false gods. Aziz tied the story to the present. "In every age, Allah sends someone down, like Abraham, to show that those things people think are great, are really meaningless. The great powers of the world, like the United States, are so proud, but they are blind to the power of Allah. When the World Trade

Center fell, Osama said, 'This was your pride, the expression of your power and success.' Allah has shown that those things can fall in the blink of an eye."

GHAZI AND AZIZ's father, Maulana Abdullah, founded and ran the Red Mosque for decades. It was the first mosque in Islamabad after the new capital was created in the early 1960s. Abdullah mentored the mujahideen during jihad of the 1980s. The Red Mosque became a way station for fighters transiting in and out of combat. Ghazi was a clean-shaven college student at the time. "The concept of jihad was not so clear to me back then," he told me. Yet the tales of ambush and intrigue tickled his imagination.

Ghazi grew close with Qari Saifullah Akhtar. Akhtar commanded Pakistan's first jihadi group, Harakat ul-Jihadi Islami (HUJI). (Benazir Bhutto's posthumously published book fingered Akhtar for his role in the October 2007 bombing of her motorcade that left more than 140 people dead.) Ghazi craved a life of adventure for himself, and asked his father for permission to join Akhtar at a camp in Afghanistan. It was around the time of his twenty-second birthday. Abdullah deferred the decision to Ghazi's mother. Ghazi told her he was "going in the way of Allah," an intentionally vague explanation, one often used by missionaries belonging to Tablighi Jamaat. Ghazi wound up at a mujahideen camp a few weeks later.

Ghazi relished his time in Afghanistan, but the experience didn't make him a jihadi for life. Before 9/11, and the ultimatums of being "with us or against us," Ghazi flitted between two worlds: the one of madrassas and jihad, occupied by his father and brother, and a more modern one. He vacationed on the beaches in Thailand. In 1998, he worked at UNICEF, the United Nations Children's Fund. That same year Ghazi received an invitation from his father to accompany him on a trip to Kandahar. Qari Saifullah Akhtar, the longtime family friend and leader of HUJI, wanted to introduce Abdullah and his sons to Osama bin Laden. "My father was curious to know what his opinions were," Ghazi said. Akhtar belonged to a small circle of non-Afghans close to Mullah Omar, the Taliban, and bin Laden, and said he could facilitate the meeting.

Abdullah and Ghazi (Aziz didn't join them, for reasons I never fully understood) flew to Quetta, and then drove across the border into Afghanistan, and on to Kandahar. Bin Laden greeted them when they arrived. A few months earlier, bin Laden had declared war against the United States, and just weeks later would order the bombings of the American embassies in Kenya and Tanzania. Now, the Saudi suggested that Abdullah and Ghazi get some rest. He promised to meet them at dawn prayers the following morning. The next day, "from breakfast until late night," Abdullah and bin Laden swapped ideas, while Ghazi, still beardless, listened. One day in the presence of bin Laden, Ghazi said, was enough for Abdullah. "He was convinced by Osama's ideas."

After the meeting with bin Laden, Abdullah and his younger son returned to Islamabad, encouraged by their new friendship and equipped with new ideas. In his weekly sermons, Abdullah exalted bin Laden, his philosophy, and his new organization, al-Qaeda. The intelligence agencies and authorities might have ignored Abdullah had he been preaching at a provincial mosque, but he attracted a flood of attention as imam of the largest mosque in Islamabad.

In October 1998, less than three months after his meeting with bin Laden, an assassin stalked Abdullah as he walked across the courtyard of the Red Mosque. Abdullah carried a bag of fruit in either hand. The assassin, who Ghazi claims to have been in the pay of the ISI, popped out from behind a wall and emptied two magazines of ammunition into Abdullah. Ghazi's father collapsed in a pool of blood and died underneath a young dogwood tree. Bin laden sent a letter of condolence.

The experience of meeting bin Laden, observing the Taliban regime in action, and then seeing his father killed had a severe affect on Ghazi. He left UNICEF and assumed control, with his brother, of the Red Mosque. Years later, when pressed to define his political and religious vision, Ghazi told me, "The ideal form of governance is Islamic governance, and it was in Afghanistan under Mullah Omar. . . . I don't like democracy. Islam is not about counting people. In democracy, the weight of one vote is the same for a man who is taking drugs and doesn't care about his country as it is for the man with a vision for the future. The majority of people are ignorant. This doesn't bring us a good system." The conversation with bin Laden had galvanized Ghazi's transformation. The death of his father changed him for good.

＊ ＊ ＊

OVER THE YEAR that I knew Ghazi, the last year of his life, I watched closely as he and his followers prepared. I wasn't sure what exactly they were preparing for, or from where they were getting the money. The worshippers who came to the Red Mosque tended to be middle-class, and with Pakistan's relative economic upturn during those years, many of them shared the wealth with Ghazi. Proceeds from Afghanistan's opium trade funded many of the Taliban groups based along the border, but it seemed unlikely that that source of money was subsidizing the Red Mosque, far as it was from the poppy fields of southern Afghanistan. But looking back, the changes I witnessed inside the mosque all indicated the looming confrontation with the Pakistan government.

I once pointed to a Kalashnikov leaning up against his computer desk.

"That's new," I said.

"No, I've always had that."

"But what about *that*?" I asked, pointing to the short, fat cylinder fixed to the underside of the barrel.

"Oh, *that*. That's a grenade launcher. A friend recently gave it to me," Ghazi said. He showed me how it worked, able to launch grenades over a wall, at a range of thirteen hundred feet. In other words, the perfect weapon to use against an encroaching force if you're holed up, surrounded by high walls inside a mosque.

Ghazi had overhauled his information and propaganda center after the "female commandos" took over the children's library. A half-dozen new computers were brought in, manned by several of Ghazi's tech-savvy disciples. Industrial-grade CD and DVD burners churned out propaganda material and footage of Taliban-led ambushes and IED (improvised explosive device) explosions in Afghanistan. In response to those who suggested that Ghazi wanted to take Islamabad back to the eighth century, he told me, "We don't want to go backward. Why would I give up my computer, my mobile phone, my walkie-talkie, and my fax machine?"

The changes weren't limited to Ghazi's armory and technology, either. (Just about the only thing that seemingly *didn't* change in the bowels of Ghazi's operations center was the "Spring Inks Color Process Chart" by Sherwin-Williams tacked up on the wall. A weird choice for wall art? Yes. But if you were a jihadi, who believed depictions of the human form were *haram*, then what better way to spruce up a room with color than a poster of paint swatches?) Security tightened around the mosque. Getting in to see Ghazi became arduous. Ghazi requested that I call at least an hour before arriving. That gave him enough time to notify the vigilante scouts pacing the sidewalks out front that a Western journalist was expected and not to attack him with a rusty shovel.

Militants with scarves tied over their faces, wearing ammo vests, and holding rifles, replaced the friendly faces of Ghazi's team of assistants who I had come to know. When the police and Rangers first surged around the mosque in early February, hundreds of armed supporters—a combination of Pashtuns from the North-West Frontier Province and the tribal areas whose sisters and daughters studied at Jamia Hafsa, and Ghazi's old students who had graduated from the men's madrassa and joined various jihadi groups—rushed to defend the mosque. A core of several hundred ruthless and well-trained militants lived in the mosque through the winter, spring, and summer of 2007. Many of them belonged to Sipah-e-Sahaba, HUJI, and Jaish-e-Mohammad. (Jaish-e-Mohammad had been accused of the two assassination attempts on Musharraf in December 2003, and the assault on the Indian parliament in Delhi in December 2001.) Musharraf admitted that a dangerous gang of militants had surrounded Ghazi, including plenty of eager suicide bombers. "I am not a coward," he said, when asked in July 2007 why he hadn't besieged the Red Mosque and crushed Ghazi's movement. "But the issue is that tomorrow you will say: 'What have you done?' There are women and children inside."

Why did they come? What was the appeal? I wanted to understand. And as threats of government bombardment increased, the more I felt I could appreciate the motivations of the young men, anxious to do battle, who never left Ghazi's side. Why did young Americans join the army? The promise of a life of travel, adventure, and a sense of purpose. The thought of fighting for something bigger than themselves. Bravery and honor. Similar reasons drove young Pakistanis to join the Islamic militias. But there was an added attraction inside the Red Mosque: Ghazi. He played the classic role of the charismatic leader to an army of brainwashed youth. I knew why they flocked to be near him: I also felt safe in his presence. With time, I began to wonder if these guys believed more in "Sharia or Martyrdom"—or in Ghazi?

Ghazi had done more than just lead an armed rebellion in the center of the capital. The more significant revolt was a social one. It took place in the hearts and minds of young jihadis. Ghazi harnessed their anger and emotions and split off from the traditional sources who had monopolized jihad in previous years. Ghazi's power grab represented a seismic shift in the leadership of religious politics in Pakistan; the traditional chiefs, though they may have agreed in principle with Ghazi about the supremacy of sharia, bucked hard against the methods Ghazi and his brother adopted.

As Ghazi's followers harassed brothel owners and policemen around town, they drew widespread condemnation. The MMA, the hard-line coalition of Islamist parties that sat in the National Assembly and governed two of the country's four provinces, distanced itself. Similarly, the examination board responsible for most madrassas in Pakistan canceled the Red Mosque's registration. And Mufti Taqi Usmani, a scholar of immense repute who acted as the *pir*, or spiritual guide, to Aziz, disowned his former pupil when the latter refused to order his students to vacate the children's library.

I asked Ghazi how he felt with the old guard turning against him. He looked unconcerned. "They are too rigid," he said. "Everywhere you look, you can see youngsters rejecting the old ones, because old people do not like change."

BY DUSK ON the first day of the standoff, I wondered if I had misjudged Ghazi all along. I considered him an opportunist and a politician, well-versed in the art of brinkmanship, but in no rush to go down in a blaze of glory himself. And yet, with my pores still stinging from the tear gas, the Ministry of Environment building still burning, and army commandos deploying around the mosque, it seemed that Ghazi might have been more than the sum of his rhetorical parts. On the Fourth of July, I sat alone on the rooftop patio of my house. (A few weeks earlier, my wife had gone to China to escape the humid summer months in Islamabad.) It was the second day of the standoff at the Red Mosque, and all American-sponsored celebrations were canceled due to fears of terrorism. I watched a different kind of fireworks show, looking out over the thick trees and rooftops between my house and the Red Mosque. Military helicopters flew overheard. Gunfire pinged away across town.

A selfish part of me wanted the standoff to go on and on. It was an exhilarating time. I relished my comparative advantage over the dozens, if not hundreds, of reporters who had parachuted into Islamabad, since I knew the mosque and the people inside so well. But I was scared, too. I didn't worry so much about an errant grenade landing on my house, but about the unpredictability of larger events that could come next. Was Ghazi right? If he was killed, would his death spark an Islamic revolution? Could it result in a violent jihadist insurgency against the government? Plus, so long as Ghazi remained alive, I knew I had some special access to him and his movement; if he died, I would be just another hostile, foreign face to the jihadis.

The possibility still existed that negotiations could defuse the crisis. Musharraf's government had signed numerous "peace treaties" with pro-Taliban militants already. Some thought they would do the same with Ghazi. The first few nights of the standoff, Ghazi had called several TV stations, suggesting his willingness to cut a deal. This seemed more like the Ghazi I knew. But the burning question remained: Was Ghazi a politician angling for a future of power on this earth, or a jihadi obsessed with fantasies about Paradise?

ON THE SECOND night of the standoff, Ghazi's brother, Aziz, was arrested trying to escape from the mosque disguised as a woman. He wore a black, head-to-toe abaya. State-run TV trotted Aziz out before the cameras and unleashed an irreverent anchorman on him. Pakistan Television broadcast the interview. If the government had hoped the interview would publicly disgrace Ghazi and his brother, erode some of their support, and coax Ghazi into surrendering, they failed. Ghazi knew the government was capable of dragging him and his reputation through the mud: he could either live a day on state-run TV and then disappear into a jail cell for decades, or live forever in the minds of the teenage jihadis he had inspired for years. The government's handling of Aziz simplified the decision.

Meanwhile, armored personnel carriers and truckloads of heavily armed soldiers constricted around the mosque. They imposed a curfew. The vendors selling prayer caps, Islamic books, and snacks to worshippers around the Red Mosque were long gone. The government announced an amnesty program for anyone who left of his or her own volition. Numbers varied, but some estimated the total still inside to be more than three thousand people. They consisted of Ghazi and his hard-core supporters, several hundred of his "female commandos," and then a large number of men who had joined the fight against the government on the first day and now found themselves trapped inside. At least one thousand people responded to the government's promise of 5,000 rupees, or around $83, and surrendered over the first couple days. Basic arithmetic would have concluded that at least five hundred to one thousand militants were still inside.

Each day, for two hours, the quarantine in the neighborhood around the mosque was relaxed, and the orders to "shoot on sight" curfew-breakers was lifted. "Mobile utility stores"—trucks loaded with milk, rice, lentils, cooking oil, tea, and other staples—made the rounds to those families who had not evacuated. They faced growing hardships from electricity and food shortages. Morning temperatures pushed well past 100 degrees, and by the afternoon, during the short period when the curfew was broken, the sun burned and the temperature reached as high as 110 degrees. No electricity meant that residents also didn't have fans or air-conditioning.

On the fourth day of the siege, I teamed up with some friends with hopes of reaching the Holiday Inn before the curfew dropped. The Holiday Inn stood less than a half mile from the Red Mosque. It was the closest relatively safe spot. An entourage of Pakistani TV reporters had camped out there for the past three nights. They speculated that the final military operation was hours away. The hotel was empty beside the few rooms occupied by journalists. One friend, preparing for the worst, toted a large canvas bag with his flak jacket and helmet. I wondered if he knew something I didn't.

In the short term, I had a medical crisis to deal with. Somehow I had acquired a nasty case of shingles that morning. So after dropping our luggage in the room, I went back to the reception desk to ask if they had any medicine—perhaps something to soothe the pus-tipped bumps spreading up my left leg. The bellboy apologized; on a normal day, they could run to the pharmacy for guests, but all the pharmacies were closed. He reached under the desk, fetched a first-aid kit, removed three bottles, and lined them up on the counter.

"You can have whichever one you want," he said.

My choices? Dettol, an antiseptic liquid used for scrubbing clothes and bathroom floors; iodine; or a third bottle, without any clear name or label, that had written across the back "P-O-I-S-O-N." I headed back upstairs with my pocked, itchy leg—and no medicine.

We had taken a room at the end of the hotel nearest the mosque and left the sliding-glass door cracked open to listen for developments. Military trucks motored up and down the road. A generator juiced the lights in the hotel since authorities had cut off the water supply and power in the area. Outside, the slightest noise, like a tree branch breaking, echoed in the eerie, black night. We held our breath. I jumped at the sound of the doorbell when room service arrived. As we looked out the window and tilted our ears toward the mosque, I wondered what would happen if one of Ghazi's suicide bombers threw himself at the commandos stationed around the perimeter. Would the impact of the blast shatter the hotel's windows? What if the militants suspected that the army was taking advantage of the hotel's roof to use as a listening post? Did they have the ability to attack it?

Later, tracer fire zoomed past the windows. I thought I could hear bullets piercing individual leaves as they raced through the trees. At one point, I asked myself what we were gaining by staying at the hotel. I arrived at only one useful result: we knew what weapons everyone was using and could have some sense of the fire exchanged. The police and the militants fired Kalashnikovs with their signature staccato *pop-pop-pop*. The army and Rangers fired machine guns, with a more rolling *tut-tut-tut*. And the Rangers and the commandos fired G3s, which made a heaving, harrumphing sound, like a fat man choking on a peanut.

When curfew broke the next morning, I went home. Actually, first I rushed to the pharmacy and stocked up on enough medicine to last for a month and to handle every possible kind of rash that had ever existed. That night, I climbed to the rooftop patio of my house and looked over the city. A massive explosion created a flash of light, immediately followed by a fireball over the mosque. A thunderous boom reverberated in my chest. The layered, multipitched chorus of gunfire grew more rapid, building toward some grand finale. I wondered if Ghazi had used his grenade launcher yet. And how the windows of the Holiday Inn were holding up.

THE POPPING AND cracking sound of gunfire made parts of Islamabad, the normally staid, sleepy city, sound like a giant bag of microwave popcorn.

Meanwhile, the intelligence agencies scoured every last room in the Holiday Inn, looking for holdouts. They expanded the cordon around the Red Mosque and imposed a media blackout. With no reporters anywhere nearby, the army assumed the job of relaying information about the fight, while simultaneously participating in it; wasn't that a conflict of interest? We expected to hear politicians fib and twist the truth, but soldiers? Aren't they the straight talkers? And yet, every word issued from the mouth of a uniformed spokesman sounded fishy, if not like an outright lie. It was nearly all the information we had.

The army spokesman was a slender man named General Arshad, and for ten days he summoned forth his inner anchorman, presidential spokesman, and trial lawyer. He had to convince the media, who could then—the army hoped—convince the public, that Ghazi and his team were irreconcilable and needed to be killed. He accused Ghazi of harboring foreign terrorists, even some "high-value" ones, a euphemism that suggested Osama bin Laden, Ayman al-Zawahiri, or other top al-Qaeda leaders might be holed up inside. As part of the authorities' attempt to brand Ghazi and his militants as extremely sophisticated, and therefore especially dangerous, Arshad told Western reporters that Ghazi's men had burrowed tunnels through which they could freely move between the Red Mosque itself and the compound that included Jamia Hafsa, the women's madrassa.

Meanwhile, Ghazi continued trying to negotiate with the government. He read the terms and conditions of his surrender to TV stations. He wanted safe passage from the mosque and immunity from prosecution. Knowing that he'd be tracked if he used the same number, Ghazi hoarded a stash of SIM cards and popped in a new one with every phone call. When the commando-led raid finally began, code-named Operation Silence, Ghazi called in to a private TV station one last time.

"I am about to die," he said. "But I will fight until my last." Those final words sounded like a reckless jihadi—and not the man I knew. Ghazi had become a victim of his own personality cult. He left himself with no exit strategy. His followers knew that even if Ghazi was awarded safe passage, they would almost certainly be arrested—and perhaps disgraced like Aziz. They weren't about to let that happen. Ghazi had led them this far. They would take it the rest of the way.

* * *

ON THE FIFTH day of the siege, I visited Shireen Mazari, the director general of the Institute of Strategic Studies in Islamabad and holder of a doctorate degree from Columbia University. Mazari had become a minor celebrity for her anti-American, anti-Indian, anti-NATO opinions, which she coupled with fervent Pakistani nationalism and an unrivaled predilection for conspiracy mongering. She wore her hair short like a female golfer, and dyed it a spectrum of magenta, fuchsia, lime green, and canary yellow, depending on the day, her mood, and her outfit. The most curious thing about her was not her hair, but the fact that she had decided to host me as a Visiting Scholar at the Institute of Strategic Studies in Islamabad during the two years I lived in Pakistan. By hosting me, she agreed to sponsor my visa, give me an office, and outfit me with business cards. Meanwhile, Mazari detected a CIA plot behind every bomb, riot, and sneeze in Pakistan.

"What's wrong with the media blackout?" she said with an irritated air when I suggested that the government was creating a credibility problem for itself. "There ought to be a limit to freedom of speech. Why is this terrorist being given so much airtime in foreign newspapers?" she asked, referring to Ghazi. Mazari admitted that she hadn't actually read the foreign coverage, but she confidently criticized it nonetheless. "A terrorist must face his actions," she said. "It's unfortunate that people are now trying to build him up."

Mazari wondered why the army didn't bomb the mosque.

"Don't you think there would be massive numbers of casualties?" I asked. "Plus, I know that the militants have an impressive arsenal of weapons that they haven't used." I told her about Ghazi's grenade launcher. "The army might be surprised by what they encounter," I said.

Mazari wrote a weekly column in the *News*, an English-language daily newspaper. Two days after our conversation, I read her column:

> Interestingly, a number of foreign journalists and analysts, especially American, were in frequent contact with Abdul Rashid Ghazi and had been allowed to view the military hardware he had surrounded himself with (and some had reported this is their stories/articles). As one of these analysts put it: Ghazi was liked by the American journalists because he

was familiar with western idiom! Given this level of superficiality, one wonders whether his action against the Chinese endeared him further.

A drive-by shooting in Peshawar a few days earlier had killed three Chinese workers. At the end of her column, Mazari suggested a possible jihadi-and-CIA-agents-posing-as-journalists nexus, part of a plot to ruin Pakistan's relationship with China. My mind reeled. This was clearly a woman who could not be trusted. And she was supposed to be my host.

THE FIRST PHASE of the siege lasted seven days. In the beginning, I would jerk awake at the sound of gunfire or an explosion across town and run up to the rooftop patio. With no clear sight-lines to the mosque, I was left listening for clues. After a week, I fell asleep telling myself that I wasn't going to spend another night in my boxer shorts on the roof, holding a paper cup to my ear and leaning toward the Red Mosque. But at a few minutes before 4 A.M., the thud of an explosion—louder than any I had heard that week—shook the windows of my apartment. I threw back the covers, grabbed a notebook, and hustled up to the roof.

The explosion heralded the beginning of Operation Silence. Commandos detonated a series of smaller bombs to demolish the walls and pave the wave for their raid. General Arshad, the army spokesman, predicted a swift operation. But Ghazi's promise to "fight until his last" turned out to be more than bluster. For two days, a few hundred commandos, backed by thousands of police and paramilitary soldiers, warred against Ghazi's jihadis, who numbered in the hundreds. Maulvi Faqir Mohammad, a Taliban commander in the Bajaur Agency of FATA, led a rally of twenty thousand fellow Taliban supporters and encouraged Ghazi to "embrace martyrdom." Eventually, after more than eighteen hours of fighting, the government declared that they had killed Ghazi in the basement of Jamia Hafsa, the women's madrassa. He was shot in the leg, refused to surrender, and was finally killed. The government paraded Ghazi's white, bloated corpse in front of television cameras.

I paused when the images flashed on the screen. Then I turned off the TV and sat in the dark. Was I allowed to mourn someone who had just led a rebellion? On the other hand, if I didn't let myself feel sad, I would be cheating my dead friend. Ghazi had taken risks time and again when he reached out to his colleagues and friends to introduce me to them. Having a reference from him was like having a backstage pass to the wild world of radical Islam. I owed it to Ghazi—and to myself—to feel remorse. It didn't mean that I supported his views. But he was a friend.

I sat down that night and wrote a story about the final days of the Red Mosque, and an ode to Ghazi. I wrote in a piece for *Slate*, the online magazine, "[Over the course of the siege] Ghazi morphed from an outspoken extremist with a perma-smirk into a bona fide terrorist." That Sunday, the piece was republished in the *Washington Post*, under the title: "My Buddy, the Jihadi." My mom, who does not regularly read *Slate* but who does get the *Post* delivered to her door, called a few hours later, near the point of hyperventilation. With my brother and father both being active-duty Marines—my dad a general and my brother a young officer, fighting jihadis in Iraq—my mom was worried about how my story would go over in their lives and careers. When it came time for security clearances and background checks, they now had to worry about my writing in the national media about being buddies with prominent Pakistani jihadis. Even after my family calmed down a bit, I continued to receive hate e-mail from readers who decided that I belonged in Guantánamo Bay, "like the rest of the terrorists." In other words, I may not ever be bound for high elected office.

One thing remained very clear, however: Ghazi's death, and the demolition of the Red Mosque, hadn't vanquished the Taliban. The episode had instead breathed further life into them, and provided their leaders with another cause to rally around. Maulvi Faqir, the Taliban chief from Bajaur, said: "We beg Allah to destroy Musharraf, and we will seek revenge for the atrocities perpetrated on the Lal Masjid."

Owing to the media blackout, many questions remained. How many people had really died? The government stated around one hundred militants had been killed, and that another ten soldiers had died. Independent estimates put the number who died inside the mosque closer to four or five hundred. But reporters were barred from visiting local hospitals. When you did the math, starting with roughly three thousand people inside the mosque on July 3, and subtracting the approximately fifteen hundred to two thousand students who surrendered, you had to think that there were at least five hundred still inside during the final push, if not a thousand. Where were they all?

Hoping to stem the rising tide of criticisms and conspiracy theories surrounding what some were calling a government-approved "massacre" inside the mosque, General Arshad led a few hundred journalists on a tour. We migrated as a herd from the army's staging ground. On the way, I spotted a woman pulling a suitcase down the road. She had probably spent the past week staying with friends who lived outside the war zone, and she wanted to return home. Sandbag bunkers, coils of razor wire, and dozens of soldiers stood in her way.

An incinerated truck sat parked in front of the mosque. Huge holes had been blasted into the walls. The area smelled like burning rubber. Photographers ran ahead of the pack, and then hurried from room to room inside Jamia Hafsa, hoping to get a clear shot before we other hacks blocked their way. General Arshad gave a short brief on the steps of Jamia Hafsa and then walked inside. Someone asked him about the "high-value" terrorists and "foreign militants." Arshad said that some of those killed looked as though "they did not belong to this area." One of the main justifications to the public for the military operation had been the presence of "high-value" targets. Yet the only explanation he now offered was that "they did not belong to this area?"

Twenty-four hours had elapsed between our tour and the last fired shots. But even as we searched long and hard for signs of death, we found hardly anything. In the courtyard of Jamia Hafsa, one of the white headbands worn by Ghazi's "female commandos" that read SHARIA OR MARTYRDOM dangled from a twig on a small, scrubby bush. The focus of the army's efforts had obviously shifted from "Silence" to "Cleanup." The army had laid out all the weapons and propaganda recovered, including pro-Taliban and al-Qaeda DVDs, books of jihadi poems, grenades, anti-tank mines, shotguns, RPGs, Kalashnikovs, machine guns, mortar rounds, soda crates filled with Molotov cocktails, gas masks, and the decorative sword Ghazi had hanging on the wall of his study. Even that didn't quite make sense. Something seemed like it was missing—or worse, planted. Where was Ghazi's favorite AK-47, equipped with the grenade launcher? And if Ghazi had pledged to fight until the end, why didn't he dip into his arsenal of heavy weaponry, the unused rockets and grenades and mines?

A brown vest with lots of pockets laid among the pile, too. A suicide jacket. When I bent down to take a closer look, one of the army's weapons specialists hurried over. "Be careful," he said. "It's still live."

Live? Was he pulling my leg? Or had they really just left a suicide jacket lying around that was one pushed button away from detonation?

Arshad walked across the courtyard, surrounded by a handful of Western reporters. It was the same courtyard where Ghazi's father had been killed nine years earlier. Arshad pointed up to the minarets and described how militants were firing on the commandos from perches up high.

"What about the tunnels, General?" someone asked.

"Tunnels? What tunnels?" he replied.

"The tunnels you told us about a few days ago."

"I didn't say anything about any tunnels," he said, calm and deadpan. "Any more questions?"

Near the entrance to the Red Mosque, we found a spot on the ground. It was damp and red, with flies buzzing around—the first sign that anyone had been wounded or killed. Empty tear gas canisters and bullet casings spread across the roof of the mosque. Ghazi's black flag with the crossed swords still fluttered from nearby lampposts.

The inside of the mosque looked like the charred, blackened interior of a charcoal grill. Arshad said that anyone who wanted to walk inside was allowed. We didn't even need to take off our shoes. A Pakistani journalist spoke up. He objected to non-Muslims being allowed inside the mosque. "This is no longer a mosque," Arshad told him. "This mosque was used as a firing place for militants against the security forces for the past fifteen days. It is not in use."

THE DECISION TO storm the Red Mosque marked another turning point for Musharraf and for Pakistan. Throughout the spring of 2007, people on Pakistani television often compared a critical day or event as "another 9/11." I had already heard it mentioned after March 9, the day Musharraf suspended the chief justice, and again after May 12, the day of the riots in Karachi. I heard it again throughout July, as the Red Mosque laid in ruins. But in a conversation I had with a young professional Pakistani man two days after Operation Silence ended, I realized that he had something else in mind when he made the comparison to September 11,

2001. Back in 2001, the United States had made a major investment in Musharraf, based on his promises to fight the Taliban and al-Qaeda living on either side of the Pakistan-Afghanistan border. In recent years, however, Washington's confidence in Musharraf had flagged. The raid on the Red Mosque, this bright computer scientist told me, would "re-up" Washington's confidence in Musharraf. It might even add another few years to his regime.

The Taliban insurgency immediately intensified. For years, the pro-Taliban fighters living inside Pakistan, near the Afghan border, had been primarily focused on Afghanistan. They now flipped their attention and initiated a ferocious campaign of suicide bombings, ambushes, and roadside bombs against military convoys traveling in FATA and NWFP. By the end of the month, more than three hundred people had been killed. By the end of 2007, the number of suicide attacks in Pakistan jumped to an all-time high of more than fifty. Local Taliban took over the shrine of a nineteenth-century mujahid in the Mohmand Agency, and renamed it Lal Masjid. Like Ghazi, they showed little respect for tradition.

Ayman al-Zawahiri, who some reporters later alleged to be very close with Ghazi and his brother, issued a short video the day after Ghazi was killed, condemning "the criminal aggression carried out by Musharraf, his army, and his security organs—the Crusaders' hunting dogs—against Lal Masjid in Islamabad." Zawahiri added, "This is a message of blinding clarity to the Muslims in Pakistan, the Pakistani Ulema, and indeed, the Ulema in the rest of the Islamic world, and this crime can only be washed away by repentance or blood.... Muslims of Pakistan: your salvation is only through Jihad." Bin Laden later released his own audiotape condemning the event and exhorting his listeners to wage jihad against Musharraf.

The government reopened the Red Mosque in late July. They had painted it a soft yellow, in hopes of starting anew. They appointed a compliant imam to lead the weekly prayers. He was ushered, under heavy security cover, to the entrance of the mosque.

Hundreds of Ghazi's dedicated followers had beat the new imam there to block him from entering. The militants climbed onto the roof carrying buckets of paint, leaned tall, wooden ladders against the lemon chiffon–colored dome, and began rolling brushes soaked in the signature Pepto-Bismol pink onto the walls.

The imam turned back and refused to take the job.

Pandemonium swept through the neighborhood. Policemen watched, helplessly, as the militants recaptured the mosque. Down the road, another crowd of policemen guarded a cluster of shops and tea stalls. In the melee, a suicide bomber slipped into the crowd of policemen. He detonated himself, sending detached body parts flying in every direction, and killing more than a dozen people.

The militants hoisted the black flag with the crossed swords from the roof of the Red Mosque. The mosque was theirs again, and they bellowed for all those below to hear: "Ghazi! Ghazi! From your blood the revolution will come!"

CHAPTER 9

"IF YOU DON'T LET US LIVE IN PEACE, WE WON'T LET YOU LIVE IN PEACE"

B Y THE TIME WE LEARNED ABOUT THE TALIBAN CHECKPOINT UP AHEAD, it was too late to turn around. On the main road leading out of Mingora, the largest city in the Swat Valley, roughly a three-hour drive north from Peshawar in the North-West Frontier Province, local militants were stopping each passing car. They searched for booze, cassette decks or CD players (used for listening to infidel music), and guaranteed that the womenfolk were properly covered. They were also looking for spies. The Taliban normally punished spies with death, and they especially suspected foreign journalists.

"What should we do?" asked Shaheen, who I had hired as a translator and guide. Shaheen looked terrified. I had only been in Swat a few hours. I couldn't believe he was asking me for advice.

I sat in the backseat wearing a brown shalwar kameez, trying to think inconspicuous thoughts. I had dyed my hair a shade of brown and draped a white-and-black-checked *dastmal*, or scarf, over my shoulder, hoping to blend in while traveling in Taliban country. I normally felt comfortable wearing local clothes. Now I just felt silly, as if I were wearing a Halloween costume.

Shaheen dialed a phone number.

"Iqbal Khan? This is Shaheen." Iqbal Khan led one of the two major pro-Taliban factions that dominated the Swat Valley. We had planned to meet him for dinner. Khan's group, Tehrik-i-Nifaz-Shariat-Mohammadia, or the Movement for the Implementation of Sharia, had been around since the late 1980s. Known as the "black turbans" because of their headwear preference, TNSM rose to infamy in 1994, when they captured the airport near Mingora and then blocked the Karakorum Highway, which connected Islamabad to Kashgar, China. They hoped this would give them some leverage as they campaigned for sharia law. Seven years later, in the fall of 2001, TNSM corralled several thousand local young men and escorted them to Afghanistan for jihad against America. When TNSM's founder, Sufi Mohammad, returned empty-handed, the boys' parents were angry. President Musharraf banned TNSM and threw Sufi Mohammad in jail.

"Shaheen brother. Where are you? I am waiting," Iqbal said. We were running twenty minutes late; Shaheen's driver had temporarily misplaced the car keys.

"We are coming, but there's a problem. There is a checkpoint up ahead. We have a foreigner in the car."

Iqbal laughed. "No problem. Those are *our* boys. What kind of car do you have? I'll let them know you're coming through. Don't worry about anything."

Upon cresting the next hill, we spotted a gang of militants mingling in front of a store. The car fell silent. One of the Talibs gestured at a Diet Pepsi advertisement hanging above the entrance to the store. The ad pictured a smiling man and woman, both holding a can of Diet Pepsi. The Talib disapproved. Women shouldn't be seen. In other parts of NWFP, Islamic vigilantes had spray-painted over billboards featuring women. This Talib looked too hard-core for spray paint. He wore a camouflage ammunition vest and held an AK-47, the butt of the gun resting against his hip. Dark hair fell to his shoulders. Instead of wasting a can of paint, I assumed that they would empty a magazine of bullets into the woman's face or just blow up the shop.

As we drove past and came around the next bend, we realized that those Talibs were just scouts. Our driver stepped on the brakes. Five flatbed trucks blocked the road. As many as fifty Talibs with black turbans, shoulder-length hair, and long beards were packed tightly on the back bed of each truck. Their rocket launchers and Kalashnikovs poked out in every direction. They looked like a frightening combination of livestock being taken to slaughter and an overstuffed vessel of Viking raiders. If one budged from his spot, he might have swiped his fellow Talib in the back of the head with a rifle barrel.

A few dozen Talibs manned an impromptu checkpoint, while a line of cars waited inspection. In the vehicle behind us, a husband, wife, and daughter looked anxious. The teenage girl fumbled to fix her head scarf to meet the Talibs' expectations.

We rolled forward in line, moving at a slow walker's pace. I unfolded an Urdu newspaper and pretended to be reading. One more car in front of us. The Talibs motioned him to the side. Our driver eased forward. The Talibs looked over the car... and then waved us through.

I discarded the newspaper, spun in my seat, and stared out the back window. Like a true voyeur, I wanted to watch, and keep watching, the Talibs for hours. To cram the image into my mind forever of them commanding a road. Then maybe I could go back later and zoom in for a closer look. At the moment of closest contact, I was too scared of being noticed to take pictures.

Analysts had long warned of "Talibanization" sweeping northwest Pakistan. A looming threat. A different kind of Pakistan. *That* Pakistan was no longer a figment of someone's worried imagination. Four hours from the capital, five trucks of militants, totally unchallenged by the police, paramilitary forces, or the army, had arrived and were in charge.

Shaheen spoke up, the first words either of us had uttered since passing the checkpoint a mile or so back. "That's him," he said. Iqbal Khan stood on the side of the road. He was tall, thin, and had a long, graying beard. He looked at the pallid color of our faces and seemed ready to burst into laughter.

"So what happened?" he asked, immediately after getting into the car.

"Nothing. They waved us through."

He sucked his teeth. "I told you," he said. "I gave them the details of your car and said you were my friends. You shouldn't worry if you are with me. These sorts of checkpoints and patrols are just for frightening people. It's a show of force."

* * *

I WENT TO Swat to see how the Taliban ran things. In the middle of July, as the Red Mosque lay in ruins, a young firebrand from Swat declared jihad against the Pakistani government on his illegal radio station. The upstart's name was Maulana Fazlullah. In the ensuing weeks, Fazlullah's suicide bombers targeted police checkpoints and military convoys. They bombed anyone Fazlullah desired, and anyone who dared oppose the Talibs. Swat, a summertime getaway for thousands of tourists every year seeking a break from the heat and humidity choking the lowlands, was known as the "Switzerland of South Asia." Now it looked more like Armageddon than the Alps.

The Talibs cautioned women against wandering around town without a male escort. They were serious. The Talibs believed that educating women was un-Islamic, and they had already bombed several girls' schools. The ladies quit shopping. Evenings in the Mingora bazaar became an all-male affair, as they took over *all* shopping duties. Men with long beards and V-necked cardigans clutched several plastic bags in each hand, sagging with pounds of apples, hunks of ill-cut meat, tubs of unsweetened yogurt, foil strips of medicine, and sometimes even a pair of women's panties or a bra.

The police were in even shorter supply. One evening in the center of Mingora, whose population numbered a few hundred thousand, I saw just two cops. They stood watch near an ice-cream shop. "There's no government here anymore. They haven't met in three months," said Shaheen. "The police don't leave their stations, and elected officials have moved with their families to Islamabad." Fazlullah and his militia filled the vacuum.

Fazlullah had been a prized madrassa student of Sufi Mohammad, the founder of Iqbal Khan's group, TNSM, and the one who had taken the young fighters to Afghanistan in the autumn of 2001, only to be thrown in jail after his botched jihad. When Sufi Mohammad prepared to marry off one of his daughters, he asked Fazlullah to be the groom. After Sufi Mohammad's arrest, TNSM lost the charismatic glue that bound it together. Fazlullah offered to hold Sufi Mohammad's spot. He had some street credibility after a few stints fighting alongside the Taliban in Afghanistan. And he was Sufi's favorite student and his son-in-law.

Fazlullah quickly began cultivating a myth around himself. Reports soon emerged of Fazlullah riding a white horse into the villages around

Mingora, spreading the backward, rigid gospel of Mullah Omar, Osama bin Laden, and other jihadi luminaries. He commandeered several radio frequencies and began a twice-daily broadcast. He used the airtime to mock the government, praise the Taliban, disparage female education, and convince local people not to have their children immunized. He alleged that a government-led antipolio vaccination campaign was an American conspiracy, with the vaccine an impotency serum, meant to sterilize and eradicate Muslims. Fazlullah's detractors dubbed him "Maulana Radio," a cute nickname that undermined his claims to be taken serious.

Fazlullah's fiery sermons bristled the other TNSM leaders like Iqbal Khan. Khan knew he was on the government's watchlist. To avoid unwanted attention, TNSM soon disowned Fazlullah. The pudgy mullah with the radio station and the horse took his brigade of foot soldiers and struck out freelance.

"THIS IS NOT a true Muslim army. It's Musharraf's army, and it's fulfilling the agenda of the Americans," Iqbal Khan said. After we picked him up we had begun snaking along a road that hugged the Swat River, heading north to Iqbal's village of Fatehpur. The river poured from the Hindu Kush Mountains farther north and meandered through the valley, nourishing apple and persimmon orchards. Fishermen waded into the river, looking unsteady from the rapids, and cast their nets.

For centuries, Swat had resisted outsiders' control. Traditionally, a local chief, known as *amir* during the British era and as *wali* during the Pakistani era, ruled over the valley, insulated from colonial dictates. During the Raj, the British termed Swat a "princely state," one of about seven hundred spread across the sprawling British Empire in South Asia. The designation involved regularly handing the amir a bag of cash, and the amir, in return, pledging his allegiance to the crown.

The chiefs had been in no hurry to scrap this arrangement, and it continued after Pakistan was formed in 1947. Swat joined the federation in 1969, under the vague moniker of a Provincially Administered Tribal Area, or PATA. In northwestern Pakistan, there were three major modes of governance. In the Federally Administered Tribal Areas (FATA), tribal customs trumped all laws besides one permitting collective punishment. In the "settled" areas of the North-West Frontier Province, people lived

In late October 2007, the Talibs in Swat prepared for their impending fight against the government by erecting donation tables where local people gave money, clothing, and food to the "mujahideen." PHOTO: JOHN MOORE/GETTY IMAGES

according to Pakistani laws drafted and implemented in the national assembly. PATA rules floated somewhere between the two. In 1985, PATA was scrapped. According to Iqbal, that year also heralded the beginning of TNSM, as they scrambled to replace the half-witted hybrid of tribal and colonial codes—a confusion that continues today—with a single, clear, and implacable one: sharia.

Long before Islam arrived in Swat, the valley had been a cradle of ancient Buddhist civilization. In the fifth and sixth centuries BC, Buddhism expanded into northern Pakistan and parts of present-day Afghanistan from neighboring India. The Gandhara civilization, which reigned from the sixth century BC through the eleventh century AD across northern India, Pakistan, and Afghanistan, was rooted in Swat and in Taxila, a town located just outside of Islamabad and recognized as a UNESCO World Heritage site. Throughout the region, followers carved statues of the Buddha into rocks and the sides of mountains. Two of the most famous of these statues once stood in Bamiyan, Afghanistan, one measuring more than 120 feet high, the other more than 180 feet. In 2001, the Taliban destroyed the statues by firing rockets and mortars at them for hours until the Buddha's faces crumbled down the side of the mountain. After the desecration of the statues, TNSM sent a delegation to Afghanistan to congratulate Mullah Omar.

Swat hosted several Buddhist statues, roughly one hundred feet tall, which militants had already tried to destroy with TNT and AK-47s. I asked Iqbal why the Talibs felt compelled to blow up the statues.

"The leadership of TNSM doesn't have anything to do with this. Young people are coming together in the *hujra*"—the traditional meeting room in a Pashtun's home—"and they might say, 'Let's go blow up the statues,' or 'There's a foreigner in Mingora who we should kidnap.' The youth are becoming more reactionary every day," he said. "We have no control of them."

We arrived in Iqbal's village of Fatehpur around dusk. The smell of baking bread wafted down the narrow roads, lined with homes and walls made of mud brick. Children scurried up and down the alleys, holding slabs of nan like armfuls of firewood.

"I'm so hungry," Shaheen said. It was the last week of Ramadan, the month during which Muslims fast from sunrise to sunset, without so much as a drop of water. Iqbal had wanted to be huddled in front of the feast when the evening call to prayer finally sounded, so that we could all break the fast. In the spirit of camaraderie born from suffering, I opted not to disclose that I had snuck in a couple of PowerBars since breakfast.

Among surrounding hills, dense with pine trees, night fell suddenly. Twenty minutes after we had begun eating inside Iqbal's home, the windows looked as if they were cloaked with a black sheet. To break the fast, we had downed glasses of pink-colored rosewater, which were soon followed by fish in a tomato gravy, tandoori chicken, peas, and count-less loaves of hearty, sweet village nan. Iqbal and I sat beside each other on the ground, at the head of a tablecloth laid out on the floor. Iqbal wore a shiny watch and his fingernails were newly clipped. Shaheen sat on my other side. A dozen of Iqbal's male relatives, wrapped in wool blankets, joined us around the tablecloth. One of them fed wood into the potbellied oven that stood in the middle of the room. An aged, toothless man mumbled in the corner. I never met the women who prepared the meal.

After dinner, men smoked their first cigarette or took their first snuff of the day.

"You want anything?" Iqbal asked me. "If you want hashish or opium, just tell me." I politely declined.

After drinking enough cups of tea to irrigate the deserts of southern Pakistan, Iqbal wanted to talk about his friends. "You know, I was the first man from this part of the country to meet Mullah Omar and Sheik Osama," he said.

"Sheik Osama?" I had never heard bin Laden referred to as "sheikh," a term usually reserved for scholars or tribal chiefs.

"Did you know that Osama has written a book of philosophy?"

I didn't.

"Come with me and I'll show you," Iqbal said.

Iqbal and I walked alone into an adjoining room. The house reminded me of a hunting lodge. Creaky floors, exposed wooden beams, crisp, inky night air. We stood in front of a yellowing cabinet, pasted with old TNSM stickers that showed two crossed Kalashnikovs and, at the bottom: SHARIA OR MARTYRDOM. Iqbal opened the cupboard, and began fetching varied items of Taliban and al-Qaeda paraphernalia.

He showed me a letter, written by Mullah Omar, thanking TNSM for organizing a relief effort to Afghanistan. (After the bombings in 1998 of two American embassies in Africa, which were linked back to bin Laden, the UN had sanctioned the Taliban.) The letter was framed and written on the official stationary of the Islamic Emirate of Afghanistan from the Office of the "Amir ul Momineen"; Mullah Omar had designated himself "Commander of the Faithful."

Then Iqbal displayed a silver 9 mm Beretta pistol, sheathed in a neoprene holster, the kind used by American soldiers. "I got this during my last trip to Afghanistan," Iqbal said. He termed the weapon as *qanimatt*, a word denoting weapons recovered from vanquished armies. He said he and his boys had overrun a U.S. forward base in Kunar Province and gotten away with several American weapons.

Iqbal pulled out a stack of pro-Taliban and al-Qaeda propaganda DVDs, labeled "Waziristan," "Iraq," "Khost," "Kunar," "Paktiya," and showing footage from IED explosions and suicide bombings in each theater of battle. I thought about my brother, a twenty-four-year-old lieutenant in the Marines. He was serving in Anbar Province at the time, trying to avoid suicide bombers and IEDs. I felt sick to my stomach.

"What about that book of Osama's philosophy?" I asked.

"Oh right, I almost forgot," Iqbal said. He pointed at two nylon knapsacks, one green and the other navy blue, lying on the lowest shelf in the cabinet. "The book is in one of those bags. They were left by a former guest who stayed here," he said. "But I promised the guest that I wouldn't touch the bags until he returned."

"Your guest sounds a little demanding," I said. I couldn't think of the Urdu word for anal. "Who was your guest?"

Iqbal looked at me, and then back down at the knapsacks. "Those bags belong to Doctor Zawahiri," as in, Ayman al-Zawahiri, al-Qaeda's number two.

I looked at my watch and decided it was probably time for us to be heading back to Mingora. We returned to the common room.

"Why don't you boys take this for the ride back," Iqbal said, presenting the Beretta.

Shaheen didn't like the idea. "We're journalists," he said. "We don't need weapons."

"What if we run into another checkpoint?" I asked.

"I could write you a letter," Iqbal said. He ripped a blank sheet of paper from a pad and began scribbling a note, in Pashto: "These people are guests of mine. Please show them respect. Iqbal Khan, District Amir, TNSM." It amounted to a get-out-of-a-Taliban-jail-free card. Iqbal was confident that the letter could guarantee our safe passage to Mingora. "But tear it up once you get there. This could get you into trouble in Islamabad."

Shaheen and I made it back to Mingora safely, without having to present Iqbal's letter to anyone along the way.

"This is our problem as Pashtuns," Shaheen said, on the drive home. "All this hospitality is great, as you can see for yourself. But these Arabs, just like you, know they can get a hot meal, sweet tea, and a warm bed at Iqbal Khan's house."

* * *

WHEN A MILITARY raid against Islamabad's Red Mosque had seemed imminent, Abdul Rashid Ghazi had dispatched emissaries throughout FATA and NWFP, wanting to know who had his back. Iqbal Khan volunteered his support. But Ghazi had really hoped to build a bridge to Maulana Fazlullah. In addition to the mythology of Fazlullah tromping into villages astride his white horse, Ghazi knew that several hundred trained militants —including foreigners, mostly Afghans and Uzbeks—acted at Fazlullah's behest. Fazlullah's mini-emirate had only expanded since then.

Shaheen and I were having second thoughts an hour before our scheduled appointment at Fazlullah's compound. Shaheen, who was in his late twenties with a thick eyebrow stitched together across the bridge of his nose, had developed good contacts in Fazlullah's camp over the years. Shaheen worked for a Pashto-language TV channel, which endeared him to the Pashtun Talibs. But this was different from Shaheen's other visits. This time he was bringing an American.

We called Iqbal Khan, hoping he might accompany us.

"You want me to come? No way," he said. "Those people are extremists."

THERE WERE TWO ways of getting to Fazlullah's compound in Imam Dehri, a village across the Swat River from Mingora. The longer and more dangerous way involved driving over a bridge and through a network of villages under Fazlullah's control. The short way entailed driving north a few miles on the road hugging the river, parking the car, and taking a small metal tram attached to a zip line over to the other side. We chose the second option.

At some point between the time when Shaheen and I boarded the tram with six Fazlullah supporters and when we disembarked on the other side, I wondered if we had made a grave mistake. The phrase "belly of the beast" popped into my head and spun around a few times. After a light push from someone onshore to get moving, the tram *whooshed* over a fast-flowing stretch of the river. Fishermen were throwing nets down below. And our car—along with our hopes of beating a sudden and hasty retreat—shrunk on the opposite bank of the river. By the time the tram squealed into the docking station in Imam Dehri, there was no point in second-guessing our decision. We had landed. No going back now.

Sirajuddin, Fazlullah's spokesman and military commander, greeted us on the other side. Shaheen reached into his pocket to pay the toll for the zip line. Sirajuddin waved his hand and plunked a few coins into the basket. "You are our guests," he said.

Sirajuddin had glacier-blue eyes and a straight, pointed nose. He wore a white prayer cap and led us through a crowd of Fazlullah's supporters. Most of them wore floppy wool caps over long, dark tresses. Fazlullah's white horse was tied to a tree. The PA system blasted prerecorded jihadi poems. Talibs mingled with assault rifles and rocket launchers slung over their shoulders. Some of them stared our way, but no one bothered us. They could see that we were with Sirajuddin. To disturb a guest of Sirajuddin—and by implication, Fazlullah—would be to disturb Sirajuddin and Fazlullah themselves.

We filed into a room and sat on the floor. A handful of Talibs crouched and listened as Sirajuddin, Shaheen, and I conversed in a mix of English, Urdu, and Pashto. The Talibs, who I gathered were the same crowd on patrol a few nights earlier, watched us with dark, piercing eyes.

"We want to live in peace," said Sirajuddin. "And we were doing that before the government said Maulana Fazlullah's sermons were provocative."

"What about the bombings against the police and army?"

"This is just a reaction," Sirajuddin replied. "If you don't let us live in peace, we won't let you live in peace."

He added, "We are fighting for Sharia. Twice, in 1994 and 1999, the government committed to enforcing Sharia in Malakand"—before an administrative reshuffle in 2001, Swat, Buner, Dir, Chitral, and Malakand districts all comprised Malakand Division—"but it never did. The people here want Islam to be a way of life. We are Muslims, but our legal system is based on English laws. Our movement wants to replace the English system with an Islamic one."

"Abdul Rashid Ghazi used to say the same thing," I said.

"There are many similarities between us. Like Ghazi, we are on the defensive," Sirajuddin said. "But Jamia Hafsa and Lal Masjid were restricted places. We have high mountains around us. This is suitable terrain for war. If the army attacks us, it will be catastrophic for them. I know every mountain, every bunker, and every cave in this area," he added. "And besides the thousands of men ready to fight for us, there are thousands of women at home who are also listening to Maulana Fazlullah on the radio, ready to make sacrifices."

"And the patrols and the checkpoints?"

Sirajuddin commanded Fazlullah's militia, which numbered around six hundred people. "You know that anything that happens in Swat is automatically blamed on us," he said. "There are no police, and the army doesn't patrol anymore. So who will maintain law and order? We had seen an alarming rise in crime, mostly murders and kidnapping. But since we began patrolling a few days ago, there has been no crime, no murders, and no kidnapping."

Sirajuddin told me about a recent operation. A gang of kidnappers had stormed into a nearby home, killing one person and snatching a couple of women. The kidnappers loaded the women into two cars and drove them west, toward Afghanistan where they could sell or trade them. When word of the plot reached Fazlullah's camp, Sirajuddin mobilized several dozen fighters into the flatbed trucks. He ordered the Talibs to bring the perpetrators back alive. The Talibs raced through the mountains, intercepted the cars, recovered (and returned) the women, and arrested the culprits.

"Today, we are going to punish them," Sirajuddin said.

SIRAJUDDIN ESCORTED US to a small room attached to the back of Fazlullah's mosque. Poplar trees shimmered in the light morning breeze. They cast shadows against the brick walls of the mosque. The room was a kind of Taliban VIP lounge. A handful of senior Taliban lieutenants, including a couple of Uzbek militants and Fazlullah's deputy, sat inside along with the union nazim, the elected official representing the area. His political future, and his life, depended on showing a friendly face at opportune times. The Taliban had already assassinated several politicians who criticized their activities.

The commanders and subcommanders appeared dressed for battle. Each wore the obligatory black turban, the tail hanging by their knees. They carried walkie-talkies, clipped near their left shoulder, to coordinate their movements. One of them, infusing the Talib look with a bit of Tron, sported knockoff Oakley Blades sunglasses. Most wore ammo vests and stuffed the pockets with extra banana clips for their AK-47s.

Since they were "on duty," it was impractical to pray all at the same time. They took turns while the others stayed alert. An Uzbek in his early twenties, with a sparse, wispy beard and long, scraggly hair, prayed in the direction of Mecca with a Kalashnikov between his legs. Most of the Uzbeks in Swat and the tribal areas came from Uzbekistan. Many of them belonged to the Islamic Movement of Uzbekistan, a jihadi outfit aligned with al-Qaeda that called for the overthrow of Uzbek dictator Islam Karimov. Unlike the Arab militants, who treaded lightly and mostly respected Pashtun customs, the Uzbeks were blamed for some of the Taliban's most brutal acts, such as masterminding the assassination of tribal elders. I had heard about the Uzbeks, but had never seen them in the flesh. I stared at the one with the AK-47 between his legs. As he prostrated himself on the ground, his forehead met the tip of the barrel. Then a crowd pushed into the room.

A short man with large gaps between his teeth stood at the front. Wavy hair fell past his shoulders. A bulky, black turban and a goofy smile. Shaheen elbowed me. "Maulana Fazlullah," he said, under his breath. No photographs existed of the man. This was the first time I had seen his face.

Ten bodyguards crushed around Fazlullah. They seemed worried that I might assassinate him. Standing near an open window on the second level of the mosque, a few yards away, a young Talib manned a machine-gun balanced on a paint-splattered ladder.

"Asallamu Aleikum," I said.

"Waleikum A'salaam," Fazlullah returned. His face twisted in another goofy smile.

He asked which newspaper I worked for, and we made small talk for a few minutes. Shaheen explained that I had known Abdul Rashid Ghazi well. Fazlullah looked pleased. He apologized for not having more time to chat. He had been observing *aitekaaf*, a meditation period at the end of Ramadan, and now he had to deliver the weekly sermon. More than ten thousand people stood on the other side of the brick wall, waiting to hear him speak. "Come back after Ramadan, and we can talk for a long time," he said. "For today, you both should feel free to go anywhere you want. You are our guests."

I nudged Shaheen. An all-access pass sounded great, but how about some backup to guard against the zealots? Surely someone around here had waited their whole life to kill an American. Shaheen relayed my request in Pashto. Fazlullah immediately agreed. He tapped one of his top lieutenants, a man named Abdul Ghafoor, to act as our bodyguard for the day.

Abdul Ghafoor, Shaheen, and I wandered the compound for an hour while Fazlullah—his voice bellowing in the background—gave the khutba. Abdul Ghafoor told us that he had been among those in the flatbed truck a few days earlier, patrolling the outskirts of Mingora. Messages crackled over the walkie-talkie attached to the collar of his ammunition vest. An extra pistol poked out of one pocket. He was thirty-two years old and earned a living as a schoolteacher. He wore purple-and-yellow Reebok high tops with a Velcro strap. He had recently graduated from the University of Peshawar with a master's degree in Islamic theology. Every day after school, and on holidays, he grabbed his gun and joined Fazlullah.

"Where do you guys train?" I asked. "Is there a firing range nearby?"

Abdul Ghafoor laughed. "Our training is passed down, generation to generation. I just taught my twelve-year-old son how to work a bullet through the chamber and how to handle a gun. This is our culture. Everyone must have a Kalashnikov."

"What are you fighting for? To create a Taliban state? The glory of Islam? Revenge for the Red Mosque?"

"This is not personal revenge," he said. "It is our religious obligation. If someone attacks Islam, then it is obligatory that we should defend Islam."

"Someone . . . like the United States or General Musharraf?"

Ghafoor nodded.

Meanwhile, Fazlullah's voice boomed over the PA system: "The government says we shouldn't do things like this public punishment, but we don't follow their orders. We follow the orders of Allah!" Fazlullah proclaimed, his voice amplified by myriad megaphones positioned throughout the compound. Men wielding rocket launchers stood on the roof, scanning the rice patties, poplar fields, and riverbanks. Fazlullah added, "When I die, the angels will ask me about my actions. Will this government save me? No! I must act for myself and for my own salvation. You people have no rights unless there is an Islamic system and government in place, based on rights and honor! Are you ready for an Islamic system? Are you prepared to make the sacrifices?"

"Allahu Akbar!" the congregation called back, raising their fists and guns into the air.

We hurried to the other side of the compound, before Fazlullah finished his khutba and the masses migrated. We skipped across a brook, leaping from one river rock to another. Up ahead, I saw the raised wooden platform where the convicted would be lashed.

SPECTATORS QUICKLY GATHERED around the platform. Some unfurled blankets, as if settling in for a picnic. There were thick, forested hills on all sides; the rushing sound of the Swat River; dozens of cars and buses parked at skewed angles. The whole scene made me think of an alternate universe's summertime music festival: Talibanapalooza. It seemed odd that the mountainsides were spotted with hotels. But they were landmarks from another era in Swat, when tourists used to line up to come here. I didn't see another guest at the hotel during my visit.

The Talibs had mastered the art of crowd control, and it was strictly prohibited to take photographs. "Those taking photos will face severe punishment," a voice on the PA system declared. I promptly stashed my camera-phone in my pocket. Hundreds of militants prowled the grounds. A few of them wielded wooden staffs, and some carried World War II–era, bolt-action rifles. But most looked prepared for serious war. Ten of them stood on the platform, holding Kalashnikovs and rocket launchers. Another lay on his stomach on the roof of a nearby shed, his eyes lined up behind the sights of an automatic machine gun. Everyone knew that Fazlullah's decision to take the law into his own hands was in blatant defiance of the government's writ: the militants' job was to repel any sudden ambush by the Pakistani army.

"Maulana Fazlullah says some of you object to this, that you are asking 'Who authorized you to do this? You are not the government.' But these punishments are permitted in parts of the country if it contributes to maintaining peace, even if there is no central Islamic government," Fazlullah's deputy said over the PA. The Talibs knew that Pakistanis complained that their court cases took too much time—and money—that they didn't have. They played this frustration to their advantage. The Taliban proffered an ideology, but more important to many people was the alternative judicial system they promised. Taliban-style justice was cruel, but speedy and free. "We have no intention to occupy the government or for any political authority," the deputy said. "This is only for peace and security."

Moments later, three vehicles—a Toyota station wagon, a 4Runner, and a Toyota pickup—appeared in the distance, speeding across a dirt road in our direction. They kicked up a giant cloud of dust. We held our collective breath. The vehicles wheeled into the middle of the circle and parked beside the platform. The pickup truck led the way. Six Talibs kneeled in the bed, pointing their guns in the air. The 4Runner followed, carrying the three accused criminals in the backseat. The station wagon pulled in last. Two men opened the back doors of the wagon and emerged wearing ski masks and camouflage jumpsuits. They had tucked the legs of their pants into black combat boots. They would dole out the lashings. One carried a thick leather belt.

We all knew that the Talibs were not planning to behead the three convicts, but I had not expected the brazen display of rocket launchers and the spectacle of a public lashing. Honestly, I didn't know what to expect. Nothing would have surprised me at that point. I wrote in my notebook: "I am nervous. I can't imagine how the criminals feel." The oldest of them was twenty-four. The Talibs frog-marched each of them onto the platform. One at a time. They received twenty-five, twenty, and fifteen lashes, in proportion to the extent of their involvement in the kidnapping and their age.

When the youngest of them, clearly still in his teens, scaled the steps of the platform, he looked as if he might collapse. His legs wobbled with fear as he waited to get his fifteen lashings, the appropriate Islamic punishment, according to Fazlullah. The boy lay facedown on the platform. One Talib held his right arm. Another Talib held his left arm. A third held both of the boy's legs so he wouldn't flop around. The punisher clutched the leather whip. He kneeled beside the boy. Every time he raised and then crashed the whip on the boy's back, the crowd called out the corresponding number of lashes as if counting the final seconds of a basketball game. The teenager's body convulsed under the crack and thud of each lash. When he finally stood up, he was shaking and drenched in tears.

And then it was over. The punished and the punishers piled into the 4Runner and the station wagon. The pickup sped out in front, and the three cars disappeared in another cloud of dust. Hardly twenty minutes had passed since they had arrived. Expedient justice, at least in the minds of the Taliban, had been served.

The PA charged back to life: "We will now pray that the infidel's system comes to an end. Vulgarity and crime can only be countered through an Islamic system."

The crowd thrust their fists and guns into the air. "Allahu Akbar!" they chanted. "God is Great."

Prerecorded jihadi poetry, in Pashto, came over the speakers. I asked Shaheen to translate the poem.

"The poem is a father, talking to his son," Shaheen said. It was a coming-of-age story, about a Talib's right of passage. "The father tells the son, 'You are now ready. You have arrived. Go to jihad.'"

CHAPTER 10

"THIS BARBED WIRE STANDS IN THE WAY OF DEMOCRACY"

TWO HOURS OF TROTTING, CANTERING, AND GALLOPING HAD MADE US thirsty. A friend of Rikki's owned a horse farm outside of Islamabad with a veranda near the stables for picnicking. (The veranda was just far enough that you didn't choke on the smell of horse poop.) Rikki, two friends, and I emptied the picnic basket: chips, salsa, tandoori chicken, nan, and a box of red wine. I punched my thumb through the perforated tab on the box, pulled out the nozzle, and filled up four plastic cups.

We each slugged our cups, and all agreed that it was the best wine we had tasted in months. While you could find liquor and beer around town—the Christian ghettos were the go-to source—wine was harder to come by. Our bootlegger had a limited selection: "red or white." The quality of his goods wasn't consistent either: if the whites hadn't turned sour from sitting on the docks in Karachi for months, and if the reds weren't sludge, then you considered it a pretty good case. So our standards quickly adjusted. Anyone who says living abroad doesn't make you a relativist—cultural, gastronomical, whatever—is lying. Wine-in-a-box tasted delicious to me.

The sun set along a spine of lush hills, bleeding into pastel tones of orange, yellow, and red. But we hadn't been relishing the cool evening and the decent wine for long before our phones began ringing. Griff, the correspondent for the *Washington Post*, got the first call. His eyes widened as he listened to the voice on the other end. He mumbled obscenities after hanging up. "Mush's really done it this time," Griff said. "He is about to declare an emergency."

We hurriedly packed up our picnic, capped the box of wine, downed whatever remained in our cups, and jumped in the car. The police were reportedly blocking roads into the city to hamper willing protesters. We were at least a fifteen-minute drive outside of Islamabad. We made it in ten. Griff and I rendezvoused with his driver in a hotel parking lot and rode around in his car the rest of the night. The ladies took the box of wine home, where they were more than happy to watch history on TV.

The capital had stirred with rumors for months that Musharraf might declare a state of emergency, or perhaps even martial law. Musharraf had never looked more uneasy. Benazir Bhutto had returned from exile two weeks earlier, with the backing and support of the United States and the United Kingdom. Musharraf was no longer the only one with a direct line to the White House. The pro-Taliban insurgency continued to spread. On October 18, terrorists displayed their lethal reach when a suicide bomber killed himself and more than 140 others on the day Bhutto returned from exile. Musharraf banked that he could convince the United States to support a martial law regime in the name of fighting terrorism.

But the real reason for Musharraf's apprehension centered around his nemesis, Iftikhar Mohammad Chaudhry. Musharraf had suspended Chaudhry, the chief justice, back in March, yet street protests and political pressure eventually forced Musharraf to cave. In July, Chaudhry was restored to the highest bench. He quickly got back to work tormenting Musharraf. In his biggest case yet, he had begun proceedings that questioned the validity of Musharraf's reelection bid, scheduled for November 15. News leaked out that the judges' decision would go against Musharraf.

On the night of November 3, Musharraf decided to do something about Chaudhry for good and announced a state of emergency. He suspended the constitution and pulled all the private TV channels off the air. The last televised image on Geo, the leading private channel, showed a document drafted by the Supreme Court judges before their imminent removal, declaring the emergency illegal and unconstitutional. It was my and Griff's first coup. We weren't sure what to do next. There had to be something to see, right? Tanks in the streets? Soldiers? When Musharraf overthrew Nawaz Sharif in 1999, people ate sweets and celebrated. Griff and I decided to drive around and look for sweets.

Aitzaz Ahsan was living on borrowed time. The police gathered at the end of his street, waiting for orders to arrest. Ahsan, the president of the Supreme Court Bar Association and leader of the lawyers' movement, called a hurried press conference. We sped in Griff's car across town — less than a ten-minute drive — to Ahsan's house.

Ahsan sat behind an oak desk in the second-story office of his Islamabad home. Rows of legal books were neatly stacked on shelves behind him and a bouquet of microphones crowded in front of his face. He was a meticulous man. He wore a gray suit and a light blue shirt. His steely gray hair was parted slightly to the right.

"This is a very fateful day for this country," Ahsan said. "Pakistan is in a deep, deep crisis. And though this country has been through many a crisis in its sixty years, this is one of the most severe."

The room throbbed with nervous energy. We wondered when the police planned to storm up the stairs and pull Ahsan out of his home. My ears were burning up. The wine kept my nerves calm, but it turned my cheeks and ears bright red.

"It is now one man against the nation. . . . General Musharraf has broken every promise he made. He has ruined and decimated every value in which civil society, and civil, liberal nations thrive. . . . General Musharraf's tenure as president and military commander will finish on the fifteenth of this month, as per the constitution. He must go home as a private citizen on that day. There is no other recourse for him under the constitution."

A man in the front row interrupted Ahsan with breaking news. "Emergency is officially imposed," he said. Ahsan was unflappable. He resumed his address. "Musharraf has behaved like a bad loser and a spoiled child. He has brought this country to shame. This is the end of the road for him. . . . The lawyers of Pakistan will not allow independent judges to be removed from their offices. Judicial structures will not be subverted!"

Afterward, Ahsan offered a reception with samosas, milky tea, and butter cookies. I slipped a few cookies into my front shirt pocket, unsure of when my next meal would come.

"Aitzaz sahib," a Pakistani journalist asked him, "you are about to be arrested. How do you feel?"

"I have been to jail many times before," he said. Ahsan had a knack for always knowing when the cameras were on. "And you can see how I look when they come to get me. But I should change out of these clothes before I go." He ran downstairs and returned five minutes later, wearing a loose-fitting shalwar kameez.

Meanwhile, the police had closed in. They now stood at the end of Ahsan's driveway. They walked up to the door, knocked, and handed over a warrant. They marched Ahsan down the stairs of his house and into a waiting police car. His supporters chanted slogans against Musharraf the whole time.

GRIFF AND I left Ahsan's home and drove across town to meet one of Musharraf's top advisers, a Georgetown-educated politician named Mushahid Hussain. Griff referred to Mushahid as "the good angel sitting on one of Musharraf's shoulders," battling some of Musharraf's other aides whose democratic pretensions were perhaps less refined. Mushahid was a smooth talker who loved old show tunes; one day at the gym, while everyone else listened to music on headphones, I witnessed him playing "Que Sera, Sera" on a miniature stereo. How would he spin the emergency to Musharraf's benefit?

Mushahid looked sad and exhausted when we arrived. He had come a long way. Immediately after taking power, Musharraf threw Mushahid—a former ally of Nawaz Sharif—in jail. A year later, as part of murky deal, Mushahid was released and became a cheerleader for Musharraf. He spent the next seven years finessing Musharraf's image in the international media and promoting Musharraf's program of "enlightened moderation." But on this November night, he watched Musharraf create, in his words, "the biggest challenge to Pakistan since 1971," referring to Bengal's secession and the creation of Bangladesh after a vicious civil war.

"Pakistan is not Myanmar," he said. "We have a robust civil society, a vibrant media, and an independent judiciary. But by taking this action, the chief of army staff"—Mushahid called Musharraf by his military title, a subtle way of distancing himself from his boss—"will end up presiding over the liquidation of his own legacy." Mushahid, who was the only member of Musharraf's inner circle to publicly criticize the emergency, flew to China the next morning.

Griff and I made one more stop before turning in for the night. We drove to the parade ground in front of the parliamentary lodges, where hundreds of police were laying roadblocks and running concertina wire around government buildings. Trucks and armored personnel carriers idled nearby. Rangers stacked sandbags in the shape of bunkers and pitched tents. It looked like they were planning to stay awhile.

As we were crossing a police cordon, a tall man with a beard, standing with his wife and daughters, stopped protesting against Musharraf long enough to direct his attention my way.

"CIA! CIA!"

He was accusing me of being a CIA officer. The CIA, he shouted, had masterminded the emergency so as to preserve Musharraf's regime. "America is destroying a nation of 160 million people to save one man!" After living in Pakistan for almost two years, I now had my first encounter with visceral anti-Americanism.

Two days later, a Pakistani friend called me, speaking in code.

"Have you heard?" he asked. "The little fish ate the big fish."

The rumor went like this: General Ashfaq Kayani, the vice chief of army staff and thus the "little fish," had apparently ousted Musharraf, the chief of army staff and thus the "big fish." The story turned out to be false, and it wasn't the first time. Back in September 2006, while Musharraf toured the United States promoting his new book, *In the Line of Fire*, the senior brass was suspected of plotting against him. An extended power outage one night convinced the nation that the army had moved against Musharraf and were rolling tanks down city streets under the cover of darkness. Ayesha Siddique, a defense analyst in Islamabad, scoffed at such breathless speculation. "A Bonapartist like Musharraf would never surround himself with other Bonapartists," she told me.

We moved and spoke cautiously during the uncertain days after the declaration of emergency. Private TV channels had no idea what they could and couldn't say on the air. The irony was that the media had flourished under Musharraf. When he took power in 1999, there was one news channel, state-run Pakistan Television. By 2007, there were so many private news channels that I didn't even know some of them existed until Musharraf blocked them out, leaving a snowy void where there should have been a newscaster. In Musharraf's address to the nation on November 3, he blamed the private TV channels for contributing to "this downslide, this negative thinking, this negative projection" of Pakistan.

Print journalists weren't spared either. Three correspondents from the *Telegraph*, a British daily, were expelled after the paper ran an editorial that called Musharraf "our sonofabitch." The phrase referred to President Franklin D. Roosevelt's characterization of the Nicaraguan dictator Anastasio Somoza in 1939: "Somoza may be a son of a bitch, but he's our son of a bitch." Something got lost in the translation. While "son of a bitch" is considered a lesser offense along a spectrum of slurs in the West, Muslims find dogs to be filthy beasts. In Pakistani vernacular, therefore, to call someone a "son of a bitch" is as bad as it gets. We walked gingerly after that.

The intelligence agencies crushed the secular forces with ease, even though they struggled with the Islamists entrenched along the western border. On Saturday night, while Aitzaz Ahsan was being carted to jail, police in Lahore placed Asma Jahangir, a leading human rights lawyer, under house arrest. The following morning, Musharraf's storm troopers raided the offices of Jahangir's human rights organization. In Karachi, leftist Baluchi leaders were yanked off the street and charged with treason. Five days after the emergency was declared, more than seventeen hundred lawyers and politicians had been arrested in Punjab alone—just one of Pakistan's four provinces.

"Ironically the President (who has lost his marbles) said that he had to clamp down on the press and the judiciary to curb terrorism," Jahangir wrote in an e-mail circulated to friends and journalists. "Those he has arrested are progressive, secular-minded people while the terrorists are offered negotiations and cease-fires." Earlier that week, Musharraf had signed another so-called peace treaty with the Taliban based in South Waziristan. He pledged to withdraw the army from the area, while the Talibs promised not to ambush any army convoys. The Talibs also returned more than two hundred captured army soldiers, in exchange for twenty-eight suspected terrorists in government custody.

Lawyers protest in Lahore in December 2007, burning the campaign posters of the pro-Musharraf party. PHOTO: NICHOLAS SCHMIDLE

With Chaudhry, Jahangir, and Ahsan detained, and most of Nawaz Sharif's party locked up, Musharraf had more or less decapitated the opposition. The lawyers' movement suddenly seemed frazzled and disjointed. Many of the leaders were on the run, not sleeping at home, and too afraid of arrest to be caught protesting. The lawyers had proved their street power earlier in the year, but could they mobilize without their beloved leaders? And more important, could they reach out to the general public to galvanize a movement that involved more than simply lawyers in black-and-white suits?

Griff and I went to the lawyers' protest spot in Islamabad. A line of police in riot gear had surrounded the bazaar to prevent the protest from spilling into the street. We met a juicer named Zulfiqar. Zulfiqar, a skinny thirtysomething man with rotting teeth, took a halved pomegranate, smashed it onto a crude emulsifier, and made juice for paying customers. A pack of protesting lawyers in formal attire wound through the narrow alleys of the bazaar. Some of the lawyers had pasted red stickers on their foreheads—MILITARY DICTATORSHIP IS UNACCEPTABLE. They chanted "Death to Martial Law," called the army robbers and thieves, and denounced the United States. They marched past Zulfiqar's juice stand two or three times, but he hardly flinched. I asked Zulfiqar why he didn't join them.

"They never stopped to ask me," he said matter-of-factly. So he kept on juicing. "I need to make money to feed my family." He pointing to his stomach and mouth.

Across the sidewalk from Zulfiqar, another family man sat behind an antiquated computer that he used to type legal documents for the lawyers. He, too, just watched as the lawyers marched by. "My heart is with the protesters, and we should chant together. But I am afraid. My family could be arrested," the typist said. "Unless the entire nation, including the common people, come out into in the streets, nothing will change."

DURING THOSE UNCERTAIN days, the biggest mystery surrounded Benazir Bhutto, the two-time former prime minister and chairperson-for-life of the Pakistan People's Party. Bhutto opposed Musharraf in public and gave the impression of siding with Nawaz Sharif, another two-time former prime minister, along with the lawyers. (Aitzaz Ahsan, the star lawyer, was a member of Bhutto's PPP. He had served as interior minister during Bhutto's first government from 1988 to 1990.) But while the leadership of Sharif's party and the lawyers languished in jail, and Sharif himself waited in exile in Saudi Arabia, Bhutto moved around Pakistan at will. This wasn't an accident or an intelligence failure. Something was brewing between Bhutto and Musharraf. The chattering classes in Islamabad and Lahore speculated over the terms and conditions of the "deal."

For months, as Musharraf's popularity crumbled at home, the White House searched for a way to facilitate a transition to civilian rule in Islamabad. The choice boiled down to either supporting Bhutto or Sharif. Few people in Washington trusted Sharif because of his links with the conservative Islamists. When Sharif tried to return from exile in September, he stepped off the plane, was handed a document outlining corruption charges he would face if he tried to stay, and was then immediately bundled off to exile in Saudi Arabia once again, just as he had been in 1999 when Musharraf toppled him. The United States hoped to bring back Bhutto without all the drama on the tarmac. The problem was that Bhutto faced a litany of corruption charges based on her and her husband's finances while she served as prime minister. Yet Musharraf desperately needed a political ally with real, grassroots support. Both sides hammered out a deal where Bhutto's cases would be discarded and Musharraf would cooperate with her.

In the middle of October, hardly two weeks before Musharraf declared the state of emergency, Bhutto had returned to Pakistan after eight years in exile. She flew into Karachi. Her party planned an extravagant parade to welcome home the two-time former prime minister, and as many as a half a million people showed up. Bhutto's supporters festooned Karachi with the PPP's red, black, and green tricolor flags. They had replastered every billboard around the airport terminal and the procession route with portraits of Bhutto's face. Hours before Bhutto was scheduled to arrive, I hopped on the back of a friend's motorcycle and made my way toward the Karachi airport. Car travel was impossible owing to the hordes of PPP supporters thronged in the streets. Along the road, giant speakers pumped Bhutto-themed techno with lyrics that repeated, "Long Live Benazir." Men with PPP flags wrapped around their shoulders like superhero capes twirled and gyrated to drumbeats and mesmerizing synthesizer riffs.

The majority of those waiting to greet Bhutto had traveled from interior Sindh, the province plagued by poverty and illiteracy, which doubled as the stronghold of the PPP. When I asked people what they thought about the supposed deal that permitted Bhutto to come back, they often stared back at me with blank eyes.

"Deal?"

"What deal?"

"Do you know that Benazir Bhutto is coming back??!!??"

"Who cares about anything else!"

I asked one senior party member, a virulent critic of Musharraf, whether Bhutto had sacrificed too much in negotiating with Musharraf. Musharraf, after all, looked like a sinking ship. "Look around," the woman said, pointing to the crowds. "Politics is the art of the possible. Benazir did what was necessary for her party, and the nation."

When her plane touched down, Bhutto shed tears, kissed the ground, and prayed. She then boarded an armored, double-decker Bhutto-mobile, where she spent the rest of the day. The security risks were paramount. A few days earlier, a top Taliban commander in South Waziristan reportedly promised to "welcome her with his men." A small, emerald-green enclosure made of bulletproof glass topped the vehicle. Bhutto stood in front, in the open, waving to her people. As the motorcade inched past, party workers hung from tree branches to steal a glimpse of their leader's face. Bhutto's top lieutenants flanked her, chatting on their mobile phones. They glowed at the prospect of their revived political fortunes. I wondered why the electronic jammers, designed to prevent close-range detonation of bombs, weren't working.

Ten hours later, the motorcade having hardly progressed to the halfway point on its journey into the center of the city, suicide bombers struck the parade. Bhutto escaped unhurt, but more than 140 people died, the deadliest terrorist attack in Pakistan's history. The carnage made for an ominous welcome.

Bhutto never publicly accused the government of trying to kill her. But her husband and many of her closest advisers fingered Musharraf and his intelligence chiefs. The accusations, as you might expect, complicated the arranged marriage between Bhutto and Musharraf. Still, neither wished to throw it all away just yet. Without Musharraf's backing for Bhutto, Bhutto's corruption cases could have reemerged at any time. And without Bhutto's backing for Musharraf, the United States might have reconsidered its support for Musharraf. Everyone was relying on everyone else.

Bhutto planned a public rally in Rawalpindi on the seventh day of the emergency. Rawalpindi sat a few miles from Islamabad, and she planned to caravan from her home in Islamabad to the site of the rally. But when she woke up that morning, swarms of riot police blocked the tree-lined street in front of her house. They looked prepared to battle an entire army of antigovernment protesters. Standing stiff and covered with ribbed hard-plastic shells over their arms and legs, they reminded me of Teenage Mutant Ninja Turtles. They—along with the concrete barriers, coils of razor wire, and the armored personnel carrier parked askew—trapped Bhutto inside her house. Down the road, school-bus-sized paddy wagons, large enough to hold hundreds of people, waited nearby. Some of the police carried assault rifles, some waved bamboo sticks, and a few clutched tear gas guns.

All the preparations seemed a bit futile, as the only people present, besides Bhutto and her cohorts locked inside the house, were journalists. Musharraf's decision to impose the emergency had already damaged his international reputation. He knew that if the Turtles started bashing on hacks and cameramen, he'd be further disgraced. So everyone just stood around. "We're out here sweating our asses off, while Bhutto is probably eating reindeer goat cheese pizza on her couch right now," an Australian photographer sniped. His comment made me hungry, so a few of us broke for an hour to dine at a nearby Chinese restaurant that sold beer.

When we showed up back at the house, Bhutto and her entourage had managed to push past one of the police cordons. The armored personnel carrier still blocked the way onto the main road, but Bhutto parked her white Land Cruiser near the APC, got out, and gave a short speech over a loudspeaker. She stood with around one hundred party leaders on one side of the barbed wire. They chanted revolutionary slogans.

"Give these crumbling walls one more push!"

"The regime cannot go on!"

"Long Live Bhutto!"

A couple of hundred journalists climbed over the APC on the other side of the wire, trying to get a clear view of Bhutto. "This barbed wire stands in the way of democracy!" Bhutto exclaimed to a rousing applause.

She reiterated what all of us saw with stunning clarity: a week into the state of emergency, the Talibs were running wild while the liberal elites in the cities were being beaten and arrested. "Our army is not fighting extremists because they are too involved crushing pro-democracy supporters," Bhutto said. "All the tribal areas are now in the hands of the Taliban. This is a battle to save Pakistan from the forces of extremism. Since Tora Bora, the Taliban have been moving inside of Pakistan, taking towns."

Days earlier, Maulana Fazlullah had conquered the center of Shangla, the district neighboring Swat. As they overran government offices and police stations, they had begun lowering the Pakistani flag and replacing it with their own. "This is not just my war," Bhutto said, as an orange sun set through the trees. "These terrorists want to destroy our people. Pakistan is in danger. And our army is not fighting!"

AFTER THE BURST of hyperactivity and protest immediately following Musharraf's declaration of the state of emergency, a new status quo settled in. The public increasingly despised Musharraf, but they seemed less and less willing to challenge his regime. One Pakistani friend—a physician, political activist, and staunch opponent of Musharraf—downloaded a ring tone that chanted "Go! Musharraf! Go!" every time someone called him. Yet he had stopped attending protests out of fear of being snatched by the intelligence agencies. Meanwhile, more than sixty Supreme Court and High Court judges were locked inside their homes under house arrest. Hundreds of lawyers and politicians remained in prison. The headless and leaderless movement was just going through the motions. The most outspoken proponents of Pakistani democracy—the United States and Benazir Bhutto—both tacitly supported Musharraf. The skyrocketing price of wheat and petrol added to the deepening public apathy and fatigue. It seemed Musharraf might escape from another crisis.

College campuses became the only bastions of resistance. Staging a hunger strike one day, and a protest the next, a loosely organized group of college and university students mounted the beginnings of a movement. Most of the activity occurred on campuses in Lahore and Islamabad and involved a small number of upper-class kids. Some of the younger ones had their parents drop them off at the protests in shiny Mercedes. Critics dismissed the students as an irrelevant pack of rich kids acting out.

But the importance of the nascent movement represented something far more than restless youth. For the first time in more than twenty years, students gathered for a cause—lifting the state of emergency, throwing Musharraf out of power, and reinstating the judges suspended on November 3—and not just an identity or an ideology. Pakistani campuses had always been highly politicized, but since the early 1980s, when student unions were banned, the major political parties—such as Jamaat-i-Islami, the Muttahida Quami Movement, the Pakistan Muslim League, and the Pakistan People's Party—had used their student wings to hustle for influence, frequently turning campuses into war zones. Paramilitary units were permanently deployed at Karachi University after a series of gun battles left several students dead. And Islami-Jamiat-Taliba (IJT), Jamaat-i-Islami's student wing, virtually ruled Punjab University in Lahore, influencing everything from the school's administration and teacher's curriculum to students' moral and dress codes.

It hadn't always been like this. In the late 1930s and '40s, the Muslim

Students Federation mobilized support among Muslim students across British India for a separate homeland: Pakistan. After the Partition in 1947, students helped Muslim refugees arriving from India to find food and housing in Pakistan. Twenty years later, a leftist student movement supplied the street power that gave rise to Zulfiqar Ali Bhutto, Benazir's father, and the founder of the Pakistan People's Party. A decade later, a right-leaning student movement, propelled by IJT, overthrew Bhutto and played the part of shock troops for General Zia ul Haq's military regime. When the pendulum swung again, and leftist groups began agitating against Zia in the early 1980s, he snuffed out student politics altogether by banning the student unions. IJT was given special status and became the sole superpower on many campuses.

In late 2007, for the first time in decades, students at Punjab University protested *against* IJT. A couple days earlier, IJT had conducted a citizen's arrest of Imran Khan, Pakistan's famed cricket hero and an outspoken critic of Musharraf, when Khan showed up at Punjab University, apparently "without an invitation" from IJT. The simple act of opposing IJT represented a revolution in itself.

Aasim Sajjad was one of the leaders of the burgeoning, nonaligned student movement. Sajjad was a tall, balding man in his late twenties with degrees from the University of Chicago and Yale. He was a young teacher, and was perhaps more responsible than anyone for the students' revived political consciousness. For six years, he had taught political economy and Marxism at the Lahore University for Management Sciences, or LUMS, one of the preeminent universities in Pakistan. LUMS was the first campus in the country where students protested against the imposition of emergency.

Sajjad lived in Islamabad. And so, by physically shuttling between Lahore and Islamabad, he also shuttled students' energy back and forth between the two cities. I saw Sajjad at a protest march in Islamabad a month into the emergency. His face showed several days' worth of stubble, and his eyes shifted quickly through the crowd. Police wearing riot gear and carrying latthis, the bamboo shafts used for crowd control, were closing in. Sajjad leaned toward me and said, titling his head in the direction of a bearded man holding a video camera, "Be careful. He works for the intelligence agencies."

Sajjad raised a megaphone to his lips and led a call-and-response.

"Until the judiciary is restored!" he called out.

"We will fight, we will fight," the crowd answered.

The students planned to march about a mile to the Islamabad Press Club. At several points along the way, they clashed with riot police. An armored personnel carrier drove up ahead but never engaged the students.

"Freedom! Freedom! Freedom!" the students chanted.

When we reached the press club, students gave one another high fives. They traded stories like wounded soldiers.

"You should have seen me!"

"I went this way, and the cop went that way!"

"He tried to hit me with a latthi, but I ducked!"

"We aren't going to let these buggers do whatever they want with our country," said one with a Fu Manchu mustache. "And we are going to make a goddamn point!"

Sajjad stood in front of the press club, holding the megaphone again. He trembled with excitement. Suddenly, they could feel a crack in the regime. A few hundred people now believed that they could outwit the system.

I asked Sajjad if the students represented the dawn of a new political culture.

"Let's put it this way: we can't go backward now. We've developed a critical mass," he said. "Pakistan's political culture is still patronage-based. But if nothing else, we've established a *competing* political culture, one reaching back to the dynamism of students politics in the 1960s and 1970s."

He then turned and yelled into the megaphone: "We are ready to face their latthis!"

THE LUMS CAMPUS in Lahore sat at the back of a quiet, upscale neighborhood with paved streets, orderly traffic, and a McDonald's. Ivy crawled up the walls of buildings, and students wearing blue jeans stood in circles, talking into their mobile phones in unaccented English. I found Sajjad in an office upstairs, bent over his keyboard typing e-mails. Wearing his tan shalwar kameez, he was probably the only person on campus in the "national dress."

Sajjad called five members of the local chapter of the Student Action

Committee, the name of their group, into the office. Sundas, an attractive twenty-two-year-old law student from Peshawar, wore tight black jeans and a high-collared jacket. Her hair fell in thick layers just past her shoulders. I asked her how she got involved in politics.

"I wasn't political before I took Aasim's class," Sundas said. "Then, on November 3, it was like I fell out of bed and was forced awake. I was like, 'What the hell!!??' All my sensibilities were offended and I suddenly realized how indecent this government had become."

Sundas said she waited a few days after the emergency for the major political parties, namely Bhutto's People's Party and Sharif's Pakistan Muslim League, to launch massive street protests against Musharraf's regime. But when the political parties didn't take any substantial action, Sundas banded together with like-minded students and they vowed to act themselves.

I asked the group if their parents knew they'd participated in the protests and the hunger strikes.

"My mother said she saw me on the evening news," one guy said. "But my father doesn't know."

"My father tried to say how he understood," another male student said. "He said he went to a rally. Once."

They all laughed.

Sundas reached into her purse to locate her ringing phone. She stared at the caller ID for a second, sighed, and put the phone back into her purse. "It's my mom," Sundas said. She hadn't answered her mother's calls for almost a week. "My mom thinks that I am just verbally supporting the movement, and doesn't know I am *this* involved. And my dad doesn't know at all."

"Will you tell them?"

"I want to hold off until after *eid* [an Islamic holiday]," she said. She didn't want to ruin anyone's holiday cheer.

"Why would they get mad?"

"There's a stigma attached to being politicized," Sundas replied. "Our parents' generation thinks that politics are bad."

IN LATE NOVEMBER, Musharraf relinquished control of the army and doffed his uniform, though he remained the president and continued to enjoy a majority of supporters in the parliament. He had described the uniform as his "second skin," and after thirty-six years of service, some thought he might wear it to his grave. In the change-of-command ceremony, Musharraf handed a symbolic baton to General Ashfaq Kayani, his friend and groomed successor. A few days later, Musharraf terminated the emergency and reinstated the constitution. What did the students have left to protest against?

Still, the issue of the suspended judges remained paramount. Chaudhry was still under strict house arrest. Two days after the emergency officially ended, the Student Action Committee in Islamabad planned to march into the judge's colony, a gated community where Chaudhry and other Supreme Court justices lived. I joined the march early, and for more than a mile, we sauntered peacefully through a residential neighborhood and a business district. A small police force walked ahead of us, at a distance. The police and the students had arranged so that, at a certain point, the students would head back in the direction where they started. If all went according to plan, the day would end peacefully. But as the student procession approached a key intersection, they reconsidered their choice: turn right and head back to where they had started, or turn left toward the judge's colony.

One or two of them started left. Soon others followed, weaving between a line of cars waiting to cross an intersection. The police scurried to catch up and position themselves in front of the students. When the students didn't budge, the police whacked them over the head and backs with their latthis. The students kept pushing. "Where are the politicians?" one student asked, referring to the opposition leaders. "We are out here getting our asses kicked, and they're at home."

Houses lined one side of the road, and a thick forest abutted the other. An armored personnel carrier trolled up and down, a lone officer's head poking out of the top. He waved a tear gas gun back and forth but hadn't fired it yet. More skirmishes broke out when students threw rocks and bricks at police officers. The police, carrying AK-47s, lowered their sights. The students ran for cover in the tress. Griff had joined me a few minutes earlier. We ran with the students and ducked behind a bush.

"*Thwap! Thwap!*" The police fired tear gas to rouse the students out of the bushes.

"*Thwap! Thwap!*"

I reached into my bag for a checkered scarf and wrapped it around my face.

"You look like a bandit," Griff said. He had tied a T-shirt around his head. The tree canopy trapped the tear gas, which hovered and burned our eyes. But at least, with the scarves and the T-shirts, we could breathe.

A student near us popped out from the bushes and fired a rock at a policeman with his back to us. The rock nailed the officer in the head. When he spun around, he looked pissed, and he charged our direction. The rock-thrower had escaped, so the only figures visible to the charging, enraged officer were two guys, looking like Mexican revolutionaries, with scarves and T-shirts wrapped around their heads. The policeman raised his stick as if he planned to beat the snot out of us. Willing to inhale a few clouds of tear gas to stave off a beating, we both immediately pulled away our face wraps, pointed to our pasty American skin, and yelled, "Journalists! Journalists!"

The policeman pivoted and chased after someone else.

THAT NIGHT, I called Sajjad to get the after-action report. Were any students injured? Arrested?

He sounded rattled and fumed into the phone. "They don't have enough latthis to stop us now. How can they say the emergency is over? Nothing has changed."

CHAPTER 11

"MADE LIKE A SANDWICH"

ONE DECEMBER AFTERNOON, I CLIMBED ONTO A CROWDED ROOFTOP IN Quetta, fifty miles from the border with Afghanistan, and wedged myself among men wearing thick turbans and rangy beards until I could find a seat. We converged on the rooftop that afternoon to attend the opening ceremony for Jamiat Ulema-e-Islam's campaign office in the dusty city in the southwestern province of Baluchistan. Jamiat Ulema-e-Islam, a hard-line Islamist party, was widely considered a political front for numerous jihadi organizations, including the Taliban. In the previous parliamentary elections, in 2002, Jamiat Ulema-e-Islam, better known as JUI, formed a national coalition with five other Islamist parties and led a campaign that was pro-Taliban, anti-American, and spiked with promises to implement sharia. The alliance, known as the Muttahida Majles Amal, or MMA, won more than 10 percent of the popular vote nation-wide—the highest share ever for an Islamist bloc in Pakistan. The alliance formed governments in Baluchistan and the North-West Frontier Province.

A cool breeze blew across the rooftop and a green kite flew above in the crisp, periwinkle sky. JUI was gearing up again for national elections, then scheduled for the second week of January, but the message this time was remarkably different from what it had been five years ago. One by one, hopefuls for the national and provincial assembly constituencies gave short speeches. Most of them spoke in Pashto, but knowing Urdu, I could understand enough to realize that they weren't rehashing the typical JUI rhetoric. No one praised the Taliban. Sharia was mentioned only in passing. Just one person, a first-time candidate in a suede jacket who probably felt obliged to prove his credentials in a party of fundamentalist mullahs, attacked the United States. Afterward, party workers handed out free plates of cookies and cups of tea.

It seemed altogether too gentle. Had JUI gone soft?

Among the several firebrands conspicuous by their absence that day was Maulvi Noor Mohammad, JUI's former representative in the National Assembly from Quetta and an outspoken supporter of the Taliban. So the next day I went to see him at his madrassa. Adolescent students, many wearing the black turbans favored by the Taliban, mingled by the metal entrance gate. Hand-painted odes and declarations of allegiance, along with paintings of JUI's black-and-white-striped flag, covered the walls surrounding the madrassa.

"[MULLAH] MOHAMMAD OMAR MUJAHID, OSAMA BIN LADEN, AND ABDUL RASHID GHAZI ARE THE GREATEST LEADERS OF ISLAM," read one.

"THE SOLUTION TO AMERICA? AL-JIHAD, AL-JIHAD," read another.

Mohammad sat cross-legged on the madrassa's cold concrete floor, wrapped in a wool blanket. He leafed through an Urdu newspaper. A pot of tea sat on a nearby ledge, beside three grimy teacups. He stroked his long, wavy white beard, and though just in his early sixties, he could have passed for twenty years older. Back in the fall of 2006, during my last visit to Quetta's hardscrabble streets, Mohammad had told me that the sole reason the Taliban hadn't defeated NATO forces in Afghanistan yet was because NATO had B-52s. When I reminded him of this statement, his proud smile bared a mouth of missing teeth. "The Taliban have more than made up for that disadvantage now with suicide bombers."

Mohammad's madrassa spread across both sides of a dirt alley in Pashtunabad, a Quetta neighborhood shrouded in mystery and speculation. Since late 2001, Afghan and American officials had alleged that much of the ousted Taliban's top leadership, including Mullah Omar, resided in or around Pashtunabad. When the Taliban ruled in

Afghanistan, Mohammad often traveled between Quetta and Kandahar to consult with Mullah Omar and his colleagues. Other JUI leaders did the same. Maulana Fazlur Rahman, the JUI chief, served as head of the Foreign Relations Committee in the National Assembly when the Taliban were starting out. Rahman used his position to lobby his own government, as well as foreign ones, on behalf of the Taliban.

But in the years since, cleavages emerged between the political leadership of JUI and its rhetorical fixation on jihad, and those militants waging jihad in Afghanistan, and increasingly, inside Pakistan. Despite the continued American presence in Afghanistan (and the Pakistani government's alliance with the United States), and the Pakistani army's destruction of the Red Mosque in July, JUI remained part of the ruling establishment by keeping its seats in the National Assembly. (Noor Mohammad was one of only a few JUI members who resigned in protest.) JUI's commitment to creating an Islamic state through democratic means had increasingly been discredited by the younger generation of militants, as well as renegade leaders like Mohammad. Moreover, their message had become overshadowed by the violence of their antidemocratic Islamist colleagues—a network of younger Taliban fighting on both sides of the Pakistan-Afghanistan border, jihadis pledging loyalty to al-Qaeda and any number of freelancing militants.

Mohammad told me that Rahman, the JUI chief, had visited three times in the previous few weeks to persuade him to enter the upcoming election on the JUI ticket. Mohammad claimed to have refused each time because he believed that JUI had drifted from its core mission: to lead an aggressive Islamization campaign and to provide political support to what he referred to as the mujahideen. "Participating in this election would amount to treason against the mujahideen," he told me.

I asked him about the others in his party, including Rahman, who had decided to run for office. Mohammad shook his head in disappointment and explained how, following the military operation against the Red Mosque rebels in Islamabad months earlier, President Musharraf put religious leaders under tremendous pressure. "Musharraf threatened to raid all these madrassas and the political mullahs got scared," Mohammad said. A sly grin snuck across his face as he added disdainfully, "Some of them were even thinking about converting from Islam."

Maulana Fazlur Rahman (no relation to Maulana Fazlullah in Swat)

Pir Zubair Shah (*left*), Maulana Fazlur Rahman, and the author, standing in the garden of the chief minister in Peshawar. PHOTO: COURTESY OF THE AUTHOR

was exactly the sort of "political mullah" whom Mohammad portrayed as running scared. Over the past year, the JUI chief had tried to disassociate himself from the new generation of Taliban wreaking havoc not only across the border in Afghanistan, as they had for years, but also increasingly in Pakistan. At the same time, Rahman tried to persuade foreign ambassadors and establishment politicians that he was the only one capable of dealing with those same Taliban. (He later denied ever offering Noor Mohammad a chance to enter the election; he added that JUI had already expelled the Taliban guru "on disciplinary grounds.")

Meanwhile, some Islamists maintained that Rahman had sold them out. That spring, a rocket whistled over the sugarcane fields that separate Rahman's house from the main road, before crashing into the veranda of his brother's home next door. No one was hurt. A few months later, Pakistani intelligence agencies discovered a hit list, drafted by the Afghan and Pakistani Taliban, with Rahman's name on it. "The Maulana is being made like a sandwich: the government thinks he is the militants' man, and the militants think he is the government's man," one of Rahman's childhood friends told me. "But in fact, more and more he is no one's man."

Earlier that fall, during one of several visits I made to Rahman's hometown, I met another of Rahman's childhood friends, Abdul Hakim Akbari, for a meal at Akbari's home. Akbari, also a lifelong member of JUI, was candid about how JUI was losing touch with the Taliban. The party, he said, was under attack.

Akbari lived in Dera Ismail Khan, situated in the southern part of the North-West Frontier Province, about one hundred miles from the Afghan border. It was a short drive from the Taliban-ruled enclave of South Waziristan. "Everyone is afraid," he told me. According to a United States National Intelligence Estimate, approved by all sixteen of America's official intelligence agencies and released in the summer of 2007, al-Qaeda had regrouped in the Federally Administered Tribal Areas adjoining the province (most potently in South and North Waziristan) and was plotting an attack on the American homeland. "The religious forces are very divided right now," Akbari said, as we feasted on plates of samosas, chicken legs, and bowls of mint chutney. "These mujahideen don't respect anyone anymore. They don't even listen to each other. Maulana Fazlur Rahman is a moderate. He wants dialogue. But the Taliban see him as a hurdle to their ambitions."

Rahman didn't pretend to be a liberal; he wanted to see Pakistan become a truly Islamic state. But the moral vigilanteism and the proliferation of Taliban-inspired militias along the border with Afghanistan was not how he saw it happening. The emergence of Taliban-inspired groups in Pakistan, such as the brigade operating out of the Red Mosque, placed immense strain on the country's Islamist community. And as the rocket attack on Rahman's house illustrated, the militant jihadis had even lashed out against the same Islamist parties that had coddled them in the past.

Toward the end of the meal, Akbari introduced me to his twenty-seven-year-old son, Tayyab, a veteran of jihad. At seventeen years old, Tayyab had crossed the border into Afghanistan and spent several years fighting alongside the Taliban against the Northern Alliance. Two years into his tour, he suffered a bullet wound while battling Ahmed Shah Massoud's forces in the sprawling vineyards north of Kabul. He opened the collar of his shirt to show me a thumb-sized scar on his chest from the bullet. Akbari looked on proudly.

Tayyab left the room to fetch a photo album. He wanted to share pictures of him and his Taliban friends. In one photo, a friend posed inside the turret of a Taliban tank. In another, taken in a Kandahar photo booth, Tayyab dressed in all black and stood beside another young man in front of a bucolic country scene painted with watercolors. The friend in the picture, Tayyab said, had recently been killed in an American air strike.

I asked him if he had any friends training in the Taliban- and al-Qaeda-run camps in nearby South Waziristan.

"Plenty," he replied.

"Do you have any desire to join them?"

"Why? They are training to fight their own people," he said, referring to those preparing for attacks inside of Pakistan. "Afghanistan is occupied by a foreign country, so jihad is allowed. But Pakistan is not ripe for jihad."

"Do you tell your friends this, those who are training?"

"Sure I do. But it doesn't matter," Tayyab said. "They are so brainwashed that they don't even listen to Islamic arguments any more."

IN THE EARLY MORNINGS, when the fronds of the sugarcane grass shimmered with dew drops and the sun burned a tangerine color low in the sky, the mosque and madrassa compound at the front of Maulana Fazlur Rahman's estate looked like it could have been pulled from a science-fiction film set. Domes of various but symmetrical proportions covered the roof, all of which was the original flat, gray color of concrete. Perhaps the architecture was most striking because of its surroundings. If you headed north past the mosque with the dimpled roof, you would drive past one-level brick "hotels" where truck drivers lunched and napped. If you headed south, you entered the dusty, frenetic streets of Dera Ismail Khan. A non-functioning stoplight stood at the busiest intersection in town.

Pir, my friend from South Waziristan, and I made numerous trips to Dera Ismail Khan that fall. We left a friend's house in Dera Ismail Khan one morning and drove the short distance to Rahman's compound. We had no sooner parked the car in front of the house when a security guard hustled over. He told Pir to move the car to another spot a few hundred yards farther away. "You never know these days," the guard said. Suicide bombers had struck several times over the previous weeks in Dera Ismail Khan, killing more than two dozen police officers in one attack. Then, of course, there was the rocket fired at the house, and the hit list with Rahman's name. No one was taking any chances.

After parking the car far enough away so that, if it blew up, it wouldn't damage Rahman's house, another guard frisked us. He carefully inspected my camera to be sure it wouldn't explode in Rahman's face. In a famous incident on September 9, 2001, in northern Afghanistan, near the border with Tajikistan, two al-Qaeda members posing as Belgian journalists had detonated their camera during an "interview" with Ahmed Shah Massoud, thus eliminating the Taliban's biggest rival in Afghanistan on the eve of 9/11. This event had not been forgotten by others in the region.

The guard escorted us into a posh drawing room. Soft, brown leather couches lined the walls, and halogen skylights dotted the ceiling. Rahman had sunk into one of the couches and was scratching his tin-colored beard when we entered. The room smelled of strong cologne. Rahman wore a pin-striped waistcoat over a shalwar kameez. I guessed his weight at around three hundred pounds. He wore an orange turban, his trademark clothing article, wrapped around his head.

Rahman grew up in the nearby village of Abdul Khel, a hovel surrounded by sand dunes and date palms. Pashtuns dominated the extremely conservative area; women, already covered head to toe in burqas, turned their backs to oncoming car traffic out of modesty. Rahman's father had eight children from two wives. Beginning in the early 1950s, the father, named Mufti Mehmood, also led JUI. He and the other party leaders, most of them mullahs, demanded Pakistan be made an Islamic state. They spread their message to lower-class Pashtuns, their base. Although Rahman was the oldest of five sons, Mehmood discouraged him from entering politics. "He said it would only disturb my studies," Rahman told me.

"Did you ever consider another line of work, besides becoming a mullah, when you were growing up?" I asked. "Did you ever daydream about being a star cricket player?"

"Never. I was from a religious family, and it was expected that I would follow the same course my father did," Rahman said.

The father had blazed a path that entangled the destinies of Afghanistan, Pakistan, and the United States—and ultimately led to the terrorist attacks on September 11, 2001. In 1979, Mufti Mehmood helped kick-start the jihad in Afghanistan when he issued a fatwa against the Soviet-backed Communist government in Kabul. Just a year later, however, Mehmood—obese and suffering from diabetes—died of a heart attack. Rahman also had diabetes. But at the age of twenty-seven, with hardly any political experience, Rahman inherited JUI and his father's jihadi enterprise.

Soon after that, Rahman spent three years in jail for opposing Pakistan's pious dictator at the time, General Zia ul Haq. When he went into prison, he was emotional, insecure, and felt that he needed to prove his commitment to those in the party who questioned his resolve. When he got out in 1985, Rahman felt more comfortable at the top of JUI and fashioned his own style of politics. He worked on cultivating his pragmatic side. He wanted to play power politics in Islamabad.

In 1993, then prime minister Benazir Bhutto named him chairman of the National Assembly's Standing Committee for Foreign Affairs, a post that "enabled him to have influence on foreign policy for the first time," Ahmed Rashid wrote in his bestselling book, *Taliban*. Most of the Taliban leadership in Kabul and Kandahar had graduated from madrassas in Pakistan aligned with JUI. Rahman referred to the Taliban paternally as "our boys." He told me that, especially in their later years, he had exerted a moderating influence on Mullah Omar. Perhaps in a few years, he suggested, more countries than just Pakistan, Saudi Arabia, and the United Arab Emirates would have recognized Omar's regime had they been given the chance. "They should have been given more time."

Rahman's links with the Taliban brought him into contact with al-Qaeda, too. In 1998, shortly after seventy-five American cruise missiles slammed into an al-Qaeda training camp in Afghanistan, Rahman issued a fatwa, or religious edict. The fatwa said that, if Osama bin Laden was killed in a U.S. missile strike, then Muslims across the world were obliged to kill any American they found.

Rahman and I had both eased into the leather couch in his drawing room, sitting side by side. When I asked him about the fatwa, he smiled, though I couldn't tell why. Did the thought of that fatwa make him happy? Was he just surprised that I had done some homework?

"You people think that anyone with a beard who says anything is giving a fatwa," he replied, speaking in Pashto. "This was not a fatwa." He said he was just making a descriptive statement, one without any moral binding. Rahman reveled in such kind of ambiguity; it was part of what made him such an effective politician.

"I didn't say that any American *should* be killed. I said that no American would be safe if bin Laden was killed, that 'Today you are creating problems in our part of the world, tomorrow these problems can come back to you.'" Rahman switched from Pashto to halting English and said, in a smug tone oozing with vindication: "This was just my political vision."

"But coming from someone in your shoes, this 'political vision' could easily be mistaken for a threat."

"That depends on you," he said. In other words, it was up to the United States to decide whether he was a terrorist—or a prescient politician. (Journalists *have* sometimes confused Rahman and Maulana Fazlur Rahman Khalil, the leader of Harakat ul-Mujahideen, and one of the signatories to bin Laden's 1998 declaration of war against the United States.) "Did what you used to say about me prove correct, or did what I used to say about the situation prove correct?" he added. "I am the same person that I was then."

But this statement, of course, hit at the heart of any debate about Maulana Fazlur Rahman. Then or now, who was he? A pragmatist disguised or a hard-core Islamist? A master manipulator? Pakistan's last hope and a bulwark against the Taliban? Or, as Noor Mohammad hinted, a sellout?

By late 2007, Pakistani politicians and foreign diplomats increasingly bought the narrative peddled by Rahman of his being the only person with credibility in both Islamabad and South Waziristan. Mushahid Hussain, the secretary-general of the pro-Musharraf faction of the Pakistan Muslim League, told me that no one could negotiate the politics of the North-West Frontier Province better than Rahman. "We know that we need a bearded, turbaned guy over there," Hussain told me one day in the locker room of an expensive hotel in Islamabad.

And it was perhaps a measure of how inextricable Islamism and politics had become in Pakistan that even the United States lined up to meet an anti-American like Rahman that fall. In September, Rahman had the first meeting with an American ambassador of his thirty-year political career. What did Rahman and Anne Patterson, the American envoy, discuss? "She urged me to form an electoral alliance with Benazir Bhutto and Musharraf," he told me a few days after the meeting. "I am not against it. But politically, because of the American presence in

Afghanistan and rising extremism, it is a bit hard for us to afford." Plus, the fact that the Americans thought Bhutto could tackle the Taliban had simply baffled him. "She has no strategy in those areas, and nothing to do with those people."

When I asked an American embassy spokeswoman if Patterson's meeting signaled a change in American attitudes, she said it "reflects our approach to democratic politics in Pakistan" and was "part of a process of talking to all those who represent political movements in Pakistan, across the spectrum."

A British diplomat based in Islamabad called Rahman "one of the most sophisticated politicians in the country." At the time I met the diplomat, in late 2007, Rahman's name was being batted around the capital city as a possible candidate for prime minister. Musharraf desperately needed allies beyond just his faction of the Pakistan Muslim League and the Muttahida Quami Movement if he wanted to maintain a majority in the parliament. Many analysts speculated that Rahman was the most pliable politician of those who had sat in the opposition benches during the previous term.

When I asked the diplomat if his confidence in Rahman would continue if the JUI chief assumed the prime ministership, he sounded cautious. He said it was hard to know if Rahman would promote a progressive social agenda and continue to fight the War on Terror as the West saw fit.

"And look, let's be frank," he said. "It would not send a good signal about the direction Pakistan was taking for someone like Fazlur Rahman to become prime minister."

THE SOUND OF an explosion punctured an otherwise pleasant evening. I had been sitting under a giant mango tree, drinking Southern Comfort with a group of friends, including a mid-level intelligence officer in the army. It was my first night in Dera Ismail Khan. While the noise of the blast jerked me upright, no one else seemed too bothered. Locals had grown used to bangs and booms. The previous night, militants had bombed a music store in the town bazaar. The sound I heard, we later determined, was the explosion from a small grenade targeting the owner of a cable TV service. Both the man and his business survived.

Musharraf's government claimed the increasingly frequent bombings were evidence of Talibanization creeping east from the Afghanistan border.

The local militants blasted shops selling un-Islamic CDs, cable TV operators, massage parlors, and other sites they considered havens of vice. A newspaper editor in Dera Ismail Khan showed me a letter he had received, signed by the Taliban, warning him not to print anything that defamed the mujahideen. They threatened to blow up his office if he didn't comply.

"Ninety-eight percent of the threats and attacks are just people settling old scores," the intelligence officer told me that night, over tumblers of SoCo on the rocks. The Pakistani Taliban, rather than being a unified, hierarchical organization, were more a loose collection of gangs operating as part of the Taliban franchise. Any bandit could grow a beard, don a black turban, call himself a Taliban, and act with impunity. (The Tehrik-e-Taliban Pakistan, an umbrella outfit subsuming most of these gangs under the control of Baitullah Mehsud, wasn't formed until the middle of December 2007.) "The militants know that Fazlur Rahman's government will not dare to do anything against someone wearing a black turban," the intelligence officer said. Rahman and his colleagues couldn't afford to discard the support of their base by throwing "Taliban" into jail. After all, they had campaigned in support of the Taliban in Afghanistan five years earlier. How could they arrest them now?

Rahman resented the allegations by those who blamed him and his party for facilitating the local Taliban. "My demands are limited to what has been said in the 1973 Constitution regarding the formulation and implementation of Islamic laws," he said. "If you want change, you need to change the constitution, and for that you need a majority in the parliament. But it takes a political struggle, not an armed one, to get that majority.... We are politicians, and we will have to go to our constituencies to get votes in an election. If there is a war going on, no one can vote."

Though the Taliban hid behind the cover provided by Rahman's party, they didn't tolerate anyone else thinking they could share the refuge. In the Dera Ismail Khan bazaar, I met a man named Hamid, the nephew of JUI's former finance secretary. Hamid owned a computer store that sold bootlegged software, computer games, educational DVDs, and Islamic CDs. "Except ones about jihad," he said. A few months earlier, Khan had received two stamped and signed letters from the Taliban. The threats inside—"Stop selling XXX DVDs or we will bomb your store"— didn't frighten him too much because, in Dera Ismail Khan those days, Hamid said "everybody gets them." But the letter warned Hamid against relying on his uncle to bail him out. "Don't think that you will be spared just because you are the nephew of a JUI leader," the letter said.

Letters like the one Hamid received illustrated more than just the growing threat of the Taliban pushing into towns and small cities in the "settled areas" of the North-West Frontier Province. (The "tribal areas" of the Federally Administered Tribal Areas had already fallen under Taliban control.) The letters also showed that Rahman and JUI were no longer the toughest Islamists on the block. In 2002, they rose to power as the "bad boys" on the political scene, with their turbans and Taliban talk. But five years later, they looked old and washed up, victims of the growing divide between the pro-Taliban leaders of yesterday and those of today. And if the high point of Rahman's career came in 2002, his low point came in 2007, during the insurrection at the Red Mosque.

From January through July 2007, when male and female rebels over-ran the children's library, then kidnapped a brothel madam, some police officers, and six Chinese masseuses, and finally holed up armed inside the Red Mosque, Rahman repeatedly tried to talk the Ghazi brothers out of their reckless adventure, but his influence inside the mosque was limited. "They are simply beyond me," he said at one point.

AFTER GHAZI AND his crew clashed with state security forces in early July, the border region burned for months with fellow Taliban militants exacting revenge. Hundreds of soldiers and policemen died in suicide blasts or in gunfights. In South Waziristan, the Taliban kidnapped more than two hundred government soldiers. In a Taliban-produced DVD I watched in Dera Ismail Khan, a teenager sawed the head off a soldier while, in the background, three of his adolescent peers chanted "Allahu Akbar."

The fact that the Taliban were now attacking the Pakistani army dovetailed, in some ways, with their attacks on Maulana Fazlur Rahman. For decades, both Rahman's JUI and the Pakistani army, especially its top spy agency, the Inter-Services Intelligence (ISI), had patronized Islamic militants who went on to fight in Kashmir and Afghanistan. Now the militants were biting many of the hands that used to feed them. In September, twin suicide blasts went off in Rawalpindi, the military's garrison city near Islamabad, killing at least twenty-five people. One ripped through a bus carrying ISI employees to work. The intelligence officer I met in Dera Ismail Khan, whose area of operations included the Taliban-ruled enclave of South Waziristan, told me that his contacts with the militants were severed long ago. "We can hardly work there anymore," he said. "The Taliban suspect everyone of spying. All of our sources have been slaughtered."

Society in the tribal areas seemed to be tearing itself apart. Tribals turned on fellow tribals who they deemed insufficiently dedicated to fighting the Americans in Afghanistan—and now to fighting the Pakistani army. But should this be called Talibanization, or was it something different? Imran Khan, the nation's former cricket hero and the leader of a political party, dismissed efforts to classify the violence as "Talibanization" and described it as a "tribal uprising." "Remember that while the Taliban were in power in Afghanistan, there was no Talibanization in the tribal areas," he said. "Today, it is more about politics. That's why people show allegiance to the Taliban. People living near the border think of the Pakistani Army as being a mercenary force for the United States. Anyone who wants to fight the Pakistani Army can go and fight alongside the Taliban."

Jihad? Revenge? Tribal uprising?

ANOTHER MORNING, I met Rahman in the bedroom of his apartment in Islamabad and asked him if acts of tribal revenge and fighting against one's own army could be classified as jihad.

"People always label a war according to their own thinking."

"How do you label it?"

Rahman took a deep breath and paused. "You should not ask such questions from me," he said and looked away.

"Why shouldn't I ask you?" I asked, playing dumb.

"Because my answer can create many problems. We, as ulema, are still debating this topic of whether or not this is jihad," he said.

Rahman took another deep breath and paused. He did this a lot. During these pauses, I pictured him imagining how his next statement would look on the front page of a newspaper.

"But personally, I believe that jihad is not fighting. It is struggle. And wherever struggle exceeds its limits, I am against it."

What about the Taliban? "Do you still consider them 'your boys' as you used to say?"

"Definitely," he replied. "But because of America's policies, they have gone to the extreme. I am trying to bring them back into the mainstream. We don't disagree with the mujahideen's cause, but we differ over priorities. They prefer to fight, but I believe in politics."

THE BICKERING AND divisions within the ranks of the Islamists were fully exposed by late 2007, when the election campaign for the upcoming parliamentary polls kicked off. One long-serving JUI member from Dera Ismail Khan confessed that Rahman and the party were going to have problems just drafting a campaign strategy. "In the last election, everything was related to Afghanistan and how innocent Afghans were being killed," he said. "But now Maulana Sahib has to answer his people when they ask him, 'What happened in our own country?'"

Since the MMA took power in the North-West Frontier Province, terrorist attacks had killed hundreds of civilians. Neither Rahman nor his colleagues had condemned any of them. Pakistan's secular media argued that his silence implied clearly enough that he supported the attacks. But with his credibility already on the wane in some jihadi circles, Rahman didn't have any other choice; if he condemned the Taliban outright, he committed political suicide.

But if campaigning on security issues seemed a futile strategy, stumping about the need for enforced sharia seemed even less promising. Maulana Fazlullah, the young renegade cleric in the Swat Valley, had already snatched that banner and made it his own.

I asked Rahman if he felt his influence threatened by Fazlullah and his ilk. The JUI chief dismissed this outright, and said that he and Fazlullah differed over style more than anything. "We in JUI are political people," Rahman told me. "We go to an area, deliver a speech, ask for votes, and come back.

"People like Maulana Fazlullah are working more at the grassroots level," Rahman said. Fazlullah spent years going door-to-door, day in and day out, often astride his white horse. Unless you lived in the Swat Valley, you had no way of knowing his strength until it was too late, Rahman said. "He just suddenly came out and surprised everyone."

When, in October, I asked Rahman if he had any control over Fazlullah, he said the negotiating efforts of the JUI leader there, Qari Abdul Bais, were saving Fazlullah and the Pakistani army from going to war. But when I met Bais, a septuagenarian with a cane, he offered this estimation of Fazlullah: "He is totally out of control."

ONE FALL MORNING in Peshawar, Rahman and I sat outside on plastic lawn furniture in the shade of a large oak tree. He rubbed a strand of chunky, orange prayer beads, and we discussed the changing leadership in the borderlands of Pakistan. In the past five years, more than 150 pro-government maliks, or tribal elders, had been killed by the Taliban. Oftentimes, the Taliban dumped the bodies by the side of the road for passers-by to see, with a note, written in Pashto, pinned to the corpse's chest, damning the dead man as an American spy or Musharraf collaborator.

"When the jihad in Afghanistan started," Rahman said, "the maliks and the older tribal system in Afghanistan ended. A new leadership arose, based on jihad. Similar is the case here in the tribal areas. The old, tribal system is being pushed to the background, and a new leadership, composed of these young militants, has emerged." He added, "This is something natural."

Rahman described the emergence of the Taliban in evolutionary terms, the result of a leadership crisis in Pakistan. He expressed respect for the secular-minded people who created Pakistan, like Mohammad Ali Jinnah, but insisted that social and religious changes over the past two decades had made such leaders much less relevant. "We have to adjust to reality. That demands new leaders with new visions."

"Do you consider yourself such a new leader with a new vision?"

"I don't consider myself as someone extraordinary," Rahman said. "I have the same feelings as everyone else in the current age. If the weather is warm, everyone feels warm. If it is cold, everyone feels cold. The difference between me and other people is in our responsibilities."

He took a long breath of the fresh fall air, continued rubbing his prayer beads, and leaned over the chair to spit into the grass. "My decisions can affect many, many people," he said. "This is why I am so careful."

Could the same man who once seemed ready to introduce Taliban-style rule in Pakistan be sincere about trying to preserve democracy from being destroyed by ruthless militants?

"I am trying to bring people back from the fire," Rahman concluded, "not push them toward it."

CHAPTER 12

"NO MERCY IN THEIR HEARTS"

IN THE LAST HOUR OF DAYLIGHT ON DECEMBER 27, JUST BEFORE
Benazir Bhutto was shot, bombed, and killed, Asfandyar Wali Khan
told me that he believed in fate. "Whatever that is, so be it."

Khan and I met at his party's headquarters in Charsadda, a town outside of Peshawar. A tall man with a gruff, wrinkled expression fixed on his
face, Khan led the Awami National Party. Observers predicted the ANP,
a Pashtun nationalist outfit, to win big in the parliamentary elections
scheduled two weeks later. The ANP's signature red flag flapped about
from every telephone pole and car antennae within fifty miles of
Peshawar. And while most parties' campaigns had been paralyzed by a
spate of suicide bombings, the work of the Taliban and al-Qaeda, Khan
and the ANP were stumping for votes around the clock. "We are the only
party whose campaign is in full swing," he told me, proudly, "and the
only one that holds public meetings at night."

Khan said he couldn't afford to stop his campaign for anything, and
distilled the choices facing Pashtuns to one between Islamic militants and
the ANP. "This election is a straight fight between those who want war

and those who want peace," he explained. "It is either fundamentalism or moderation."

Yet even bigger things than winning an election occupied Khan's thoughts. The international image of his people, the Pashtuns, needed to be rehabbed, as well as the very structure of their culture. "At this moment, if you talk about Pashtuns, the world thinks he is a terrorist, has a beard to his navel, hair to his shoulders, and holds a Kalashnikov," said Khan. "Islamic fundamentalism is destroying the basic fabric of Pashtun society." Pashtuns, who numbered more than twenty-five million, had been renowned as fierce fighters for centuries. They lived along the Pakistan-Afghanistan border and had repelled British armies, Sikh armies, Soviet armies, and now American, NATO, and Pakistani ones, too. Almost all of the Talibs were Pashtuns.

Khan argued that Pashtuns were not naturally brash, militant people—that this was an impression that had been created by the Taliban. His grandfather, Khan Abdul Ghaffar Khan, had even earned the nickname "Frontier Gandhi" for his role in leading the Pashtuns in a nonviolent resistance movement against the British Raj during the 1930s and '40s. The elder Khan's organization became known as the Red Shirts, which explained the ANP's current color scheme. Ghaffar Khan had opposed the Muslim League, the main group lobbying for the creation of Pakistan, and supported Gandhi's Congress Party instead. He believed the guiding rationale for the creation of Pakistan, that religious identity should determine the country where a person lived, was flat wrong. Yet he wasn't exactly a pluralist either. Ghaffar Khan contended that ethnic identity was most important for establishing one's identity, and he called for the creation of an independent Pashtunistan. A year before the birth of Pakistan, fellow Muslims physically attacked him—leading to his hospitalization—for being, in their minds, anti-Muslim, underscoring the long-running tension between ethnic nationalists and Islamists.

Just as violence colored the run-up to the creation of Pakistan in 1947, it also marred the run-up to the elections in 2008. Sixty suicide bomb attacks had killed more than 770 people in Pakistan in 2007, according to a report by the Pakistan Institute of Peace Studies. The majority of the attacks targeted police, paramilitary units, and soldiers in the NWFP and FATA, but the militants occasionally set their sights on politicians, too. In the village of Sherpao, bombers had tried to assassinate the serving interior minister, Aftab Sherpao, while he prayed inside the village mosque.

The most dramatic assassination attempt came on October 18, when two suicide bombers struck Benazir Bhutto's motorcade in Karachi, detonating their explosions within seconds of each other. While barely missing her, they killed 140 others. From then on, Bhutto confined most of her campaigning to her home province of Sindh. When she came to Peshawar for a rally on December 26, many stayed away fearing violence and thousands of seats remained empty in the stadium where she addressed the crowd. A teenager was arrested trying to enter the rally with 450 grams of explosives hidden underneath his jacket.

AFTER WE HAD enjoyed several cups of green tea, Asfandyar Wali Khan stepped outside and melted into a red sea of supporters waiting in the parking lot of the ANP headquarters. Khan climbed into a red SUV and, trailed by another twenty cars, most of them red, too, they drove to a rally. We followed.

At the site, Khan mounted a makeshift stage in the clearing of a village. "We are locked in a war for survival," Khan announced. Hundreds of men sat on chairs before him, wearing wool blankets to fight off the evening chill.

MEANWHILE, LESS THAN a hundred miles away in Rawalpindi, Bhutto was leading a rally in Liaquat Garden. The park was named after Pakistan's first prime minister, who had been killed by an assassin there in 1951. "The country is in danger," she said to her followers. "Bomb blasts are taking place everywhere. . . . I appeal to all of you to vote for us to save the country." After the rally, Bhutto loaded into her white, armored Land Cruiser and pulled away. Her supporters crowded the car, so she poked her head through the sunroof to wave. She wore a blue shalwar kameez, a white head scarf, and a candy-cane-colored garland around her neck. As she rose into view through the roof, a gunman wearing sunglasses stepped closer and fired. Moments later, a suicide bomber detonated his charge.

As I SAT listening to Khan, a flood of text messages arrived on my mobile phone. They shared conflicting reports of Bhutto's condition. I could hear Khan speaking in the background, but my mind was in Rawalpindi.

"Bhutto assassination attempt."

"Bomb at BB rally. BB escaped."

"BB injured in bomb."

"Hospital reports that Benazir is killed."

A man sitting in the front row interrupted Khan mid-sentence: "Asfandyar Sahib, Benazir Bhutto is dead from a suicide bomber."

KHAN RELAYED THE news over the PA system. He then bowed his head in respect and exited the stage. The all-male crowd of Pashtuns dispersed. They looked confused, scared, and lost, and buzzed with conspiracy theories already. They had come to hear Khan, but they left thinking only of Bhutto. In the end, the Talibs and their al-Qaeda affiliates had derailed Khan's campaign, too.

My friend Shaheen from Swat and I ran to the car and sped back to Peshawar. Neither of us spoke on the way. I stared out the window in shock. A gloom settled over the back roads that wind through the dark forests of NWFP. What came next for Pakistan? I felt much as I had on a few other occasions over the last couple of years. I thought back to May 12, when police stood by and watched as armed activists of rival political parties killed one another and returned Karachi to its gangland days. And to the Red Mosque siege, when Islamic militants launched a rebellion against Musharraf's government in Islamabad, and at least one hundred people died. And to October 18, when hundreds of thousands of Bhutto supporters spilled into the streets of Karachi to welcome her home and seemed destined to lift the PPP to power. How could Musharraf possibly hold on now?

And what would the immediate reaction of the people be? Although Bhutto's critics, and even some of her supporters, felt she was compromised by her negotiations with Musharraf, she remained the most loved politician in the country. The drawing room analysts in Islamabad, Lahore, and Karachi, who sniped at Bhutto on talk shows and in newspaper columns, had little effect on street politics anyway. The rural areas mattered. And Bhutto's stronghold of interior Sindh was always itching for a reason to rebel. People there already believed that the military establishment had it in for the Bhutto family and the PPP. Bhutto was the only leader in Pakistan with nationwide appeal. She symbolized the unity of

Pakistan, and without her the federation was weak. Some speculated that her assassination would trigger a revolution.

As we neared the city limits of Peshawar, a line of empty passenger buses streamed out of the city. Rioters would surely set them on fire if they stayed. Stranded bus passengers stood on the side of the road, thumbing for a ride. Shopkeepers pulled down their metal shutters. They stayed closed for days. Musharraf had already declared a three-day mourning period.

We had planned to drive through the middle of Peshawar, but a policeman stopped us near the entrance to the city. Just a few hundred yards behind him, a flaming car obstructed the road.

"What's going on up there?" Shaheen asked him.

"They are shooting and burning everything they see. When they see your car, they will burn it, too," the officer said. As we made a U-turn, the officer yelled out, "They are Pashtuns. They have no mercy in their hearts."

I HAD SPENT most of that December on the road, traveling to each of the four provinces to get a sense of public opinion ahead of the parliamentary elections, then scheduled for early January. Musharraf had lifted the state of emergency in the middle of December, though the target of his wrath—Iftikhar Mohammad Chaudhry, the former chief justice—was still a prisoner within the walls of his own home, encased by hundreds of police and intelligence agents. Elsewhere, the Taliban insurgency raged and the security forces seemed unable to do anything about it. The public held Musharraf responsible for everything bad. Military rulers were supposed to bring order and stability. Musharraf was doing neither.

The price of wheat and other basic subsidies ballooned beyond the public's meager means. A cancerous apathy spread throughout the country. "Why are you asking me about elections when I have no food?" replied a man packing neswar, a snufflike tobacco product for sale, when I stopped by his stand one afternoon in late December. He sat cross-legged beside a pit where he ground the neswar, and then stuffed it into small plastic bags. He said he made the equivalent of less than $3 a day. "Spring comes and spring goes, but there is no change in my life. I am still hopeless. Elections are still very far away."

"They are only two weeks from today," I said.

"I don't know if I will be alive in ten minutes, so why should I care about elections in two weeks? If anyone brings me a sack of flour, I will vote for them."

Meanwhile in Quetta, the parched city in Baluchistan, army and paramilitary units rolled through the streets. The tribal insurgency had spread beyond the remote hills in the eastern part of the province and now affected the city. Locals in Quetta felt that they were under occupation. "It's like Baghdad," one resident said.

An armored personnel carrier sat just outside the entrance to my hotel in Quetta. Machine-gun barrels poked out of sandbags at major intersections. Heavily armed convoys patrolled the streets every evening after sundown. Two weeks before I arrived, a top commander from the Baluchistan Liberation Army was killed, setting off a wave of riots and guerrilla attacks on security forces that left dozens dead. When I asked a slum dweller in Quetta named Naiz whether he considered the dead BLA commander a fallen hero, he answered, "We don't live in circumstances where we have time to dream of heroes. Independent Baluchistan is our hero."

On my first night in Quetta, a soldier standing behind a stack of sandbags near the center of town took a bullet in the face, fired from a passing motorcycle. He died. The intelligence agencies, police, and paramilitaries raided BLA strongholds throughout the province. They cordoned off Naiz's slum and took twelve of his fellow tribesmen. This was all what passed as normal. Since the insurgency heated up in late 2005, hundreds of young Baluchi men had simply "disappeared," kidnapped by the intelligence agencies. Their whereabouts were unknown.

A politician from one of the nationalist parties told me that six thousand Baluchi men were missing. The man beside him described how his cousin had been kidnapped by Anti-Terror Force troops in front of his four nephews in a city park.

"How did the four kids"—aged between four and eight—"know the identity of the kidnappers?" I asked. "That they were Antiterror Force and not some other agency?"

"In America, your children play with toys. That's what they know," he said. "Our children know about the intelligence agencies and the army. This is what they grow up on."

* * *

MANY PEOPLE IMMEDIATELY accused Musharraf and his team of orchestrating Bhutto's murder. "One general killed Zulfiqar Ali Bhutto, and now another has killed his daughter," said Wajid, a man in his late sixties who I met in Peshawar the morning after the assassination. His eyes welled with tears. "We, the common folk, are ready to go to Islamabad. We are ready to die. Just please, please tell Musharraf to stop killing our talented people!"

An e-mail surfaced that only added fuel to the fire. Bhutto had sent an e-mail to her U.S. spokesman, Mark Siegel, saying: "Nothing will, God willing, happen. Just wanted u to know if it does in addition the names in my letter to Musharraf of Oct. 16nth"—former Punjab chief minister Chaudhry Pervez Elahi, former ISI chief Lt. General (ret.) Hamid Gul, former deputy chairman of the National Accountability Bureau Hassan Waseem Afzal, and former Intelligence Bureau chief Brigadier (ret.) Ijaz Shah—"I wld hold Musharaf responsible. I have been made to feel insecure by his minions and there is no way what is happening in terms of stopping me from taking private cars or using tinted windows or giving jammers or four police mobiles to cover all side cld happen without him."

The government scrambled to deflect the accusations, but the incompetence of the investigation undermined its position. An FBI special agent familiar with Pakistan told *The New Republic*, "Hundreds of photos [of the crime scene] should have been taken. All the blood stains and bomb residue should have been swabbed, and shell casings and bomb fragments should have been mapped to 'freeze frame' the scene." Instead, the site was hosed down and cleared of debris.

A bumbling government spokesman said that Bhutto had died from hitting her head on the sunroof lever, not from being shot at close range by an assassin or finished off by a suicide bomber. Though the assertion struck many as outrageous, the medical reports later corroborated the claim. There were apparently no bullet wounds. The PPP refused to allow an autopsy, which could have answered many questions.

The biggest question—who did it?—lingered. The most plausible culprit, and the one fingered by the government, was Baitullah Mehsud, the leader of the Pakistani Taliban. Mehsud had reportedly said back in October, as Bhutto planned her return from exile, that he would "welcome her with his men," though he later denied having said this.

Regardless, it seemed to me that whoever had tried to kill her the first time would keep trying until they finally did.

The day after the assassination, the Interior Ministry released what they described as damning evidence against Mehsud, a recording of one of his phone conversations with a lieutenant, whom he called "Maulvi Sahib." The conversation apparently took place in South Waziristan.

"Asallamu Aleikum," said Maulvi Sahib.

"Waleikum A'salaam," said Mehsud.

"Chief, how are you?"

"I am fine."

"Congratulations, I just got back during the night."

"Congratulations to you. Were they our men?" asked Mehsud.

"Yes, they were ours."

"Who were they?"

"There was Saeed, there was Bilal from Badar and Ikramullah."

"The three of them did it?"

"Ikramullah and Bilal did it."

"Then congratulations," said Mehsud.

"Where are you? I want to meet you."

"I am at Makeen"—a town in South Waziristan—"come over, I am at Anwar Shah's house."

"Okay, I'll come."

"Don't inform their house for the time being."

"Okay."

"It was a tremendous effort. They were really brave boys who killed her."

"Mashallah"—Praise Allah. "When I come I will give you all the details."

"I will wait for you. Congratulations, once again congratulations."

"Congratulations to you."

"Anything I can do for you?" Mehsud asked.

"Thank you very much."

"Asallaam Aleikum."

"Waleikum A'salaam."

The tape's credibility was suspect. Besides sounding scripted, I wondered how they could get audio tapes of Mehsud, admitting that his boys had killed Bhutto, but not enough intelligence to actually arrest or kill Mehsud.

An enterprising Pakistani journalist traveled to Makeen, South Waziristan, to see if things checked out. His discovery? There was no phone service in the town.

PETER BERGEN, a journalist and terrorism analyst at the New America Foundation in Washington, D.C., described the magnitude of Bhutto's assassination as "the Kennedy assassination and 9/11, rolled into one." Terrorists had proven that one attack could destabilize a nuclear-armed country of 160 million people. Like the bullet that killed Lincoln, Kennedy, or Dr. King, the blast also destroyed a sense of progress and hope. After two previous terms in office, hampered by allegations of corruption, I had wondered whether Bhutto could come back a third time and lead Pakistan down the road to prosperity. Judging by the past, she and her party's populist rhetoric simply didn't mesh with their actions, namely their record of corruption. But her presence meant more than her deeds. And without an educated, liberal woman vying for power, one less obstacle now stood in the way of Pakistan becoming the bigoted basket case its naysayers often described it as.

Bergen's comparison to the Kennedy assassination and 9/11 was apt in yet another way. A flood of conspiracy theories followed. The most serious one placed Musharraf or one of his cronies in the middle of the conspiracy, ordering the hit. But that didn't make sense to me. How could he have gained from this? Maybe, he hoped, his domestic and international supporters would redouble their demand for a strongman in light of the ensuing chaos. In reality, Musharraf slid further out of favor with the West and lost more popularity at home. And if the intelligence agencies had worried that Bhutto's party might win the elections, the PPP now seemed almost guaranteed to sweep the poll, carried by a sympathy vote.

The economic damage resulting from the assassination was startling. The Karachi Chamber of Commerce printed a statistic that roughly $130 million in revenue disappeared every day in Karachi alone when strife paralyzed the city (and its port), not including damages to property. In 2007, I witnessed the city in this state for at least ten days. After the assassination, foreign investors' confidence eroded even more. Some stores stayed closed for more than a week, with both merchants and shoppers taking cover from the sounds of sporadic gunfire.

Back in Peshawar, rioters burned cars—and anything else flammable and available—throughout the night. The morning after the assassination, I headed to the bazaar to find that, besides the indispensable and fearless butcher and milk shops, all the other businesses were boarded up. You could hear footsteps in the alleys of the usually hectic market. Children played cricket in the empty streets. One money exchanger sat on a stool in front of his shop, resting a shotgun across his lap in case vandals tried to loot his store.

I met an elderly wrinkled man named Alam, guarding his street corner. Alam wore a tattered blanket over his shoulders. He had sat there throughout the morning, while angry mobs burned a motorcycle, ransacked the chamber of commerce building, and threw stones at police just a few feet away. Yet, even as the sound of gunfire clattered nearby, Alam didn't dare leave the kiosk where he sold neswar. The thirty bags, stacked neatly on the box beside him and worth a total of about $1.50, constituted his entire inventory and livelihood. Only when the police began chucking shells of tear gas at the protesters, and a cloud of gas engulfed Alam's business, did he decide to run. "I was vomiting the whole time," he said.

I arrived about a half an hour after the police fired the tear gas, and chemicals still hung in the air, burning my eyes.

"How many bags of neswar have you sold today?" I asked Alam.

He brushed aside my question. "I am not concerned with money today. I only worry about keeping my corner."

Lawlessness and anarchy prevailed for days, as rioters rampaged through city streets up and down the country, torching buildings and looting banks. In Bhutto's home province of Sindh, mobs burned eleven offices of the Election Commission, torching all the voter registration information stored inside. Businesses that could pull down their shutters and pray for the best did. Some people who ran their businesses on open street corners, like Alam, were forced to flee at times. Alam had left his bags at the mouth of Peshawar's main bazaar. In the confusion and the clouds of tear gas, no one had robbed his stash. He counted himself lucky.

"Opportunists are everywhere these days," Alam said. "You have to watch out. You could lose everything you own in just an hour or two."

An armored personnel carrier parked in front of a billboard showing Benazir Bhutto and her father, Zulfiqar Ali Bhutto, in the Karachi neighborhood of Lyari, several days after her assassination. PHOTO: NICHOLAS SCHMIDLE

Across the street, two young boys—no more than twelve years old, their faces, hands, and clothes filthy—picked through the debris from a burned out motorcycle. They were collecting sooty pieces of scrap metal that they could later resell for, according to them, about 20 rupees, or 30 cents, a kilogram. I asked the taller of the two how much he had gathered so far.

He stopped rummaging for a second to hold out his plastic sack with a straight right arm. "Two, maybe three kilos," he said. He looked pleased with his find.

ON DECEMBER 30, the fourth day after the assassination, the People's Party called a press conference to announce the contents of Bhutto's will, in which she had named her successor.

According to the party's organizational tree, Makhdoom Amin Fahim, the vice chairman, should have been next in line to lead the PPP. Fahim, a feudal lord from interior Sindh, ran the party while Bhutto sat out in exile. In many ways, he was the perfect substitute for her: the political classes in Karachi and Islamabad all knew that he spoke for Bhutto, and yet, owing to his loyalty and lack of personal charisma, he posed no threat to her legacy. At the press conference in Naudero, a small town in northern Sindh, Fahim joined Asif Ali Zardari, Bhutto's husband, and Bilawal Zardari Bhutto, Bhutto's nineteen-year-old son, at the head table. The three men wore black clothes to show their mourning, and sat in high-back chairs. Bilawal, an Oxford student with thick black eyebrows, whose Facebook page showed photos of him dressed as a devil on Halloween, sat in the middle, behind a wall of microphones. Fahim sat quietly to Bilawal's left, watching his power slip away. Zardari, who did most of the talking, sat to Bilawal's right.

Great anticipation surrounded the press conference, not only because the PPP was to announce Bhutto's successor, but because every decision they took would immediately impact the stability of the country. What would they do about the elections? Nawaz Sharif had already announced his intent to boycott; if the PPP followed suit, the polls would be totally discredited. What about the unrest? At Bhutto's funeral, mourners had chanted, in Sindhi, "Break Pakistan!" while interior Sindh burned. The main road running north and south through the province had been blocked by mobs. They hijacked, and then torched, any cars or trucks that tried to pass. Looters ravaged several banks. The army, who usually let the Rangers handle civil unrest, was deployed to Sindh to restore law and order. If the PPP sympathized with the militant Sindhi nationalists, it could deepen the ethnic tensions in the country—and lead to civil war.

Zardari, Bhutto's corruption-plagued widower, appealed for calm. "We want Pakistan. We want Pakistan," he said, in Sindhi, at the press conference. He added, "Our struggle is not with the Pakistani army." Zardari was an extremely controversial and divisive figure. Besides allegations of graft, he was also accused of having a hand in the assassination of Bhutto's brother, Murtaza, in Karachi in September 1996. After years in his wife's shadow, never given the chance for public rehabilitation, he looked eager to assume the mantle of power. The moment he began speaking at the press conference, camera bulbs flashing, it was clear that a new era of the PPP had begun. Amin Fahim and Aitzaz Ahsan, arguably the two most public personalities of the PPP during Bhutto's exile, would play little role in that new era. This one was staying in the family.

"Rise to power Bilawal! We are with you!" supporters chanted.

"Yesterday, Bhutto was alive! Today, Bhutto is alive!"

Bilawal, resting a photograph of his mother on his lap, leaned into the microphones. On the verge of tears, his body quivered. He kept his comments brief. He promised to "stand as a symbol of the federation" and follow in the footsteps of his mother. Caste and lineage mattered more than anything else in Pakistani politics, especially in Sindh; so long as Bilawal evoked his mother's memory, he could cover his own lack of political experience. He had even changed his named from Bilawal Zardari to Bilawal Zardari Bhutto, to silence doubts about his dynastic rights.

"My mother always said," Bilawal concluded, "democracy is the best revenge!"

WITH ELECTION DAY and the chance to seek revenge through democracy still weeks away, many of Bhutto's angry, grieving supporters in Sindh continued to seek revenge through vandalism. When I arrived in Karachi on New Year's Eve, the seaside metropolis was finally limping back to normal after four days of intense rioting and looting. It felt like the first day after a blizzard, but instead of snowdrifts there were blackened husks of vehicles. More than nine hundred cars, buses, and trucks had been torched in Karachi alone. Countless private shops and government buildings had been razed throughout Sindh. The Indus Highway, running north and south through Sindh, looked like an apocalyptic repo lot, lined with burning cars stretching for hundreds of miles.

Shocked by the violence, investors had panicked, and when the Karachi Stock Exchange opened on the morning of January 31, it was down big. Long lines streamed out of gas stations, where pumps had been closed for days. Shopkeepers tentatively opened up, while keeping their metal shutters halfway down in case they needed to close in a hurry. Around lunchtime, a rumor spread throughout the city that Farooq Sattar, a leading politician from the Muttahida Quami Movement, Bhutto's rival party in Karachi, had been assassinated. The rumors proved false, but the city of fifteen million, already spooked and edgy, immediately withdrew back into its shell. Gas pumps were turned off and shopkeepers pulled their shutters down. Normalcy would have to wait at least another day.

I called up Hafeez, the activist from Nawaz Sharif's faction of the Pakistan Muslim League who I traveled with during the riots back in May. Hafeez had recently been named the PML (N) candidate for a national assembly seat in Karachi. I wanted to see how Bhutto's assassination had affected the campaigning and political dynamics on the ground. Members of Musharraf's faction of the Pakistan Muslim League totally stopped campaigning out of fear. Many pro-Musharraf candidates, including members of the MQM, had gone into hiding.

From the moment Bhutto was declared dead, the political jostling began. It included internal disputes between Fahim and Zardari, and national ones, too. "We are the only ones who can still run a public campaign," Hafeez said, referring to Sharif's PML (N). The night of the assassination, Sharif had rushed to the hospital and, on the verge of tears, renewed his pledge to topple Musharraf. Cuddling up to the PPP, and the fact that he was the most prominent face of the opposition, boosted his popularity beyond measure. But could he and his party—or anyone else for that matter—translate that into votes?

Hafeez and I headed to Machar ("Mosquito") Colony, a slum built on top of a swamp. Two days earlier, a teenage boy from Machar Colony had been shot and killed by Rangers. The slum was located in Hafeez's constituency. He wanted to offer a funeral prayer with the family before they buried the teenager. A small fire burned in a mound of trash just behind us, and the slum smelled like sewage and an old fish market. When the residents recognized Hafeez from his campaign posters, they rushed to him, complaining about the lack of electricity, water, and trash removal.

"I take one bath a week, if I am lucky," one man said.

Hafeez, who stood more than six feet tall, towered above the crowd and made lofty promises.

"Nawaz Sharif can provide for you!"

Gunfire suddenly rang out a few hundred yards away. Everyone scattered. Hafeez and I jumped into his car and sped off. I wondered how those people, watching their candidate scram, would vote.

We drove to another spot in the constituency where, the day after Bhutto's assassination, Hafeez had organized a memorial. A goat walked down the street wearing a T-shirt. "I can't leave the PPP alone right now," Hafeez said. They were riding a wave of sympathy, and Hafeez knew he would lose the election if he didn't take the initiative. That meant both leading the agitation against Musharraf and sympathizing publicly, and whenever possible, over Bhutto's death. "I've tactfully cut into the PPP by sponsoring events in Benazir's honor and then inviting PPP supporters," he said. "I make them come to *my* events. Benazir didn't just belong to the PPP, just like they don't own the memory of Zulfiqar Ali Bhutto. We, the people of Pakistan, own the Bhuttos and their memories."

But like so many other crises in Pakistan, Bhutto's assassination had aggravated the nation's long-simmering ethnic tensions. Most of the violence that followed her death occurred in Sindh, and most of it was directed at non-Sindhis, primarily people from Punjab and the North-West Frontier Province. One Pashtun trucker watched 190 of his trailers seized and burned along the Indus Highway. And the PPP's decision to tap Bilawal as the new head of the party promised to alienate voters in other provinces who didn't subscribe to the dynastic politics sanctioned by Sindhi customs and feudal traditions. Never mind the fact that Zardari, who planned to run the party until Bilawal came of age, was perceived as a sleazy crook. "Zardari will damage the PPP's national appeal more than anything," said Hafeez. "They will end up confining themselves to interior Sindh."

A FEW DAYS LATER, I went to the PPP office in Lyari, a People's Party stronghold in Karachi and the site of ethnic riots the previous May, where a memorial was being held for Bhutto. The road leading into the neighborhood was muddy and rutted. It hadn't rained for months. The pools of slush were sewage. Chalk graffiti on one wall said, in Urdu: GO! GO! TO THE KARACHI AIRPORT! GO! The chalking dated back to Bhutto's return from exile in October. We arrived at the local office to find roughly one hundred women sitting on the floor, weeping and reading the Quran in Bhutto's memory.

"Oh Benazir, Princess of Heaven, we are sorry that your killers are still alive," they chanted.

When the ladies paused, I asked one woman to assess the impact of Bhutto's murder on the Sindhi people. "There is no representation of Sindhis in the federation without Benazir, so Sindhi nationalism will be reignited," she said.

She wanted to say something else. Wiping tears from her eyes, she added, "We have become orphans."

"THE FEAR FACTOR SPOILS THE FUN"

In August 2008, I went back to Pakistan. I arrived exactly seven months after being expelled. What's that old saying? The snake bites you once, it's the snake's fault; snake bites you twice, it's your fault. But it seemed pretty safe. *Smithsonian* magazine gave me an assignment to write about a Sufi festival in Sindh. A politically benign piece about Muslim mystics. The kind of story that the Pakistani government complained there weren't enough of. My itinerary would keep me in Islamabad, Karachi, and rural Sindh. No ventures into NWFP, Baluchistan, or radical madrassas. How bad could it be?

The Pakistani ambassador to the United States, Husain Haqqani, invited me to his office in Washington to pick up my visa and share a cup of tea. I had applied two months earlier. The process normally took just a few days, but since I had been "blacklisted," Haqqani needed the approval of the intelligence agencies in Islamabad before issuing the visa. Such things take time, I was told. To his credit, Haqqani took a personal interest in pushing my visa through. He now had just one request: "Please don't get in trouble again."

"But sir, no one told me exactly what I did to get kicked out the first time."

"Well, just keep a low profile," Haqqani said.

I raced home and bought a plane ticket. I felt giddy. I e-mailed one of my best—and most trusted—friends in Karachi to let him know that I would be there in a few weeks. Could we meet for dinner? He wrote back a few days later. Just one cryptic, disconcerting line: "Don't contact me and don't ask why."

Unsure what that meant, I e-mailed his girlfriend, who responded: "Do not get in touch with me again."

A bad omen? A warning? I wasn't sure what to make of the e-mails. I tried to ignore them, but they pinged around in the back of my head until the time I arrived, throughout my trip, and still, to this day.

I REACHED ACROSS the counter as the immigration official in the Karachi airport flipped back and forth through my passport. She inspected the several Pakistani visas inside from previous trips. "Not that one," I said, "Or that one... *definitely* not that one.... Yes, that's the one." While she leafed through my passport, I wondered if she was just buying time, waiting for the ISI operatives to show up and detain me. I grew more anxious the longer she held the passport, before she finally stamped it, flashed a hollow smile, and handed it back to me. "Next!"

My friends and fellow reporters thought it miraculous, and even I had a hard time believing that I could be kicked out in January and then welcomed back in August. I took a deep breath, but the airport smelled like sweat, so I quickly exhaled. In the seven months I had been away, a lot had changed. In February 2008, the Pakistan People's Party, formerly led by Benazir Bhutto and now headed by her widower, Asif Ali Zardari, had won a plurality of seats in the parliamentary elections. The poll results had handed President Pervez Musharraf a major defeat, as his allies in the parliament were drubbed. But Pakistan's transition to civilian government wouldn't come overnight; it involved steadily eroding Musharraf's power base by chipping away at his control over the army, parliament, and the presidency. His retirement from the army in December, followed by the poll results in February, symbolized a sort of soft, yet incomplete, coup. All he had left now was the presidency.

The violence had continued and the entire security calculus changed since I left. Bombers now targeted embassies and cafés. In the spring, terrorists had attacked a pizza place in Islamabad popular with foreigners, leaving the impression that no place was safe anymore. Our friends had stopped going out. Meanwhile, in NWFP and FATA, the Taliban and al-Qaeda battled with Pakistani security forces, attacking checkpoints, munitions factories, and military bases. The militants' tactics became even more macabre: one day in late February, they killed a police officer, waited until later that day when mourners gathered for his funeral, and struck again with a suicide bomber, killing another forty people. Grassroots efforts to challenge the Talibs were violently discouraged, too. In March, a suicide bomber detonated himself among a council of elders gathered to draft a strategy against the militants, killing forty-two people.

The PPP-led government, ostensibly hoping to separate the local Talibs from the "irreconcilable" al-Qaeda elements, tried to negotiate with the militants. The government claimed that it was not negotiating from a position of weakness, but they didn't fool anyone. The Talibs had the upper hand. Baitullah Mehsud, the warlord in South Waziristan, accused by American and Pakistan intelligence of Bhutto's assassination, invited several Pakistani journalists to his jihadi compound for a tour and press conference one day, an act that reminded everyone of the government's ineffectiveness against him. Maulana Fazlullah, the Taliban chief in Swat, was less brazen, but nonetheless still alive, shuttling between Bajaur, Dir, and Swat. Abdul Rashid Ghazi's disciples threatened a newspaper editor with death for publishing cartoons that maligned Ghazi's sister-in-law, suggesting that she taught jihad in her classrooms at Jamia Hafsa. Just weeks earlier, thousands of their female madrassa students had congregated at the Red Mosque and vowed to produce "babies for jihad."

One of the new government's biggest challenges was reigning in the intelligence agencies, particularly the ISI, which continued to operate beyond the purview of the elected leaders. A week before I arrived, the PPP-led government announced its plan to wrest the ISI from the army, thus placing the spy agency under the command of the Interior Ministry, a civilian-run institution. But days later, the government reversed its decision, caving in to pressure from the military. The incident proved that while a president in a business suit may uniquely symbolize the replacement of a military dictatorship, the military's two main intelligence agencies, ISI and Military Intelligence (MI), remained the true arbiters of power—regardless of who was the president or prime minister.

Amid the escalating insecurity and confusion, local and international investors feared the worst and fled with their money. The economy was tanking. The rupee had lost nearly fifty percent of its value against the dollar since January. The price of gasoline had jumped above $5 a gallon, in a country where most annual incomes are capped at $1,000. The composite index of the Karachi stock exchange had fallen more than 40 percent since April. Electricity shortages led to rolling blackouts; in the heat of summer, lights and air conditioners shut down for four, five, sometimes six or more hours a day. Hordes of beggars—previously unseen in Islamabad—now loitered around busy intersections. Women shrouded in black rags clicked their fingernails against the glass of passing automobiles and extended an upturned palm.

I thought back to the question my grandfather had put to me more than a year earlier, when he asked, genuinely curious, "What's wrong with that place?" I realized that I was no closer to offering a comprehensive answer now than I had been back then. That bothered me. The political, social, economic, and religious dynamics embedded in Pakistan seemed to become more and more complicated—and volatile—with time, and less and less solvable. But I disagreed with those who said that ethnic tension, the Taliban, economic crises, years of military dictatorship, the lack of a cohesive identity and so on would eventually lead to Pakistan's breakup. That would almost be too linear and neat: creation, extended crisis, and then dissolution. It seemed more likely that Pakistan would continue to exist in a perpetual state of frenzied dysfunction; alive, but always appearing to be on the verge of perishing.

BY THE MIDDLE of the summer of 2008, with public confidence in the new government flagging, the politicians needed a boost. Impeachment proceedings seemed like they could turn things around, so the first week of August, Zardari set his sights on Musharraf. The PPP and the PML faction headed by Nawaz Sharif jointly filed a charge sheet against the former commando. According to the sheet, Musharraf stood guilty of subverting the constitution and overthrowing the judiciary on November 3, 2007, selling Pakistani citizens to the United States for bounties, as well as some shady involvement in Islamabad's only McDonald's; the fast-food joint had been built in a federal park, technically off-limits for construction during his time in office. The two sides faced off, flexing and posturing and calling each other's bluffs. Finally, on August 18, Musharraf announced that he'd be addressing the nation on TV.

At 1 P.M., Musharraf's mug showed up on screens around the country. He wore a dark gray suit with a gray-and-white-striped necktie. Almost everyone suspected that he would resign in the speech from his last remaining office, but forty minutes into it he had given no such indication. Having touted his achievements while in power—such as resuscitating an economy on the verge of bankruptcy and saving Pakistan from becoming a failed state—he then blustered about the infamous and murky charge sheet. (The charge sheet was never released to the public, and only snippets were leaked.) "No charge sheet can stand against me," Musharraf said. "[My opponents] cannot prove a single charge."

But then Musharraf softened his tone and the speech took a sentimental turn. "Pakistan is my love," he said. "Now and always, my life is for Pakistan." Musharraf admitted that if he stayed in office, "institutions will be endangered." And so, after more than eight years in power, he continued, "having consulted with my legal and political advisers, I have decided to resign from my post." He took a long pause, relishing his final moments in the spotlight. He bid the country Allah's blessings, raised both fists above his chest, and, for the last time as president, proclaimed, "Long live Pakistan." Private TV channels immediately panned to shots of people celebrating in the streets of Lahore, Karachi, and Multan, stuffing one another's mouths with sweets and dancing awkward, joyous jigs.

I headed over to the PPP headquarters that afternoon to meet with Zardari. When I arrived, a line of black pickups, detailed for politicians' security, were parked out front; Nawaz Sharif, Maulana Fazlur Rahman (of the JUI), and Asfandyar Wali Khan (of the ANP) were inside congratulating Zardari. Owing to the constant bomb threat, most of the homes in Zardari's neighborhood had built high blast walls, some as tall as forty feet. Police outposts, covered with lime green plastic shades and patterned with psychedelic blue and fuchsia flowers, popped up in the surrounding streets. A crowd of local journalists positioned their cameras near the driveway entrance, waiting for Sharif, Rahman and Khan to emerge. A banner, staked into a slice of grass out front, read: CONGRATU-LATIONS TO ASIF ALI ZARDARI FOR LEADING THE MOVEMENT TO FIGHT AGAINST THE WORST DICTATORSHIP.

I walked through two metal detectors on the way inside and ran into Maulana Fazlur Rahman in the hallway. He was wearing his signature orange turban. We had met several times previously—I wrote a profile about him for the *New York Times Magazine*—and his face lit up when he saw me. He asked me where I had been, where I was living, and what I was doing. "You know," I said, "two days after my story about you came out, I was deported."

"Yes, I heard about this," Rahman said, before smiling a smug grin. "But our government has let you back in. And just in time to see Musharraf get kicked out." We both laughed.

I waited for Zardari in a side room, decorated with framed photo-graphs of Benazir Bhutto and Zulfiqar Ali Bhutto. A vase of pink gladio-las rested on a glass table beside a sofa. Zardari charged through the door and into the room. He apologized for being late, ran his hand through his hair, and collapsed onto the couch. He wore black slacks with a cream-colored shirt. Soon after taking a seat, he unbuttoned the top two buttons of the shirt, reached in, and twisted a tuft of his chest hair.

Zardari had spent more than eleven years off and on in prison since marrying Bhutto in 1987. He had endured torture, with scars to prove it on his neck and tongue from being cut with pieces of glass. According to the mythology promoted by the PPP, the experience hardened his resolve and illustrated his commitment to democracy. (The intelligence agencies had apparently offered him bail if he promised to keep Benazir out of the country, propositions he refused time and again.) With Musharraf now officially out of the picture, Zardari sounded like a man who felt nothing less than destiny had handed him the presidency. He wanted to share a jailhouse anecdote with me.

"I was sitting in prison once, looking at the poverty, looking at the problems of the nation, and thinking, 'How are we going to bring the country out of this mess?'" Zardari told me. "I am aware that the popula-tion growth is 3.6 percent. I *know* that the figures are all wrong. I *know* that everyone thinks the population today is around 160 million. But I put it at 180 million," he added, again twisting his chest hair and looking at the ceiling. "I know where the state is going. You don't have to be Einstein to understand that." Two weeks later, Zardari was the president of Pakistan.

On Wednesday, forty-eight hours after Musharraf bid farewell, photographer Aaron Huey, his wife, Kristen, our translator, Waheed, and I began our journey to the Sufi festival that *Smithsonian* had assigned me to cover. (Waheed, for the record, is not his real name.) The festival marked the death anniversary of Lal Shahbaz Qalander, a Muslim mystic who died in the thirteenth century and whose shrine continues to attract hundreds of thousands of devotees every year. The shrine sits in Sehwan, a town almost two hundred miles north of Karachi. The annual *urs*, as the festival is known, spanned three days; urs, an Arabic word meaning "marriage," symbolizes Sufis' sense of their cosmic union with the Divine. I hoped the story would reveal a side of Islam—joyous, celebratory, nonviolent—previously unreported in Pakistan. The Taliban might have the guns, but the Sufis had the numbers.

Waheed, a thirty-one-year-old journalist based in Karachi, rented a white Toyota Camry for us and volunteered to drive. We had barely left Karachi's city limits when he received a mysterious phone call. The person on the other line claimed to work at the Interior Ministry's secretariat in Karachi and be named Ahmed Ali. He peppered Waheed with questions about me: "Where is Nicholas?" "What is he doing?" "Where can I meet him?" Waheed immediately detected something odd, tipped off by the fact that "Ahmed Ali" used a mobile phone; such official business, Waheed said, is almost always conducted on landlines. Waheed hung up and called a senior bureaucrat in the Interior Ministry in Islamabad. The man's secretary answered the phone. Waheed rehashed the conversation. "Neither that person, nor that office, exists," the secretary said, confirming our suspicions. "It's probably just the agencies."

I had expected some harassment by the ISI ever since my good friend in Karachi wrote me an e-mail saying, "Don't contact me and don't ask why." Maybe I should have read more into it. Just the previous night, as Waheed and I had made plans on the phone, I heard various taps and buzzes during our conversation.

"Did you hear that?" I asked Waheed.

"Hear what?" he said.

Clearly, someone else had been eavesdropping. But what scandalous nugget of information did they pick up? That I requested a Camry for extra legroom? That we planned to leave after breakfast? That before heading out of Karachi, I needed to change a few hundred dollars into rupees? That I was heading to a Sufi festival, trying to write a story that exposed the lighter side of Pakistan?

Slightly spooked by the call, but undeterred, we continued driving north on the highway into the heart of Sindh. Patches of a flowing bush that resembled stunted willow trees lined the road. Water buffaloes soaked in muddy canals. Naked kids splashed beside them. Camels rested in the shade of mango trees.

About an hour later, my phone rang. It displayed the same number on the caller ID as the one from "Ahmed Ali."

"Hello?" I answered.

"Nicholas?"

"Yes."

"I am a reporter from the *Daily Express* newspaper. I want to meet you to talk about the current political situation," he said. "When can we meet? Where are you? I can come right now."

Covering the mouthpiece with my palm, I turned to Waheed and whispered, "It's the same guy."

"Hang up," Waheed mouthed.

"Can I call you back?" I said, and hung up. My heartbeat raced. Images of Daniel Pearl, the *Wall Street Journal* reporter who was kidnapped and beheaded by Islamic militants in Karachi, flashed through my mind. In January 2002, Pearl had been lured into trusting someone who turned out to be a wanted terrorist. Some people accused the Pakistani intelligence agencies of involvement in Pearl's murder, as the *Wall Street Journal* reporter was researching the possible link between the ISI and a jihadi leader with ties to Richard Reid, the so-called shoe bomber who tried to blow up an airplane flying from Paris to Miami in December 2001.

My phone rang again. A reporter from the Associated Press told me that her sources in Karachi said the ISI was searching for me. I had assumed as much. But why? What did they want? And why, if they had nothing nefarious in mind, were they requesting a meeting while pretending to be people that didn't exist?

Everyone in the car sank into thought. Aaron, generally an excitable fellow, was the first to speak. "Dude, this is getting intense," he said. "I need to get Kristen out of here." While I was thinking kidnap, Aaron was thinking ambush; a year earlier, he had been embedded with DynCorp in southern Afghanistan when the Taliban launched a sophisticated assault on his unit. And Kristen worked at an international think tank, where her duties included tracking instances in Pakistan of "disappearances"—usually at the hands of the intelligence agencies—and political murders. We later joked with Kristen about her becoming a subject of her own research.

Waheed scrambled to call every senior politician, bureaucrat, and police officer he knew in Sindh. He reached Zulfiqar Mirza, one of Zardari's closest pals and business partners. He informed Mirza that, just two days earlier, I had met with Zardari. Mirza promised his full cooperation. The police, he said, would provide us with an armed escort the remainder of our journey—even to the urs. An hour later, we rendezvoused with two police trucks at a gas station near the town of Nawabshah. Both trucks carried four men holding AK-47s. In the lead truck, a man stood in the bed armed with a mounted machine gun.

The presence of the police had just begun to have a calming effect when I took another phone call, this time from a friend in Islamabad.

"Man, it's good to hear your voice," he said, sounding relieved.

"Why?"

"Local TV stations say that you've been kidnapped in Karachi."

With that, the stakes suddenly seemed far graver than just being deported. Who was planting these stories? And why? To foreshadow their intent? Just to threaten me? There was no shortage of fatal "car accidents" involving people in bad standing with the intelligence agencies. And surely, with some of the high-tech toys the ISI had acquired from the United States after 9/11, they could track a phone call with some precision. I took the planted stories as a hint that I should leave. As soon as possible.

The only problem was that we had traveled several hours north of Karachi already. Waheed had an idea. A friend of his ran the police force in northern Sindh. We would go to Sukkur, a city in northern Sindh, rest for the night at the policeman's compound, try to figure out what was happening, and make a plan to get back to Karachi safely.

WE ATE EGGS and parathas for breakfast the next morning. I ate more than normal to store up, like a camel drinks water before it ventures across the desert. I had survived the day before on a diet of Mountain Dew. Tension had otherwise killed my appetite.

That morning, three English-language dailies printed the following report:

> Nicholas Shamble, US based journalist went missing from Karachi.... Shamble is the editor of the US based magazine Smithsonian and had been visiting Pakistan more frequently. The source further said that Shamble used to work on terrorism and other issues of Pakistan.... It has also been learnt by the source that Shamble had been deported from Pakistan some two years ago.

Despite having butchered my last name and personal details, the article clearly referred to me. Okay, I said aloud. I can take a hint. You don't want me here. I am leaving.

Our gentle, unassuming host, the policeman, joined us at the breakfast table. Waheed filled him in on the details of our drama. The more he listened, the more his eyes widened. "This sounds serious," he said. I hated it when he said that because people in uniform aren't supposed to sound surprised by anything. Waheed reminded him that I was the reporter who had been kicked out seven months earlier. Our host leaned in, lowered his voice, and asked me, "So tell me, seriously. Is the ISI supporting the Taliban?" Before I had a chance to answer, the officer received a phone call from the local ISI office, requesting to see him. "I gotta go," he said. We needed to get moving, too. We never learned why the ISI called our host.

Our ultimate destination that day was the Karachi airport. But on the way, we planned to stop in Sehwan. We had traveled halfway around the world to see the shrine of Lal Shahbaz Qalander. We would do our damnedest to get there, even under police protection. We could use Qalander's blessings, after all.

We drove through the day. That afternoon, as the setting sun burned the color of a Creamsicle and lit the sugarcane fields on the horizon, I turned to Waheed, hoping to lighten the mood. "It's really beautiful here," I said.

Waheed nodded, and his eyes stayed glued on the road. "Unfortunately, the fear factor spoils the fun of it," he said.

By then we could see the buses clogging the highway, red flags poking from the windows and flapping hard in the wind as the drivers raced for Qalander's shrine. (The "Lal" in Qalander's name means "red" in Urdu.) The railway ministry had announced that thirteen trains would be diverted from their normal routes to transport worshippers. Some devotees pedaled bicycles, red flags sticking up from the handlebars. We roared down the highway in the company of two trucks—five guys per truck—of Kalashnikov-toting police. A caravan of armed pilgrims.

THE CAMPSITES BEGAN appearing about five miles from the shrine. Our car eventually mired in a human bog, so we parked it and continued on foot. The alleys leading to the shrine reminded me of a carnival fun house—an overwhelming frenzy of lights, music, and aromas. I walked beside a man blowing a snake charmer's flute. Stores lined the alley, with merchants squatting beside piles of pistachios, almonds, and rosewater-doused candies. Flies swarmed on the sweets, only to be swatted away with dirty rags. Fluorescent tubes the size of baseball bats glowed like light sabers, leading lost souls to Allah, and perhaps a snack along the way.

Drummers pounded away as celebrants swathed in red pushed a camel bedecked with garlands, tinsel, and multihued scarves through the heaving crowd. A man skirted past, grinning and dancing, his face glistening like the golden dome of the shrine nearby. "*Mast Qalander!*" he cried. The ecstasy of Qalander.

The camel reached a courtyard packed with hundreds of men jumping in place with their hands in the air, chanting "Qalander!" The men threw rose petals at a dozen women who danced in what appeared like a mosh pit by the shrine's entrance. Enraptured, one woman placed her hands on her knees and threw her head back and forth, like she was bobbing for apples. Another bounced and jiggled as if she were astride a trotting horse. The drumming and dancing never stopped. Not even for the call to prayer.

I stood at the edge of the courtyard and asked a young man named Abbas to explain this dancing, called *dhamaal*. Dancing is central to Sufism—think of Turkey's whirling dervishes—but dhamaal is particular to South Asian Sufis. "When a *djinn* infects a human body," Abbas said, referring to one of the spirits that populate Islamic belief (and known in the West as "genies"), "the only way we can get rid of it is by coming here to do dhamaal." A woman stumbled toward us with her eyes closed and passed out at our feet. Abbas didn't seem to notice, so I pretended not to either.

"What goes through your head when you are doing dhamaal?" I asked.

"Nothing. I don't think," he said. A few women rushed in our direction, emptied a water bottle on the semiconscious woman's face, and slapped her cheeks. She shot upright and danced back into the crowd. Abbas smiled. "During dhamaal, I just feel the blessings of Lal Shahbaz Qalander wash over me."

LATER, WE FOLLOWED a group into a tent next to the shrine packed with dancers and drummers. A tall man with curly, greasy, shoulder-length hair kept a beat on a keg-sized drum hanging from a leather strap around his neck. The intensity of his eyes, illuminated by a single bulb that dangled above our heads, reminded me of the jungle cats that stalked their nighttime prey on the nature shows I watched as a kid on TV.

A man dressed in all white linen lunged flamboyantly into a clearing at the center of the crowd, tied an orange sash around his waist, and began to dance. Soon he was gyrating, with his limbs eventually trembling with such fierce and tight control that, at one point, it seemed that he was moving only his earlobes. Clouds of hashish smoke rolled through the tent and the drumming filled the space with a thick, engrossing energy.

I stopped taking notes, closed my eyes, and began nodding my head. As the drummer built toward a feverish peak, my mind—and body— drifted unconsciously closer to him. Before long, I found myself standing in the middle of the circle, dancing beside the man with the jiggling earlobes.

"Mast Qalander!" someone called out. I knew that the voice came from right behind me, but it sounded distant. Anything but the drumbeat and the effervescence surging through my body seemed remote. From the corner of my eye I noticed Aaron high-stepping his way into the circle. He had thrown off his visor and passed his camera to Kristen. Moments later, Aaron's head was swirling as he whipped his long hair around in circles. Clearly, we both had some energy to burn.

In his day, Qalander preached to all the faithful, regardless of creed, and invited them to create a spiritual bond with the Divine. Now, more than seven hundred years later, if only for a few minutes, it didn't matter whether I was a Christian, Muslim, Hindu, or atheist. In that moment, I understood why pilgrims braved the great distances and the heat and the crowds just to be near the shrine. While spun into a trance, I forgot about the danger, the phone calls, the reports of my disappearance, and the police escort.

Later, one of the men who had been dancing in the circle approached me. He gave his name as Hamid and said he had traveled more than five hundred miles by train from northern Punjab. He and a friend were traversing the country, hopping from one shrine to another, in search of the wildest party. "Qalander is the best," he said.

I asked him why.

"He could communicate directly with Allah," Hamid said. "And he performs miracles."

"Miracles?" I asked, with a wry smile, having reverted to my normal cynicism. "What kind of miracles?"

Hamid laughed. "What kind of miracles?" he said. "Take a look around!" Sweat sprayed from his mustache, onto my face. "Can't you see how many people have come to be with Lal Shahbaz Qalander?"

I looked over both of my shoulders at the drumming, the mayhem, the dhamaal, and the sea of red. I stared back at Hamid and tilted my head slightly to one side, acknowledging his point. At the same time we both muttered: "Mast Qalander!"

IT WAS GETTING LATE, and we still had a lot of distance to cover. If we made good time from Sehwan, we could be back in Karachi by 2 A.M. There was a flight to Dubai at 5:30 A.M. Perhaps I could make it.

Then we realized that we were nearly out of gas. We had planned to fill up in Sehwan, but all the pumps had closed because of the urs.

Waheed guessed that we could go about fifteen miles with our supply. Dadu, the nearest town with a pump, stood twenty-five miles away. We didn't have another option. Along with our police escort friends, we drank another round of Mountain Dew and headed out. We threw a rope in the trunk just in case we needed a tow.

Waheed eyed the gas gauge nervously as we cruised along a very dark, ill-paved road. Scrubby desert unrolled on either side of the street, lit by our headlights and then spreading like black ink for miles. The authorities normally discouraged any travel after sunset. Highway bandits roamed throughout interior Sindh. "Dude, people told me *never* to drive on this stretch of road at night," Aaron said. "Dadu is supposed to be a super sketchy place." At least we had an escort, right? I looked ahead at the police truck leading the way, and realized that, on one of the most notoriously bandit-infested roads, our two-vehicle escort had dwindled to one . . . and, unless my eyes were deceiving me, no one in the truck was carrying a gun. The two guys in the bed and the two guys in the cab were clutching latthis, the bamboo thatches used for crowd control.

We laughed at the absurdity of our "armed" escort and sounded like a gaggle of delirious madmen until Waheed announced, "The tank is now on E." We were literally running on fumes. Then we hit a hole. Not a normal-sized hole, but more like a crater. We heard a loud sound of breaking metal. I prayed to Lal Shahbaz Qalander. There, on the bandit road, in the middle of the night, with a police escort comprised of hungry guys holding sticks, we had cracked the axle of our Camry. We waited for an hour as the police radioed for a mechanic to come. The mechanic slid underneath the Camry. "It should get you to Karachi. Just don't drive fast," he said. "And there's a gas station just around the bend."

Between a stop for dinner, another for tea, and the cracked axle, we finally approached the city limits of Karachi at 9 A.M. on Friday. I intended to reserve a flight over the phone and camp out at the airport until the plane departed. It seemed safe there.

But if the past day or two had been weird, things were about to get a lot weirder. As we were waiting at the police outpost at the edge of town for the Karachi city police to decide if they would escort us into the center of the city, a hatchback with tinted windows and two stubby, black antennae eased beside our Camry. The man in the front passenger seat

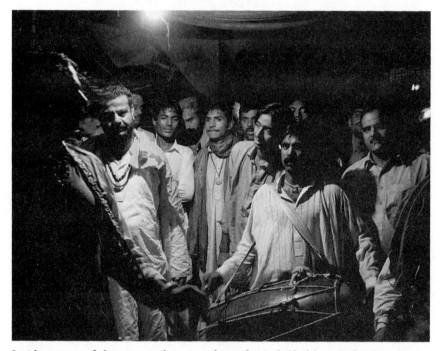

Inside a tent of dancers at the annual *urs* for Lal Shahbaz Qalander. Photo:
Nicholas Schmidle

stared, and then they drove off. "Agencies," said Waheed, who looked
bleary and ready to sleep. We called Zulfiqar Mirza, the Home Minister,
but he didn't answer. Neither did anyone else who had been so coopera-
tive two days earlier. The Karachi police chief, when we finally reached
him on the phone, yelled at Waheed and accused him of being "an
opportunist." "Who are the foreigners that are with you? I'll bet you don't
even know who they *really* are! Are you willing to work with anyone, just
to make some money?"

The police chief's rant, coupled with the undeniable observation that
suddenly no one wanted anything to do with us, suggested that someone—probably the intelligence agencies—had told these people to stop
cooperating, which left me feeling thoroughly uncertain about everything. Fat, gloomy clouds hung over the city.

I called a couple of travel agencies. They said all departing flights were
booked for days. When a bus passed on one side and honked its horn, I
jumped in my seat. I had never felt more alone and paranoid in my life.

* * *

I EVENTUALLY CALLED the U.S. consulate in Karachi. I had been in touch with them as the stories were breaking about my disappearance to let them know I was okay, but now I was asking for help. They told me, for the first time, that they knew that I was being tracked by the intelligence agencies, but couldn't say whether the agencies were spying on me to protect me from a threat, or whether the agencies were themselves the threat. They sounded concerned, though. An American diplomat recommended that I check into a hotel and stay off the streets. She said she'd arrange my departure.

Three hours later, a Pakistani employee of the consulate, referred to by the American woman as the Facilitator, knocked at the hotel room door and showed his ID. I said good-bye to Aaron and Kristen. (Waheed had already gone home.) The Facilitator and I got into the elevator. When the elevator door opened on the lobby floor, he called the driver waiting outside on his cell. "We are coming out," he told him.

A black, bulletproof Range Rover, with dark tinted windows, idled near the entrance. The guard, a tall, serious-looking Pakistani with a pompadour, stepped out and scanned the parking lot for suspicious movements while I loaded my luggage through the back hatch's opened Kevlar door. Once I had sat down and pulled the door shut, it made a sucking sound, like being trapped inside a freezer. A few hours earlier, the diplomat had noted that most "incidents," such as bombings and assassinations, occurred on the road leading from the center of town to the airport.

The bulletproofing made the inside of the car nearly soundproof. The air-conditioning blew cold. No one spoke. I told a few jokes. Not real jokes, with punch lines, just jokes from the night before, about us driving through the middle of interior Sindh with a cracked axle, accompanied by a police truck full of guys holding bamboo sticks. My escorts in the car howled with laughter.

We arrived at the airport three hours early to guarantee I didn't get bumped off an already overbooked flight. I had checked into flights countless times in Karachi, but the Facilitator stayed with me as I cleared immigration, customs, and multiple security checks. I used my cell phone to call home to my dad, the Marine general. I tried to tell him the story of our night, and the planted stories of my disappearance, but both times I began, the phone mysteriously cut off. "I'll call you when I get to Dubai," I said, having decided it would be better to be physically outside of Pakistan before I accused the Pakistani intelligence agencies of conceiving a plan to kidnap me. My flight boarded on time. The Facilitator stood in the lounge until the terminal gate closed.

I FOUND A bar in the Dubai airport and downed a stiff drink. For the first time in more than forty-eight hours, a part of me—the part that wouldn't put anything past the ISI—relaxed. I was sleep deprived, but the terminal's neon consumerism kept me awake. Buzzed from the alcohol and drained from exhaustion and fright, I couldn't muster much more than a flat, stale sadness.

I felt sad for Pakistan, and the people there who couldn't just leave. My friend Waheed had taken a huge risk in agreeing to work with me after I had already been deported once. Sure, he was well connected and had lots of friends. But we both knew the agencies could do whatever they wanted. Prime ministers and presidents had died mysterious deaths. No one was immune.

When my wife and I had been kicked out in January, I had left feeling jealous of anyone who got to stay, to watch, to live in this fascinating country as it wrestled against military dictatorship, vied to enact the rule of law, and struggled to form a single, unified national identity. I was particularly envious of all the foreign journalists who had not been kicked out, who could still travel anywhere in Pakistan, doing their work. Why did I have to go home? But I also knew all along that I should be able to get back. Stay away a few months and let the air clear. That's all it would take, I thought.

This time was different. I left in a bulletproof car. I knew, sitting in Dubai, that unfortunately I was done with Pakistan for a while. I needed a lot more time away from the intelligence agencies. And I had left most of my optimism about Pakistan back at the urs. Really, what was there to look forward to? Musharraf was gone, but the military was still in control. Elections had brought a democratically elected civilian government, but average Pakistanis felt no more empowered than they did before. Despite the populist rhetoric of the PPP, poor people still couldn't afford basic commodities like wheat and tea, never mind "luxuries" like electricity. Pakistan stood on the verge of bankruptcy, in almost every sense.

But what was the agencies' problem with me? Who knows, maybe they thought I was someone I was not. Maybe they felt threatened by me. I know, it's kind of a silly, self-aggrandizing thing to say. But why would they plant stories in the newspapers that I had been kidnapped?

Maybe after a few years I will feel comfortable enough to go back. Maybe by then they will have forgotten about me. Nicholas who? Schmidle? Any relation to Nicholas Shamble? That would be a conversation I'd look forward to. I just hope I can remember how to speak Urdu when the time comes. I wonder what the place will look like then.

NOTES

Most of this book was compiled through personal interviews and observations. That being said, I relied heavily on previous scholarship, reporting, and research to frame my opinions and analysis. I owe a great deal to the *New York Times* and the *Washington Post*, in addition to the *Daily Times*, *Dawn*, and the *News*, all English-language newspapers in Pakistan. I also made a habit out of reading *Jang*, an Urdu-language daily newspaper, particularly the opinion pages. Below, I have listed some books and articles that were especially helpful, and which I would recommend for anyone wanting to read more.

INTRODUCTION: LAND OF THE PURE
The best book-length introduction to Pakistan—and Chaudhry Rahmat Ali—is *The Idea of Pakistan* by Stephen P. Cohen (Washington, D.C.: Brookings Institution Press, 2004).

For more on Daniel Pearl's kidnapping and murder, read *Who Killed Daniel Pearl?* by Bernard-Henry Lévi (Hoboken, N.J.: Melville House, 2003), and *A Mighty Heart* by Pearl's widow, Mariane Pearl (London: Virago Press, 2004).

CHAPTER 1: "TO THESE GUYS, YOU ARE ALL INFIDELS"
For a clear account of the early history of Islam, and an explanation of the Sunni-Shia split, read Reza Aslan's *No God But God* (New York: Random House, 2005).

Hassan Abbas dedicates several pages to Sipah-e-Sahaba in *Pakistan's Drift into Extremism* (New Delhi: M. E. Sharpe, 2005). This book, along with Husain Haqqani's *Pakistan: Between Mosque and Military* (Washington, D.C.: Carnegie Endowment for International Peace, 2005), Gilles Kepel's *Jihad* (London: I. B. Taurus, 2004), and Steve Coll's masterful *Ghost Wars* (New York: Penguin, 2004), document the growing Islamization in Pakistan during the 1980s.

The most comprehensive list of militant groups in Pakistan is Mohammad Amir Rana's *The A to Z of Jehadi Organizations in Pakistan* (Lahore, Pakistan: Mashal, 2005).

Vali Nasr covers the roots and history of sectarianism in Pakistan better than anyone in his article "International Politics, Domestic Imperatives, and Identity Mobilization: Sectarianism in Pakistan, 1979–1998." *Comparative Politics*, Vol. 32, No. 2 (January 2000), 171–90.

CHAPTER 2: "SELL YOUR LUXURY GOODS AND BUY A KALASHNIKOV"

Oskar Verkaaik, a Dutch scholar, has written two books about the MQM that proved extremely helpful: *People of Migrants* (Amsterdam: V U University Press, 1994) and *Migrants and Militants* (Princeton, N.J.: Princeton University Press, 2004).

CHAPTER 3: "DON'T SPEAK ENGLISH IN PUBLIC"

Coll's *Ghost Wars* is the authoritative text on the relationship between Islamabad and the Taliban. Ahmed Rashid's *Taliban* (New Haven, Conn.: Yale, 2000) is also informative.

Pervez Musharraf's autobiography *In the Line of Fire* (London: Simon and Schuster, 2006) recounts the conversation with Armitage.

To read more about the Pashtuns, go to Olaf Caroe's *The Pathans* (Oxford, U.K.: Oxford University Press, 1958). I learned a lot about South Waziristan from Akbar S. Ahmed's *Resistance and Control in Pakistan* (Cambridge, U.K.: Cambridge University Press, 1983). And for more on the Pakistan-Afghanistan border in general, read Ainslie T. Embree's *Pakistan's Western Borderlands* (New Delhi: Vikas, 1977).

CHAPTER 4: "LEFT ALONE IN A CAVE OF TIME"

For anyone wanting to understand the history of the Deobandi madrassa, Barbara Daly Metcalf's *Islamic Revival in British India: Deoband, 1860–1900* (New Delhi: Oxford University Press, 1982) is a must-read. Coll, Abbas, Haqqani, and Rashid also discuss the role of the madrassas in supporting the Taliban and supplying young men for jihad in Afghanistan and Kashmir.

CHAPTER 5: "IT JUST SOUNDS AWKWARD TO CALL MYSELF
A PAKISTANI"
Although it is almost thirty years old, the best primer on contemporary Baluchi
nationalism is Selig Harrison's *In Afghanistan's Shadow* (Washington, D.C.:
Carnegie Endowment for International Peace, 1981).

An exceptional book about Central Asia in general, and which describes the
contest between the Russian and British empires for control of Baluchistan better than any, is *The Great Game* by Peter Hopkirk (New York: Kodansha, 1990).

To appreciate how the English used to conduct espionage, check out Henry
Pottinger's *Travels in Beloochistan and Sinde* (Oxford, U.K.: Oxford University
Press, 2002).

CHAPTER 6: "WHAT WAS WRONG WITH PAKISTAN?"
The staff at the *Daily Star* in Dhaka were more instructive than any book I had
previously read about Bangladesh. Badruddin Umar's *The Emergence of
Bangladesh* (Oxford, U.K.: Oxford University Press, 2006) helped me understand the economic dynamics leading up to Bangladesh's independence.

CHAPTER 7: "WE HAVE ACCEPTED THE CHALLENGE"
The *Washington Post* covered the lawyer's movement better than anyone. To
understand Musharraf's sense of his own place in Pakistani history, read his autobiography, *In the Line of Fire*.

CHAPTER 8: "THE BLOOD OF OUR MARTYRS WILL NOT
GO TO WASTE"
Saleem Shahzad's reports in *Asia Times Online* helped me grasp the importance
of Abdul Rashid Ghazi and to understand his jihadi network.

CHAPTER 10: "THIS BARBED WIRE STANDS IN THE WAY
OF DEMOCRACY"
James Traub has written an interesting profile of Aitzaz Ahsan for the *New York
Times Magazine*, published on June 1, 2008.

For a thorough understanding of the Pakistan People's Party and its genesis,
read Philip E. Jones's *The Pakistan People's Party: Rise to Power* (Oxford, U.K.:
Oxford University Press, 2003).

Vali Nasr provides a fascinating account of Jamaat-i-Islami and its cam-
paign to control university campuses in *The Vanguard of the Islamic
Revolution: The Jama'at-i Islami of Pakistan* (Berkeley: University of California
Press, 1994).

CHAPTER 11: "MADE LIKE A SANDWICH"

For those curious to know more about Maulana Fazlur Rahman's family and JUI, read Sayyid A. S. Pirzada's *The Politics of the Jamiat Ulema-i-Islam Pakistan* (Oxford, U.K.: Oxford University Press, 2000).

CHAPTER 12: "NO MERCY IN THEIR HEARTS"

In her posthumously published *Reconciliation* (New York: HarperCollins, 2008), Benazir Bhutto discusses the bombing of her motorcade on October 18, 2007, and her suspicions of who was trying to kill her.

For a measured, well-reported account of Bhutto's assassination, read Peter Bergen's "The Killer Question," published in *The New Republic* on January 30, 2008.

EPILOGUE: "THE FEAR FACTOR SPOILS THE FUN"

For more on Sufism in Sindh, Sarah D. Ansari's *Sufi Saints and State Power: The Pirs of Sind, 1843–1947* (Cambridge, U.K.: Cambridge University Press, 1992) is indispensable.

Acknowledgments

This book would have never been possible without support—financial and otherwise—from the Institute of Current World Affairs. Despite having only a couple of published articles to my name, the institute sent me to Pakistan for two years with three basic instructions: learn Urdu, don't come home, and write about what you see. The experience changed my life. Thanks to Peter Byrd Martin, who served as director of ICWA when I was selected as a fellow in 2005, and to Phillips Talbot, the namesake of my fellowship, who visited me in Lahore a few months after his 92nd birthday. Special thanks to Steve Butler, who directed, supervised, edited, and oversaw the majority of my fellowship. His encouragement and guidance proved invaluable.

The foreign press corps in Pakistan frequently pointed me in the right direction, and always helped salvage my sanity. Special thanks to Griff Witte and Emily Bliss, Ben Sand and Maria Ma, Declan Walsh and Sophia Frias, Aryn Baker, Kim Barker, Warrick Page, Andy Drake and Chiade O'Shea. Thanks to Mailis Orban and Nicole Ruder for their friendship, and to Zubair Indris, who opened his home and his stables to us on numerous occasions. And thanks to Barry Newhouse, who spent months trying to collect a debt on my behalf.

I am immensely grateful to all of the Pakistanis who helped guide, advise, and translate for me along the way. Special thanks to Pir Zubair Shah for his wisdom and friendship. Shaheen Buneri, Abdul Rahman Achakzai, Shahzad Jillani, Wajadan, Rashid Bokhari, and Rafi Nasser all assisted me on multiple occasions. Many others were generous with their time, thoughts, and analyses, including Hamid Mir, Zaffar Abbas, Mushahid Hussain, Saleem Shahzad, Rahimullah Yusufzai, and Zahid Hussain. Bishaw Das, Tusher Hasan, and Julfikar Manik were extremely helpful while I stayed in Bangladesh. Nooruddin Bakhshi and Javed Ahmed Khan were both indispensable in Afghanistan. My apologies to those I haven't mentioned by name. Some of you would probably prefer it that way.

Thanks to Naseem for teaching me Urdu, to Saeed Khan for letting me live in his house, to Shabana and Akeel for their hard work, and to Mardan for taking great risks in protecting Rikki and me from snooping intelligence agents. All of you helped make our apartment in Islamabad feel like home.

Shireen Mazari kindly offered to host me at the Institute of Strategic Studies in Islamabad, even while it seemed that she never wanted me there. Husain Haqqani and Khalid Hasan worked tirelessly to get me back into Pakistan in August 2008, for which I am also grateful. (Sadly, Hasan passed away in February 2009.) Arshi and Moazzem Hashmi, Stephen Cohen, Christine Fair, and Marvin Weinbaum were all helpful in the weeks and months before I moved to Pakistan.

Thanks to all of those who published my work over the years. Readers of *Slate*, *The New Republic*, *Truthdig*, *Boston Review*, the *Washington Post*, *Virginia Quarterly Review*, *Smithsonian*, the *New York Times Magazine*, and the Institute of Current World's Affairs monthly newsletters may find some parts of this book familiar; portions were previously printed in all of these outlets. Very special thanks to June Thomas at *Slate*, Ted Genoways at *Virginia Quarterly Review*, Peter Scoblic at *The New Republic*, Tom Frail at *Smithsonian*, and Scott Malcomson at the *New York Times Magazine*. Many others have facilitated jobs, foreign trips, introductions, and experiences that have proved helpful and confiding along the way, including Erin O'Connell, Randy Gangle, Frank

Hoffman, Ralph Peters, Carole O'Leary, Ahmed Iravani, Daniel Burghart, and Svetlana Savranskaya.

Parag Khanna began encouraging me to write this book before I had even spent a day in Pakistan, and his sage advice over Skype conversations guided me through the early stages. Thanks to Andrew Stuart for his early confidence in me, and to Carl Bromley for his interest in this book. Parag, Nir Rosen, and Doug McGray were all instrumental in talking up this book to editors and agents.

A very special thanks to Doug McGray, who has been a friend, editor, and mentor for years. Doug and Griff Witte both read early chapters of the manuscript, and I am grateful for their comments and suggestions. Many thanks to Victoria Rowan, who taught me invaluable lessons about book writing.

Special thanks to Nadia Schadlow and the Smith Richardson Foundation, who invested in me long before anyone else considered it, and whose support made writing this book possible.

The New America Foundation opened their doors to me the moment I arrived back in the United States after being deported, for which I will be forever grateful. Special thanks to Steve Coll and Steve Clemons for their support.

Rafe Sagalyn, with his trademark composure, helped conceptualize this book from an otherwise haphazard proposal over a long weekend less than a week after my deportation. At Henry Holt, David Patterson's energy and dedication to this project made meetings and edits a pleasurable and stimulating experience.

Many thanks to my family—sorry for keeping you up late at night worrying about us in Pakistan. Much love and gratitude to Joyce and Ed Jutkus, Mae and Bob Schmidle, David Bohan, Kathy Bohan, and Ashleigh Bohan. Thanks to my brother, Christian, for being my best friend and for putting up with me. My mom and dad, Pam and Bob, always supported my dreams to be a writer. Thanks to you both for your love and for teaching me the importance of always wanting more.

Above all, thanks to Rikki, who agreed that a honeymoon in Pakistan sounded like a good idea. Your love and humor motivate me day after day. I adore you.

Index

Note: Page numbers in *italics* refer to photographs

Aaj TV, 125
Abdullah, Maulana, 62, 138
    assassination of, 141, 153
    bin Laden and, 140–41
    founding of Red Mosque, 140
Afghanistan, 85
    Soviet invasion and jihadists in, 19, 30, 48, 58, 78–79, 101, 140, 159, 194, 196
    Taliban in, *see* Taliban, in Afghanistan
    U.S. invasion in 2001, 20, 41, 48, 75, 191
Afridi, Latif, 55
Afzal, Hassan Waseem, 211
ahle-Hadith, 18
Ahmadinejad, Mahmoud, 5–6
Ahmadiyyas, 102, 111
Ahmed, Hafez Khalil, 63–64
Ahmed, Iajuddin, 106
Ahsan, Aitzaz, 122, 175–76, 178, 179, 180, 216
Akbari, Abdul Hakim, 194

Akbari, Tayyab, 194–95
Akhtar, Qari Saifullah, 140
Al-Badr force, 108–9
Ali, Imam, 17, 18, 24
Ali, Chaudhry Rahmat, 6–8, 10, 102
Al-Markazul Islami, 100, 101, 102, 112
al-Qaeda, 9, 10, 43, 48–49, 50–51, 59, 135, 141, 168, 194, 196, 197, 222
    propaganda, 163–64
Amin, Maulana Mohammad, 67–68
Another Day of Life (Kapuscínski), 122
APMSO (All Pakistan Mohajir Student Organization), 34–35
Armed Forces Journal, 80, 84
Armitage, Richard, 42
Arshad, General, 148, 150, 152, 153
Ashura, 23, 26
Associated Press, 227
Ataturk, Kemal, 70
Ata-ur-Rahman, Dr., 62
Ausaf, 47
Awami League, 102, 106, 115
Awami National Party (ANP), 54–55, 123, 124, *125*, 127, 205–6, 207
Aziz, Khalid, 49, 54

Aziz, Maulana Abdul, 11, 44, 62, 133, 141, 144, 201
  arrest of, while escaping the Red Mosque, 145, 148
  described, 138–39
  sermon of, 139–40
Aziz, Shaukat, 71–72
Aziz, Tariq, 3

Bais, Qari Abdul, 203–4
Baluch, Moyheddin, 88
Baluch, Shakeel Ahmed, 95–96, 97
Baluchis, 33, 34, 85, 86, 123
Baluchistan, 3, 7, 69–99, 190
  Gwadar deep-sea port, 70–71, 79, 89, 91–97
  history of, 84–87
  nationalists, 72–83, 84, 88–90, 92, 97, 178, 210
  social development indicators, 71
  workshop for mullahs from, 56–58, 63–68, 65
Baluchistan Liberation Army (BLA), 73–74, 81, 88, 210
Baluchistan National Party, 75, 76
Baluchistan Provincial Assembly, 77
Baluch Students Organization (BSO), 70, 88
Bangladesh, 10, 100–16
  constitution of, 108
  history of, 33, 102–3, 107–8, 176
  Islamism in, 105, 107–12, 115
  National Assembly, 108
  parliamentary elections, 102, 103–4, 106, 109
  state of emergency in, 106–7
Bangladesh Nationalist Party, 106, 108
Bareilvi, 18
Bengalis, 33
Bergen, Peter, 213
Bhutto, Benazir, 79, 121, 197, 198–99, 225
  assassination of, and its aftermath, 8, 10, 45, 205, 207–9, 210–19, 215, 222
  corruption charges against, 181, 182, 213
  Musharraf and, after return from exile, 180, 181, 182–83, 184, 208

Musharraf regime's role in assassination of, 211–13
  October 2007 bombing of motorcade of, 140, 182, 207
  Pakistan People's Party and, 180, 181, 187, 208, 211, 213, 219
  return from exile, 174, 181–82, 211
Bhutto, Bilawal Zardari, 216, 217, 219
Bhutto, Murtaza, 216
Bhutto, Zulfiqar Ali, 34, 77–78, 185, 210, 215, 219
Biman Airlines, 105–6
bin Laden, Osama, 10, 12, 59, 62, 101, 197, 198
  Ghazi and, 13, 140–41, 154
  Iqbal Khan and, 163, 164
Binori Town madrassa, 62, 101, 138
Bishwa Ijtema, 112–14, 113
Bizenjo, Hasil, 93, 95, 97
Blair, Tony, 12
"Blood Borders," 80
Britain, 17–18, 45–46, 58, 74, 206
  Baluchistan and, 85
  Benazir Bhutto and, 174
  Partition of India and exiting the subcontinent, 33, 85–86
  Swat Valley and, 160
Buddhist statues, Taliban's destruction of, 19, 161–62
Bugti, Akbar Khan, 73, 76, 79, 87–89
Bugti, Jamil, 89
Burma, 85, 86
Bush, George W., 138–39

Center for Emerging Threats and Opportunities, 61
Central Intelligence Agency, 5, 48, 80
Chaudhry, Iftikhar Mohammad, 117–30, 134
  attempt to return to Karachi and resulting riots of May 2007, 117–30
  described, 121
  under house arrest, 179, 188, 209
  proceedings questioning Musharraf's reelection bid, 174
  restoration of, 174
  state of emergency and, 174, 179
  Student Action Committee's march to community of, 188–89

suspension as Chief Justice, 117, 120, 153, 174
China, 135
    Gwadar deep-sea port and, 91–92, 135
Chittagong, Bangladesh, 111
Congress Party, Gandhi's, 206
Crane, Charles, 5
Curzon, Lord, 46

Darul Uloom al-Muhammadia, 59–60
Darul Uloom Deoband (or Deoband University) (madrassa), 18, 58
Dawn, 6–7, 32
Dawood, Aga Suleiman, 89–90, 98
Denizens of Alien Worlds: A Study of Education, Inequality, and Polarization in Pakistan (Rahman), 61
Deobandi, 18, 58
Derrida, Jacques, 59, 65–66

Egypt, 105
Elahi, Chaudhry Pervez, 211

Fahim, Makhdoom Amin, 215–16, 218
Fazlullah, Maulana, 159–60, 165–70, 183, 203–4, 222
Federally Administered Tribal Areas (FATA), 47–48, 160, 194, 206
    Taliban control in, 42, 154, 201–2, 222

Gall, Carlotta, 76
Gano (the People's Forum), 115
Gardner, Howard, 64–65
Gaza, 105
Geo TV, 121–22
    state of emergency and, 174–75
Ghafoor, Abdul, 169
Ghazi, Abdul Rashid, 11–13, *14*, 44, 50, 101, 104, 131–55, 166, 168, 222
    accused of terrorist plot in 2004, 137–38
    bin Laden and al-Qaeda, 13, 135, 140–41, 154
    death of, 150–51
    education of, 138
    jihadists and, 140
    negotiations with Pakistani government from Red Mosque, 148

    pro-Taliban movement in Pakistan and, 11–12, 132, 133, 141, 150, 151
    rebellion at Red Mosque, 11, 135–37, *137*, 142–54, 201
Gilani, Sheikh, 12–13
Gul, Lt. General Hamid, 48, 211
Gwadar, Baluchistan, 69–71, 79, 88, 90–99
    history of, 95, 96
    plans for modern deep-sea port in, 70–71, 79, 89, 91–97, 135
Gwadar Development Authority, 71, 96

Hafeez (of Pakistan Muslim League), 218–19
Hamas, 105
Haq, General Zia ul, 18–19, 23, 78, 185, 197
Haq, Ijaz ul, 23
Haqqani, Husain, 220–21
Harakat ul-Jihadi Islami (HUJI), 14, 62, 140, 143
Harakut ul-Mujahideen, 62, 198
Haroon, Hamid, 32
Harrison, George, 105
Hasina, Sheikh, 106
Hazaras, 19
Hezbollah, 105
Hindus
    in Bangladesh, 104, 105, 111–12
    of Gwadar, 96, 97
Holiday Inn (Islamabad), 146, 147, 148
Hossain, Kamal, 114–15
Huey, Aaron and Kristen, 226, 228, 233, 235
Human Rights Commission of Pakistan, 81, 84
Hussain, Mushahid, 176–77, 198
Hussain, Abbas, 64–65
Hussain, Altaf, 30, 31–33, 34–35, 36, 38–40, 118, 126
Hussain, Imam, 17, 18, 24, 25, 26
Hussain, Saddam, 18

Imamia Student Organization, 25
India, 103
    Partition of 1947, 30, 33, 86, 185
Indian Mutiny of 1857, 58
Indian Parliament, 2001 assault on, 143

Institute of Current World Affairs, 4–6
Institute of Strategic Studies, Islamabad, 83, 149
intelligence services, Pakistan, 8, 58, 193, 225
  Baluchistan nationalists and, 80–82, 84, 97, 210
  ISI, *see* Inter-Services Intelligence (ISI)
  lawyer's movement and, 120
  Military Intelligence (MI), 81–82, 84, 97, 223
  in Quetta, 75–76
  Red Mosque and Ghazi, 138
  Special Branch, 83
  Taliban and, 43, 46–47
International Center for Religion and Diplomacy (ICRD), 63, 64, 97
International Court of Justice in The Hague, 89, 90
International Islamic University, 2
Inter-Services Intelligence (ISI), 2, 53, 59, 97, 141, 201–2
after September 11, 42–43
Zardari government and, 222–23
In the Line of Fire (Musharraf), 107, 120, 177
Iqbal, Mohammad, 6, 7
Iqbal Khan, 157, 158, 160, 161, 162–64
Iran, 5–6, 24, 25
Islamic Revolution in, 18, 24
shah of, 18, 78
Iraq
  -Iran war, 18
  sectarianism in, 20
Iraq war, 138
Islamabad, Pakistan, 131–32, 132–33, 222
  Red Mosque, *see* Red Mosque (Lal Masjid)
  state of emergency and, 174
Islamabad Press Club, 186
Islamic Movement of Uzbekistan, 168
Islami-Jamiat-Taliba (IJT), 184, 185
Ismaelis, 96

Jabbar (Baluchi activist), 73, 74
Jafri, Husain, 18
Jahangir, Asma, 178, 179
Jaish-e-Mohammad, 62, 143

Jamaat-i-Islami, 29, 62, 105, 106, 107, 108, 109, 110–11, 115, 184
  student wing, 184
Jamaatul Mujahideen Bangladesh (The Bangladesh Mujahideen Party), 110
Jamia Hafsa (all-female madrassa in Islamabad), 12, 131–32, 144, 150, 152, 166, 222
Jamiat Ulema-e-Islam (JUI), 29, 49, 63, 190–94, 196–97, 200, 201
Jang, 36
Jinnah, Mohammad Ali, 5, 6, 8, 18, 35, 90
jirga (tribal council), 55, 77, 89
Jyllands-Posten, 40

Kabir, Shahriar, 107–8, 110–11
Kalat, 84, 86–87
  Khans of, 84, 85, 86, 87, 89, 90, 95, 97, 98
Kamaruzzaman, Muhammad, 108–10, 115
Kandahar, Afghanistan, 140–41, 192
Kapuscínski, Ryszard, 122
Karachi, Pakistan, 9, 117–30
  Anti-Violent Crime Cell, 119
  after Bhutto's assassination, 213, 217
  Bhutto's return from exile and, 181, 208–9
  lawyer's movement and, *see* Chaudhry, Iftikhar Mohammad; lawyer's movement
  MQM and, 29–33, 35–40, 117–18, 119, 122–26
  riots of May 12, 2007, 123–30, 134, 153, 208
Karachi Chamber of Commerce, 213
Karachi Stock Exchange, 217, 223
Karachi University, 34, 184
Karakorum Highway, 135, 157
Karbala, battle of, 17, 23
Karimov, Islam, 168
Kashmir, 7, 10, 19, 45, 58, 59, 105
Kayani, General Ashfaq, 177, 188
KGB, 79
Khalil, Maulana Fazlur Rahman, 198
Khamenei, Ayatollah, 24
Khan, Ahmed Yar, 90
Khan, Asfandyar Wali, 205–8, 224, 225

Khan, General Ayub, 34
Khan, Hayatullah, 47
Khan, Imran, 185, 202
Khan, Iqbal, 157, 158, 160, 161, 162–64
Khan, Khan Abdul Ghaffar, 206
Khan, Khodadad, 85
Khan, Naseer, 84–85
Khan, Nori Naseer, 85, 86
Khawaja, Khalid, 12–13, 44
Khelafat Majlish, 100, 102, 106, 108, 115
Khomeini, Ayatollah, 18, 24, 25
Kissinger, Henry, 102, 103
Kumaili, Allama, 23–27
Kurds, 84

Lahore University for Management
    Services (LUMS), 185–87
Lal Masjid, see Red Mosque (Lal Masjid)
lawyer's movement, 10, 120–30, 134
    arrests during state of emergency, 175,
        176, 184
    Karachi riots of May 12, 2007 and,
        123–30, 134, 153, 208
    during state of emergency, 179,
        179–80, 183–84
Lebanon, 105
Liaquat Ali Khan, 33, 34
Lindh, John Walker, 50

McDonald's, 224
madrassas, 12, 21–22, 23, 42, 55, 56–68,
    191, 192, 197
    in Bangladesh, 111, 115–16
    Binori Town madrassa, 62, 101, 138
    Jamia Hafsa, see Jamia Hafsa
    workshops, 56–57, 63–68
"Madrassas and the Modern World," 57
maliks (tribal elders), 47–48, 49, 204
Mao Tse-tung, 103
Marri, Khair Baksh, and son Balach, 79
Marri tribesmen, 79, 89
Marxism, 55, 78, 111
Massoud, Ahmed Shah, 87–88, 194, 196
Mazari, Shireen, 149–50
Mehmood, Mufti, 196–97
Mehsud, Baitullah, 45, 200, 211–12, 222
Mehsud tribe, 45
Mengal, Akhtar, 75, 76–77, 79, 80–83, 84,
    88, 97

Mengal, Ataullah, 77–80, 82
Mengal tribe, 76–77, 78, 89
Migrants and Militants: Fun and Urban
    Violence in Pakistan (Verkaaik), 36
Millat-i-Islam Pakistan (Islamic Nation),
    23
Ministry of Environment, Pakistan, 136
Mir, Hamid, 43, 44
Mirza, Zulfiqar, 228
MMA (Muttahida Majles Amal) (United
    Action Front), 23, 49, 54, 190, 203
    Ghazi and, 144
mohajirs, 30, 31, 33, 34–35, 123
Mohammad, Maulvi Faqir, 150
Mohammad, Maulvi Noor, 191–92,
    193
Mohammad, Prophet, 9, 16
    cartoons depicting, 9, 40
Mohammad, Sufi, 157, 159
MQM-Haqiqi (The Real One), 33, 35
MQM (Muttahida Quami Movement),
    29–33, 35–40, 117–18, 119, 122–26,
    127, 184, 199, 217, 218
    founding of, 30, 35
Musharraf, Pervez, 10, 23
    assassination attempts on, 143
    autobiography, 107, 120, 177
    Baluchistan nationalists and, 73–74, 75,
        78, 79, 84, 97, 133–34
    Benazir Bhutto and, see Bhutto,
        Benazir
    Chaudhry and lawyer's movement, see
        Chaudhry, Iftikhar Mohammad;
        lawyer's movement
    Ghazi and the Red Mosque, 44,
        131–32, 135–37, 142–54
    Gwadar deep-sea port and, 70–71, 79
    impeachment charges against, 223–24
    Karachi riots of May 12, 2007 and,
        126–27, 153
    the madrassas and, 12, 59, 192
    overthrow of Nawaz Sharif, 175
    religious militias banned by, 22–23
    relinquishes control of the army,
        187–88, 221
    resignation from presidency, 224
    state of emergency in Pakistan, 174–88,
        209, 223
    TNSM and, 157

Musharraf, Pervez (continued)
   U.S. relationship after 9/11, 42–43,
      46–47, 59, 120, 121, 154, 174, 182,
      184, 224
Muslim Brotherhood, 105
Muslim League, 206
Muslim Students Federation, 185
Muttahida Majles Amal (MMA)(United
      Action Front), 23, 49, 54, 190, 203
   Ghazi and, 144
Muttahida Quami Movement, see MQM
      (Muttahida Quami Movement)
"My Buddy the Jihadi," 151

Naqvi, Mohsin, 65–66
Narail, Bangladesh, 104–5
Naseer Khan, 84–85
National Intelligence Estimates, U.S., 43,
      194
National Party, 72–73, 93, 95
New Republic, The, 103, 211
New York Times, 42, 86
New York Times Magazine, 2, 103, 225
"Next Islamic Revolution?, The," 103
Nirmul Committee, 108
Nixon, Richard, 103
Non-Objection Certificate (NOC), 83,
      90–91, 98
Northern Alliance, 194
North-West Frontier Province (NWFP), 7,
      45, 72, 160–61, 190, 194, 206
   public lashing in, 171–72
   Taliban's control in, 2, 154, 156–72,
      198, 199–201, 203, 222
"Now or Never; Are We to Live or Perish
      For Ever?" 7–8, 102
nuclear weapons, 8

Omar, Mullah, 20, 42, 140, 141, 162,
      163, 191, 192, 197

Pakistan, 199
   history of, 6–8, 33, 206
   intelligence services, see intelligence
      services, Pakistan
   map, xiii
   parliamentary elections of 2008,
      190–91, 199, 203, 205–7, 209, 213,
      216, 217–19, 221, 236

   state of emergency, see state of emer-
      gency in Pakistan
   violence leading to 2008 elections,
      206–7, 210
   see also individual politicians, parties,
      geographic areas, and issues
Pakistan Institute of Peace Studies, 206
Pakistan International Airlines, 88
Pakistan Muslim League, 88, 123, 124,
      184, 187, 198, 218, 223
Pakistan People's Party (PPP), 52, 77, 123,
      218–19, 223
   Benazir Bhutto and, 180, 181, 187,
      208, 211, 213, 219
   founding of, 185
   student wing of, 184
   successor to Benazir Bhutto and,
      215–17, 219
   Zardari-led government, 221, 222–26,
      236
Pakistan Petroleum Company, 87
Pakistan Television, 145, 178
pan, 9–10
Pashtuns, 29, 30, 31, 33, 35, 45, 51, 54,
      75, 85, 123, 127, 164, 196, 206
   ANP and, see Awami National Party
      (ANP)
Patterson, Anne, 198–99
Pearl, Daniel, 12–13, 16, 62, 227
Pearl Continental Hotel, Baluchistan, 71
Pirzada, Sharifuddin, 121
Pottinger, Sir Henry, 84
Powell, Colin, 43
Predator drones, 51
Provincially Administered Tribal Area
      (PATA), 160, 161
Punjab, 7
   arrests during 2007 state of emergency,
      178
Punjabis, 33, 34, 88, 97
Punjab University, 184, 185

Qalander, Lal Shahbaz, 226, 232
Qasim, Mohammed bin, 17
Quetta, Pakistan, 75–76, 83–84, 88, 127,
      190–92

Rafi (journalist), 15

Rahman, Maulana Fazlur, 192–204, *193*, 224, 225
Rahman, Sheikh Mujibur, 102, 108, 115
Rahman, Dr. Tariq, 61
Rahman, General Ziaur, 108
Rahman, Qari Shafiqur, 15–16, 19–22, 158
Rajpar, Mohammad, 91–92
Rana, Amir, 61
Rashid, Ahmed, 197
Red Mosque (Lal Masjid), 11, 13, 20, 44, 135–55, 166, 194, 222
  described, 134–35
  founding of, 140
  mujahideen during jihad of 1980s and, 140
  Operation Silence, 148, 150, 153, 192
  rebellion at, 11, 135–37, *137*, 142–55, 201, 208
  reopening of, 154–55
  sharia courts inside, 132
Red Shirts, 206
Reid, Richard, 227
Roosevelt, Franklin D., 178
Rosen, Nir, 76
Rumsfeld, Donald, 61
Russian Empire, 85

Sajjad, Aasim, 185–87
Sandeman, Robert, 85
sardars (chiefs), 76, 77, 78, 79, 85, 89
Sattar, Farooq, 28–39, 118, 122, 217
Saudi Arabian intelligence services, 48
Schmidle, Nicholas (author), *193*
  deportation notice in January 2008, 1–4, 225
  family of, 11, 151, 164, 235–36
  ICWA fellowship, 4–6
  Pakistan intelligence agencies and, 83–84, 97–98, 226–29, 234–37
  return to Pakistan in August 2008, experiences after, 220–21, 224–37
Schmidle, Rikki (wife), 2–3, 133, 144, 173, 236
September 11, 2001, 42–43, 139–40, 196
Shafiqur Rehman, Qari, 15–16, 19–22, 158
Shah, Ijaz, 211

Shah, Pir Zubair (journalist), 45–46, 47, 49–55, *193*, 195–96
Shaheen (translator and guide), 156–57, 159, 162–69, 172, 208–9
Shahidul Islam, Mufti, 100–102, 104, 112, 114, 115
  bin Laden and, 101
Shakur (fisherman in Gwadar), 96–97
Sham, Mahmood, 36
Shams (Pakistan People's Party activist), 51–52, 53
Shankar, Ravi, 105
sharia, 131, 166, 190, 191, 203
  Red Mosque and, 132
  TNSM and, 157
Sharif, Nawaz, 79, 121, 124, 175, 176, 179, 187, 216, 218, 223, 224, 225
  attempt to return from exile, 180
Shazia, Dr., 56–57
Shi'ites, 16–27, 27
Siddique, Ayesha, 177
Siegel, Mark, 211
Sikander, Dr. Abdul Razzak, 62–63
Sindh, 7, 72
  Benazir Bhutto and people of, 181, 207, 208, 214, 216, 217, 219
  highway bandits in, 233
Sindhis, 33, 34, 123
  in Karachi, 30
Sipah-e-Mohammad, 22–23
Sipah-e-Sahaba (Army for the Companions of the Prophet), 14, 16, 19–25, 143
Sirajuddin (spokesman for Fazlullah), 166–67
Slate, 151
Smithsonian, 220, 226
Sohrabi, Majid, 69–71, 72, 94
Somoza, Anastasio, 178
Soviet Union, 103, 135
  invasion of Afghanistan, *see* Afghanistan, Soviet invasion and jihadists in
state of emergency in Pakistan, 174–88, 223
  arrests of lawyers and politicians, 175, 176, 178, 179, 184
  college campuses during, 184–87
  Musharraf announces, 174

state of emergency in Pakistan *(continued)*
    private TV channels and, 174, 177–78
    rumors of Musharraf's ousting, 177
    Taliban insurgency during, 178, 183
    termination of, 188, 209
Student Action Committee, 186–87,
    188–89
Sufis, 17
Lal Shahbaz Qalander festival, 220, 226,
    229–32, 234
Suhrab Goth neighborhood, Karachi,
    29–30, 31
Sui gas plant, Baluchistan, 73, 87
Sundas (law student), 187
Sunnis, 16, 17–20, 23
    dominant sects in Pakistan, 18
Supreme Court Bar Association, Pakistan,
    175
Swapan (Bangladeshi activist), 115–16
Swat Valley of North-West Frontier
        Province
    history of, 160, 161–62
    Taliban control in, 156–72, *161*, 183,
        222

Tablighi Jamaat, 112, 140
Tagore, Rabindranath, 107, 110–11
Taliban, 2, 9, 10, 19–20, 194–95,
        199–201, 206
    in Afghanistan, 19–20, 58–59, 64
    Ghazi and pro-Taliban movement in
        Pakistan, 11–12, 132, 133, 141, 150,
        151
    intensification of insurgency in Pakistan
        in 2007–2008, 8, 154, 174, 183,
        201–2, 209, 222
    Jamiat Ulema-e-Islam and, 190, 191,
        193, 194, 197, 200, 201, 202–3
    in North-West Frontier Province, 2,
        154, 156–72, 198, 199–201, 203, 222
    in Quetta, 75
    tribal leaders replaced by, 204
    in Waziristan, 41–55, 178, 182, 201,
        222
    women and, 133, 158, 159
Taliban (Rashid), 197

Tariq, Azam, 22
Tehrik-e-Taliban Pakistan, 200
Tehrik-i-Nifaz-Shariat-Mohammadia
        (Movement for the Implementation
        of Sharia) (TNSM), 157, 159, 161,
        162, 163
    Fazullah and, 159–60
Telegraph, 178
Tora Bora, Afghanistan, 49
Turabi, Allama Hassan, 25

UNICEF, 140, 141
United States
    anti-Americanism, 135, 191
    Bangladesh independence and, 103
    Benazir Bhutto and, 174, 180–81,
        198–99
    Chinese role in Middle East and, 92
    invasion of Afghanistan in 2001, 20, 41,
        48, 75, 191
    Musharraf regime and, *see* Musharraf,
        Pervez, U.S. relationship after 9/11
U.S. consulate, Karachi, 235–36
Urdu, 33–34
Usmani, Mufti Taqi, 144
Uzbeks, 167, 168

Verkaaik, Oskar, 36

Washington Post, 121, 151, 174
Washington Times, 92
Waziristan, North and South
    al-Qaeda in, 194, 195
    Durand line, 45–46
    Taliban in, 41–55, 178, 182, 201, 222

Yunus, Muhammad, 106

Zardari, Asif Ali, 182, 216, 217, 218, 219,
        221, 223, 224–26, 228
    corruption charges against, 181, 216,
        219
Zawahiri, Ayman al-, 51, 52–53, 164
    Ghazi's death and, 154
Zia, Khaleda, 106, 108

About the Author

NICHOLAS SCHMIDLE is a fellow at the New America Foundation. He writes for the *New York Times Magazine*, *Slate*, *The New Republic*, *Smithsonian*, and the *Virginia Quarterly Review*, among other publications, and received the 2008 Kurt Schork Award for freelance journalism. As a fellow of the Institute of Current World Affairs, he lived and reported in Pakistan for two years. Schmidle is a graduate of James Madison University and American University. He lives in Washington, D.C., with his wife.